# Freedom & Tyranny:
# Social Problems in a
# Technological Society

Consulting Editor

# MARVIN BRESSLER

PRINCETON UNIVERSITY

# Freedom & Tyranny:

## Social Problems in a

## Technological Society

Edited, with Introductions, by

# Jack D. Douglas

UNIVERSITY OF CALIFORNIA, SAN DIEGO

**Alfred · A · Knopf** / NEW YORK

THIS IS A BORZOI BOOK
PUBLISHED BY ALFRED A. KNOPF, INC.

Copyright © 1970 by Alfred A. Knopf, Inc.

Library of Congress Catalog Card Number: 74-105653

Manufactured in the United States of America

First Edition

987654321

# Frontispiece

In 1921 I believed—and I shared this belief with most of my contemporary physicists—that science produced an objective knowledge of the world, which is governed by deterministic laws. The scientific method seemed to me superior to other, more subjective ways of forming a picture of the world—philosophy, poetry, and religion; and I even thought the unambiguous language of science to be a step towards a better understanding between human beings.

In 1951 I believed in none of these things. The border between object and subject had been blurred, deterministic laws had been replaced by statistical ones, and although physicists understood one another well enough across all national frontiers they had contributed nothing to a better understanding of nations, but had helped in inventing and applying the most horrible weapons of destruction.

Max Born, Physics in My Generation

# Preface

The United States has become a technological society. In fact, the United States has become *the* technological society, the prototype for all of the technological societies rapidly evolving around the world.

Slowly, but seemingly inevitably, the entire earth is being knit into one giant technological society. Radiating out from the center of technological innovation and postindustrial production, the forces of technology are increasingly determining the shape of our everyday lives and bringing all sections of the earth into greater interdependency. A global communication net will soon bring us into almost instantaneous contact with all parts of the world. In the not too distant future, it is conceivable that this communication net will become the foundation for a global system of production and distribution of goods.

The growth of science and technology to this position of dominance presents us with great promises and great threats. Through the use of automated production and atomic power, technology promises us unlimited wealth and power, but it also threatens us with the unlimited destruction of thermonuclear war. Technology promises us freedom from drudgery and physical suffering, but it also threatens us with the most efficient tyranny man has yet known.

The evidence of the last century shows clearly that we have learned how to use science and technology to steadily improve our physical standards of living. The evidence also shows that, at least within Western societies and increasingly within the other developing nations, there has been no Marxian "immiseration" resulting from our form of technological production: both the rich and poor have benefited from our technologically produced wealth.

But this evidence also indicates that the threats to our personal freedoms are profound. Our traditional personal freedoms, our civil rights were built largely on private ownership of the decentralized means of production, an educated citizenry capable of understanding complex problems of government decisions, and liberal forms of pluralism in government and private life which prevented the concentration of power in any one part of the society. The technological society thrives on centralization, massive size, and expert decision making—all of which have served to undermine the foundations of our traditional freedoms and their direct threats to these freedoms appear to be growing at an accelerating rate as technology itself grows at an accelerating rate.

As the threats of technological tyranny have grown, the attacks on the technological society, and sometimes on technology itself, have grown in severity and moral fervor. There is now a massive literature devoted to what Manfred Stanley has called the technicist projection. Jacques Ellul, Herbert Marcuse, and many others believe that we already have a technological society in which the centralized forces of the system (or the structure) control our daily lives through corporate and government planning and manipulate our support for this planning through mass-media propaganda and through the testimony of "experts" in behalf of this planning.

As will be apparent in my essay, "Freedom and Tyranny in a Technological Society," the validity of these attacks can be questioned, especially their projections of an inescapable, ironclad, and rapidly approaching technological tyranny. There is also every reason to take these arguments seriously. How our personal freedoms have already been affected, and what the effects are of mass-media propaganda on our thinking are some of the profound questions facing us today. Since nothing could be of greater importance to most of us than our personal freedoms, it is of vital importance to continually reexamine these questions concerning freedom and tyranny in our society.

It will be especially important in the years and decades ahead for sociologists and other social scientists to provide the kinds of information and analyses that we need to make wise decisions concerning the uses of science and technology. It will also be of vital importance for all members of our society to be aware of the fundamental issues involved if we are to have any realistic hope of controlling science and technology to increase and protect our personal freedoms instead of allowing them to destroy our freedoms with ruthless efficiency. If we are to achieve the needed kind of public awareness, then we must begin with the educated. It is the purpose of this volume to present these basic issues to college students in such a way that they can understand the issues and will be stimulated to search for the answers.

**J.D.D.**

La Jolla, California

March 1969

# Contents

# PART IV
# The Control of Information
# and Power in
# the Technological Society

# PART V
# The Tyranny of Experts
# in the Technological Society

# PART VI
# The Future of Freedom
# and Tyranny in
# the Technological Society

# PART I

## General Introduction

# Freedom and Tyranny
# in a Technological Society

JACK D. DOUGLAS

This essay serves as an overview of the basic issues presented in the whole volume. It begins with a brief historical treatment of the rise of science and technology as a basic revolutionary force in the Western world. The relation between science and technology and economic activity has been a basic concern of sociologists and other social scientists for a hundred years. There are still important disagreements, but there is little disagreement over the importance of the issues involved ; and while it is widely believed that economic forces in the Western world are related to science and technology, it is important to realize that science and technology have become ends in themselves.

Not only do science and technology contribute to economic prosperity and development, but economic development contributes to them. For a growing number of people in our society, it is this contribution of economics to technology and science which is most important. In any event, this interdependency between economics and the

*3*

scientific-technological complex assures us of the continued growth of science and technology as basic forces in our society. Science and technology have become the basic form of knowledge in the Western world. They are the ideal form of knowledge toward which all other forms must strive if they are to be taken seriously and given prestige in our society. Because of this, science and technology have become the basic determinants of education and thus basic determinants of every major institution.

These facts have led many serious scientists and social philosophers to believe that we have already achieved a state in the development of the technological society in which technology and science have tyrannical control over every major part of our society. The more extreme critics believe that we are approaching the society pictured in Orwell's *1984*.

When we actually examine the great mass of complex information relevant to weighing this argument, we see there is evidence both for and against it. As argued in this essay, there is every reason to believe that the more extreme critics have overstated the case. In some ways, they have become the victims of their own moral fervor, but there is still reason to take these critics and their messages seriously.

We must become increasingly aware of the possible dangers of the technological tyranny. We must become aware of the ways in which science and technology give rise to a large and growing class of experts who have profound influence on the directions of our social policies. We must recognize that expert knowledge is a necessity in the technological society but that it also has dangerous implications. We must exercise our freedom both in understanding such problems and in seeking to solve them in order to protect ourselves from the possibilities of a technological tyranny.

If we can do this, then technology and science can provide us with the knowledge necessary to build a world of greater wealth and, hopefully, of greater freedom for all.

> now a significant number of our most thoughtful scholars seems to fear that a third mandala is rising . . . the labyrinth with the empty center, where the investigator meets only his own shadow and his blackboard with his own chalk marks on it, his own solutions to his own puzzles. And this philosophical threat is thought to be matched . . . by the physical threat considered as originating from a blind, aimless, self-motivating, ever-growing engine of technology.
>
> It therefore is not surprising that those who think of our culture and our persons as caught between these two tendencies find little comfort in the beauty of scientific advances, in the recital of coherence-making forces, or in promises that the lamp of science will light the way to a greater society. Not until their doubts are allayed will there be any hope for achieving the rapprochement needed for finding a more positive and valid place for science in our culture.
>
> Gerald Holton, *Science and Culture*

The most basic and pervasive change in Western society over the last several centuries has been the development and increasing dominance of the scientific and technological world view—a complex set of cognitive and normative criteria specifying the realm of "reality" and the appropriate ways of knowing and dealing with that "reality." Beginning with Medieval and Renaissance naturalism and rationalism, synthesized into nineteenth-century positivist thought, and modified by twentieth-century relativistic thought, this world view is now accepted by the great majority as the one legitimate way of knowing and dealing with reality.

This rationalist-scientific-technological world view developed independently of practical economic activities until the sixteenth and seventeenth centuries. The early association between capitalism and the scientific-technological world view did not begin with a belief on the part of the entrepreneurs that they needed the help of the scientists or technologists in solving their practical problems; on the contrary, it was the propaganda work of such men as Sir Francis Bacon, especially in his work *Magna Instauratio,* that convinced men of the practical benefits of science.

However, long before this practical relationship developed between capitalism and the scientific-technological world view, there was a distinct and growing relationship between the two, based on their common association with Protestantism, especially Puritanism. These apparent associations[1] between Puritanism and capitalism and between Puritanism and science Max Weber[2] and Robert K. Merton[3] theorized as certain complex shared ideas among the "spirit of capitalism," Puritanism, and the scientific world view. This shared-meanings theory has been sharply attacked in recent years.[4] The associations among the three now seem to have been more the result of allied relationships. It must be remembered that the early rationalist world view, which was closely allied with the developing scientific world view, was important in undermining the traditional authority of the Church. Catholic counterreformationists viewed the rationalist-scientific world view with increasing suspicion, though the early creators of the rationalist-scientific world view had been Catholic. Thus the Protestants and the scientists allied, and the Protestants allied with the urban capitalists who were making increasing use of this scientific world view.

Through this early relationship with Protestantism, capitalism and the scientific-technological world view became more closely linked. But the crucial link, that of practical necessity, developed primarily in the latter part of the seventeenth century, partly as a result of Bacon's effectiveness in convincing men that science could be useful economically and partly as a result of the effective application of science to economic activities, especially agriculture. These complex supporting relationships between science and economic activity have been well summarized by Richard Foster Jones in his classic study *Ancients and Moderns*.

There were also certain social correlatives of the scientific ideas mentioned above that, especially in the puritan era, receive vigorous expression because congenial with attitudes arising from other sources. These sprang almost entirely from the utilitarian element in scientific thinking and from the lowered intellectual gifts demanded of experimenters. The farmer, artisan, and mechanic, because they were in contact with natural things and were unhindered by an intellectual principle of exclusion, rise in importance and receive considerable recognition. The *democratic implication* in this situation can hardly escape notice . . . Certainly science contributed something to that stream of democratic thought and feeling which, arising in the Reformation, was gathering force among the Puritans. The emphasis placed by Bacon upon the material benefits which his philosophy would bestow upon man could not but introduce or re-enforce the social motive of the public good, for this philosophy made such a goal seem quite feasible. A specialized version of this social conception is revealed in the appearance of a humanitarian spirit which found in the prospective blessings of science the hope and the means of bettering the condition of the poor. . . . During the mid-seventeenth century the social utility of science is recognized; the beneficent results of scientific activity are contrasted with the evils of war; and the heroes of science supplant those robed in martial glory.[5]

Over the centuries the ties between science and technology and economics have grown even greater. The crucial link has proved to be between industrial (and postindustrial) means of production and applied science rather than between capitalism and science or technology. Since World War II, it has become a common article of faith on all sides of the various "curtains" that the three prime goals—health, prosperity, and security—of any industrial, and especially any postindustrial or electronic, society can be achieved only through the effective use of scientific and technological knowledge. Modern man has come to feel intensely dependent on science and technology for his prosperity, his security, his very existence. The concomitant fears of dependency and control over one's life, held by alienated intellectuals and many other segments of the public, have been repressed by the general public. Scientists have become the high priests of the dominant world view; they alone can provide the cherished goals through their "miraculous" control of the "secrets of nature," even though they themselves have come to feel more and more uncertain about the bases of scientific knowledge.[6]

The industrial-technological society has become dependent on science and technology, but, at the same time, science and technology have become increasingly dependent on industrial societies for the vast economic and social support they need in order to grow. While it is true that they have become dependent for their individual material wealth on the industrial society, both in the private and the public spheres, this form of vulgar dependency, the sellout made so much of by traditional leftists, is hardly significant compared to their more idealistic dependency. Until recently it was common practice for scientists and technologists to sacrifice their financial self-interests to the goals of science and technology. But it would be impossible for scientists and technologists to function and advance scientifically without immense contributions of wealth and work to their projects by the industrial society. In fields like elementary particle physics, for example, development is dependent upon experimental results that can be achieved only by particle accelerators that cost hundreds of millions of dollars and can be built only by a highly industrialized society. Science at the most idealistic level—science pursued entirely for the sake of building the truth about reality—has become highly interdependent with the industrial-technological society.

This interdependency has been important in making the scientists as well as the technologists the servants of power, the creators and tenders of the technological base of society. The scientists have even helped to create and support this position by creating and institutionalizing the value-free definition of science.

> Along this spectrum, science is not in conflict with the disciplines of the older tradition of humane learning. On the contrary, it shares with them a common set of problems. It is impossible for either kind of scholarly knowledge, in a free constitutional system, to be translated directly into political decisions. In Western nations, the theologians have long since been forced to learn how to let lawyers and administrators serve as the intermediaries between their abstract truth and the politicians who exercise supreme authority. The scientists are newcomers to the status of being established with public support, and are not yet altogether persuaded that they need to develop a clear constitutional theory of their relation to political authority.
>
> The scientists have one advantage: in theory it has been rather more clear to them than to most of the theologians that they can develop their kind of knowledge only by freeing themselves from assumptions about human purposes and values. Thus they have protected themselves, to some extent, from the temptations of power and the dangers of political control. By the very nature of their discipline, they remain dissenters, with no interest in founding a new political dogma. But they need a great deal of money from the government, and what they do with it has an obvious impact on public policy. Even as dissenters, they must be established, and the future status of their estate must be developed with care if we are to adjust our constitutional system to modern technology without losing our freedom.[7]

## The Rise of the Technological Society

The scientific world view, I suspect, eventually would have achieved its dominant position independently of its involvement with technology and industrial production primarily because science, at least in its early positivistic form, was as much an absolutist form of thought as Christian theology and was partly an outgrowth of that earlier religious absolutism.[8] In this way science met many of the same needs as our traditional religions.

The early battles between science and religion were fought and won by scientists, at least among the intellectuals, without appealing to the utilitarian values of science. Even many of the later battles, such as the great nineteenth-century battle over evolution, were fought and won quite independently of utilitarian considerations. The scientific world view is an end in itself for Western man, a generalized perspective that orders experience in the most acceptable way, and, as such, a form of thought to which a great majority of Western men have become emotionally and normatively committed.

But there can be little doubt that the practical values of science, worked out in technology, have been a primary reason for the rapidity with which the scientific-technological world view has become dominant in public communication over the last hundred years. Scientific thought became the public (or least common denominator) form of communication, the normatively prescribed form of thought, because it alone among the major forms of reasoning was objective enough, pure enough from subgroup values and commitments, and dependent enough on the more nearly universal experience of sense perception, to serve as the arbiter of the endemic conflicts resulting from our social pluralism.[9] Yet even this reason for the spreading influence of scientific thought seems to have been greatly influenced by its technological success in solving practical problems. Scientific thought, as applied through technology,[10] worked and the common man was loathe to argue with success.

As Galbraith has argued, the simple factors of massive investment, complexity and inflexibility of decision making, and long lead times (between planning and marketing) resulting from the modern technological means of production have come more and more to determine the general nature of our society, especially the growing interdependency between industry and government, growing planning, and the ever growing use of official controls and propaganda (advertising) to control consumer market responses. Galbraith believes that these changes in turn have the more lasting effect of changing our social values and beliefs.

I am also concerned to show how, in this larger context of change, the forces inducing human effort have changed. This assaults the most majestic of all economic assumptions, namely that man in his economic activities is subject to the authority of the market. Instead, we have an economic system which, whatever its formal ideological billing, is in substantial part a planned economy. The initiative in deciding what is to be produced comes not from the sovereign consumer who, through the market, issues the instructions that bend the productive mechanism to his ultimate will. Rather it comes from the great producing organization which reaches forward to control the markets that it is presumed to serve and, beyond, to bend the customer to its needs. And, in so doing, it deeply influences his values and beliefs—including not a few that will be mobilized in resistance to the present argument. One of the conclusions that follows from this analysis is that there is a broad convergence between industrial systems. The imperatives of technology and organization, not the images of ideology, are what determine the shape of economic society.[11]

Galbraith also argues that there are very serious, and sometimes very dangerous, consequences of this social commitment to the technological means of production, such as the cold war arms race.

The industrial system has not become identified with the weapons competition by preference or because it is inherently bloody. Rather, this has been the area where the largest amount of money to support planning was available with the fewest questions asked. And since armies and cannon have always been in the public sector, government underwriting in this area had the fewest overtones of socialism. But the space race shows that underwriting outside the area of weaponry is equally acceptable.[12]

One of the most crucial effects of this scientific-technological revolution on our society has been the increasing dominance of science and technology on formal education, particularly higher education. Scientific thought has gained steadily in education, especially in colleges and universities, for the important nonutilitarian reasons we have already discussed. The traditional dependency of higher education on business for support (and governing through business trustees) and the traditional job orientation of most American education have led to the rapid dominance of scientific and technological training in universities and colleges. Government support, going almost exclusively to science and technology, has accelerated this process and has helped to turn philosophy into linguistics, linguistics into mathematics, psychology into rodentology, sociology into methodology, and music into computer cacophony.

Many intellectuals are convinced that we already live in a society dominated by technique and that we, especially we Americans, are already one-dimensional men secretly controlled by the technocrats and our own false consciousness. The most brilliant presentation of this position has been made by Jacques Ellul in his work *The Technological Society,* which has been best summarized by John Wilkinson. (See pp. 48–59 in this volume.)

Ellul, like Galbraith, believes that the dominance of technology can be guaranteed only through the continual use of systematic, monolithic—saturation—propaganda encapsulating all individuals through multi-media messages in their daily lives. The technological society *must* tyrannize the mind through propaganda, and by doing so, it creates a satisfied population in which propaganda itself is valued. (See Jacques Ellul's article in this volume, pp. 116–125.)

Herbert Marcuse has carried this argument to its extreme—and made it popular—by arguing that this tyranny of the technological society is not only here but has already made almost all Americans happy with it. (See Herbert Marcuse's "The New Forms of Control" in this volume, pp. 33–47.)

## Failures of the Technicist Projection

Although there is a great deal of prima facie evidence to support the argument that we are moving rapidly in the direction of some form of technological tyranny, which Manfred Stanley has called the "technicist projection," there seems to be as much, and possibly more, evidence against the basic assumptions of the technicist projection. The assumption that Western society, especially American society, is monolithic in any way, even in the language used, appears absurd on prima facie grounds. Pluralism of class interests, work life, styles of life, political affiliations, foreign policies, race, languages, ethnic cultures and identifications, sectional cultures and identifications, religious beliefs, and so on, are all apparent in our society. Unlike almost all other major intellectual figures who accept the technicist projection, Herbert Marcuse has lived intermittently for over thirty years in American society, though he has clearly never been of American society in the sense of sharing the common identities of our society. Probably because of this experience, however limited, Marcuse agrees that pluralism exists but believes that it is ineffective in counterbalancing the monolithic majority position. He argues that this apparent pluralism cancels out real pluralism. If this criticism means that no countervailing force has yet risen that is strong enough to destroy the society or to produce a violent takeover of the federal government, the Marxist's beloved revolution, then it is true: this society does still exist and has not yet had the successful revolution. Yet this is hardly what

Marcuse has in mind, for revolutions in the Marxist sense of the term are rare indeed and total destructions of society from within even rarer. What Marcuse means is that our pluralism prevents any effective change in the unilinear directions of both domestic and foreign social policy in our every-day social practices. But I submit that this too is absurd on prima facie grounds. Anyone who believes that the federal government policies and practices over the last several years have not changed vastly in economic matters, in racial matters, in foreign-aid matters, in Vietnam, and so on is either being obtuse or assumes that he knows something profound that transfigures all of these apparent realities but something which we mere mortals are unable to comprehend because we have been so successfully brainwashed into false consciousness by the social monolith. This latter position is, indeed, Marcuse's position.

There is also evidence against the other basic assumptions of the tech-nicist projection. It is apparent that science and technology, as represented in technique, are not considered as autonomous goals or goals valued in themselves by most members of our society. If they are, then our society must certainly not value them very highly, for it is not willing to put any significant amount of time, effort, or money into them for their own sake. The federal government under Eisenhower was unwilling to put even small amounts of money into the simple technical tasks of launching a satellite until sputnik appeared as a threat to security. No federal administration has ever attempted to justify spending money on such scientific-technologi-cal projects as moon rockets, SSTs, and accelerators on the grounds that these are interesting problems in technique.

The evidence concerning the issue of whether science and technology are leading us toward ironclad tyranny or toward greater individual free-dom is extremely ambiguous. Even the fundamental problems of deciding what constitutes relevant evidence and how this evidence is to be used in deciding between theories of such vast scope and ambiguous structure have hardly been attacked by the proponents of these conflicting positions, much less solved in some way that most proponents can accept. As a result, whether one foresees gloom and doom or bright utopias arising from the steady advance of the scientific-technological world view seems at this time to depend primarily upon one's general moral orientation or even one's ideological mood toward our modern society.

Almost all of those sharing the technicist projection are older European humanists, even classicists or theologians, who have many personal, even professional, reasons to resent the scientists and technologists. Some of them, especially Marcuse, were obviously committed Marxists or neo-Marxists long before they took up the technicist projection, and they seem to have taken it up as a cudgel to be used against their arch enemies: the capitalistic-war-mongering-imperialist Americans. When evidence is presented that seems obviously to disprove some point they make, then they respond by either shifting the basis of the argument or by using the old leftist tactic of arguing that the apparent contradiction is really the strongest possible evidence in favor of their position. On the other hand, while there are some American scientists and technologists—for example, Norbert Wiener—who warn of the dangers of science and technology, most of the blithe spirits presaging utopia are American scientists and technologists, such as B. F. Skinner.

There seems to be a fundamental assumption underlying both these points of view which makes their proponents so certain of their contradictory conclusions: both sides have already assumed the necessity of some form of tyranny and the impossibility of human freedom. Their main dispute is simply over which kind is better. Those sharing the technicist projection survey the juggernaut of history and see technological tyranny developing ineluctably out of centuries of Western thought. The technicist projectors have assumed, then, that man is already subject to tyranny, that he is not free to control this development or even to know it is happening to him. They see man as necessarily controlled by unconscious forces, especially by the unconscious meanings or effects of technological propaganda which creates false consciousness so that man believes the opposite of the truth. Presumably, only they, the technicist projectors, have escaped this brainwashing effect of propaganda, and therefore only they can serve as an elite in deciding what is really true and can act to suppress this false consciousness by suppressing the (falsely) free speech of those who are really the suppressors through the mechanism Marcuse calls "repressive tolerance." [13] If this sounds like the foundation for a terrifying tyranny to us, this is only because we suffer from the false consciousness produced by the propaganda of real tyrants practicing "repressive tolerance."

Those who foresee utopia as growing out of the development of science and technology also assume some form of historical necessity, but their necessity drives man blindly on toward a technological utopia—his essential goodness or reasonableness allowing him to make the right choices. The assumptions and projections of the technological utopians are immensely more rosy and cheerful than are those of the technological projectors, the technological Jeremiahs; for most men would certainly prefer to be happy subjects of benign technocrats than miserable subjects of evil technocrats. If everything, including the expectations of technological utopia or technological Armageddon, is determined by the necessities of the grand sweep of historical evolution, then man should be happy that history has lulled him into such a pleasurable state of acquiescent optimism. Perhaps the next wave of history will silence the would-be tormentors by making these technological Jeremiahs the next victims of repressive tolerance.

That is the crucial point. If we have no freedom, no choice in decisions that help determine the course of history, then any criticism of past and present events is irrelevant, serving no purpose other than a vapid expression of emotion; if we have no freedom, then it is absurd to morally blame any of us for acquiescing in a bland, comfortable unfreedom or to morally exhort us to seek greater freedom; if we have no freedom either because of historical necessity or because of false consciousness induced by saturation propaganda, then we have no responsibility for the present or the future or for the tolerant oppression of would-be oppressors; if we have no freedom, then pity those who have not yet been adapted by natural means or by "therapeutic" control to the comfortable unfreedom. In fact, one of the earliest and most influential technological Jeremiahs, Oswald Spengler, made the most reasonable conclusion that could possibly be made from that tyrannical position. He acquiesced in the rising tide of materialistic technology and advised the vast number of readers of *The Decline of the West* in the 1920s to do the same, preferably by becoming technicians (engineers) and serving the tyrannical state. In the succeeding years many of his fellow Germans followed this "reasonable" course religiously.

Nothing could be more absurd than to deny the existence and efficacy of human freedom. To deny freedom is to make the very denial absurd.

In an age in which cultural relativism is common knowledge, we can hardly believe in any absolute freedom of man. The physical and social contexts in which we live—our existential situations—do appear to serve as constraints even on the things we normally think about and the way we think, much less the choices we make. But this is also an age in which we have become aware of how cunning we human beings are in managing our public social appearances—to the very purpose of being more free of those would-be social constraints. And this is an age in which more than a hundred years of positivistic and behavioristic rhetoric about predicting and, thence, controlling human behavior has been revealed as nothing more than a blind faith, with no substance. Even more, this is an age in which the proud certainties of positivistic science have fallen on uncertainty. This is an age in which the terrifying freedoms of solipsism and nihilism are realistic dangers.

While it is important for us to continue to analyze freedom and constraint, it is clear that we must assume the existence of freedom and the possibility of determining the historical development of technological society. Indeed, both the technological Jeremiahs and utopians seem to believe we have this freedom to determine the course of social development.

Whether science and technology will lead to freedom or to tyranny will depend primarily on the adequacy of our knowledge and on the choices of allegiance the technological experts make in the crucial years immediately ahead when we shall be creating the basic structure of the first world-wide technological society.

## The Rise of the Mass Knowledge-Based Society

The steady increase in application of the scientific-technological world view has increasingly made ours a knowledge-based society—that is, a society in which scientific-technological information is the legitimate basis of action and, at least for a growing part of the population, a goal in itself. This has produced a steady increase in knowledge occupations and in the percentage of our national product devoted to them,[14] which in turn increases the commitment to the scientific-technological world view.

The massive, complex information needed to make legitimate decisions in the knowledge society produces several important changes: it helps produce our omnipresent committee decision making system and our corporate production system;[15] it leads to their creation and increasing dependence on them for decision making, since no man alone can make effective use of the vast amounts of information available.

For our purposes here, the most important result of this development is an increasing dependency on experts for our decisions. Experts are defined as men having the knowledge we don't have (unless we're one of them) but whom we feel we need to make decisions legitimately (that is, scientifically) in a given area of action.

## The Standardization of Everyday Life and the Rise of Expertise

Our faith in and social dependence on scientific knowledge, and thus on experts, has actually far outstripped the real possibilities of science and technology. First of all, as Thomas Kuhn,[16] Boguslaw,[17] and others have emphasized, scientific—or even technological—reasoning cannot be directly applied to our everyday lives as we now live them. The kinds of situations we face and the decisions we make are almost always emergent —or existential. We make decisions in great uncertainty (we even value this, as seen in some forms of gambling). We know that very often we must make rapid decisions on the basis of dimly perceived ideas—intuition, if I dare say so. In these situations of everyday life, science, as normally defined by natural scientists, cannot be validly applied to decision making: that is, precise prediction is impossible; and, in fact, any formalized attempt to predict will be less successful than commonsense predictions. At the most, scientific and technological thought can provide us with partial information which we can then use to construct a reasonable decision.

But given the persistent, strong feeling of need for expert (scientific) decisions in an ever expanding realm of activities, there are two courses of action that have increasingly been taken in our society.

First, everyday life can in fact be standardized or controlled so that it becomes subject to presently available scientific analysis, prediction, decisions, and planning. This is what is happening as education becomes increasingly standardized so that given practices are seen to produce given results on standardized tests. As Galbraith has argued, this is what our massive public opinion control industry is supposed to do: advertising and public relations combined with public polling make expertise work. Expertise also works by using ex post facto validation: that is, it trains millions of students to believe that expertise is true, so they then "see" it at work in their practical lives.

This course of action, however, is difficult to follow in our democratic society. (It is easier in the communist, scientific-technological societies.) For this reason, scientific rhetoric is created to bridge the gap between felt need and scientific possibilities. The public demand leads the expertise entrepreneur[18] to create a commonsensically plausible set of technical terms, quantitative measures and methods of analysis, and formalized theories for any area in which the market demand is great, thereby offering high rewards in prestige, power, and money.

Expertise or scientism is distinguished from expert or scientific knowledge by its reliance on the rhetoric of science to convince its practitioners and their audiences rather than on results. Regardless of the intentions of the practitioners—which I for one generally consider half pure and half venal—the public felt need leads the public to accept the information presented in the symbolic forms of science as being science.

The control which the experts have over the relevant information and the felt ignorance of all nonexperts make the presentational devices extremely effective: what is made to look like science will normally, but not always, be accepted as science if there is also a great feeling of need for such expert help. Only bad dramaturgical devices will defeat the goals of the rhetoric.

Regardless of how or why a given discipline becomes socially categorized as a science, once it is so categorized the public makes even more demands on the expert practitioners of this new science, and the more pressing are the problems the science is supposed to solve. Thus there are greater incentives than ever, both rewards and punishments, especially the fear of being proved a fake, for presenting expert knowledge as more scientific than can be effectively demonstrated to be the case—that is, for constructing expertise.[19]

At this point especially, experts are under great pressure to present their conclusions as scientific knowledge. The expertist is now trapped by the social definition of himself that he has helped to create. Whereas the experts had been tentatively discussing the errors in their data and theory, they now come increasingly to treat their data and theory as if it were scientific knowledge (especially in public)—and soon the distinction is lost. They move from being simply experts to being expertists.

One good example of this loss of distinction is found in the way the social scientists commonly handle official statistics on crime, suicide, and so on. At first they only discussed the problems, because they realized how very unreliable the statistics were. But they generally concluded that "we must get on with the task, so we must make use of the only quantitative data available to us." A scientist at this point would concentrate on getting highly reliable information and only then going on. But the expert feels the public demand to be overwhelming—it is the background rule which is covertly determining his strategy. The official statistics become as-if knowledge. Soon there is no more question. This conspiratorial silence of experts can go on for decades before the issue is reopened. Even then, the conspiracy of fearful experts can lead to oblivion for a critical work,[20] unless it shows a new way to maintain the front of the "scientific expert."

The growing transformation of the social scientists (and other groups taken by the public to be "experts" on man and society) into surveyors, methodologists, systems analysts, mathematical modelists, and computer simulators could have dire consequences in propagating social science expertise. All of these quasi-mathematical techniques are fundamentally expertist even when their creators and users have the purest intentions. None of them add anything to the social data. Indeed, they appear to create the data in their own image, in accord with the presuppositions of the mathematical ideas involved, as Aaron Cicourel has argued so excellently.[21] These techniques also pose a great danger because they presuppose certain kinds of answers to any social problem to which they are applied. It is this which creates the great expertise power of systems.

And so it is that a designer of systems, who has the *de facto* prerogative to specify the range of phenomena that his system will distinguish, clearly is in possession of enormous degrees of power (depending, of course, upon the nature of the system being designed). It is by no means necessary that this power be formalized through the allocation of specific authority to wield nightsticks or guns.

The strength of high-speed computers lies precisely in their capacity to process binary choice data rapidly. But to process these data, the world of reality must at some point in time be reduced to binary form. This occurs initially through operational specifications handed to a computer programmer. These specifications serve as the basis for more detailed reductions to binary choices. The range of possibilities is ultimately set by the circuitry of the computer, which places finite limits on alternatives for data storage and processing. The structure of the language used to communicate with the computer places additional restrictions on the range of alternatives. The programmer himself, through the specific sets of data he uses in his solution to a programming problem and the specific techniques he uses for his solution, places a final set of restrictions on action alternatives available within a computer-based system.

It is in this sense that computer programmers, the designers of computer equipment, and the developers of computer languages possess power. To the extent that decisions made by each of these participants in the design process serve to reduce, limit, or totally eliminate action alternatives, they are applying force and wielding power in the precise sociological meaning of these terms.[22]

## The Government Bureaus and the Social and Behavioral Sciences

It is important to note that the public demand for expertise on man and his society has been placed upon government officials who in turn provide the incentives for the experts on man. They make the incentive structure more effective and provide the funds and the goals. By licensing certain of the experts they provide the greatest possible incentives to expertise. The license not only makes the expert responsible for possible mistakes, but socially certifies his expertness, thereby making him more accountable for rendering scientific help.

Most of the "sciences" of man and society have been more involved with the government bureau complex from their beginnings than sociologists have realized. Sociology, for example, was largely created by the moral statisticians, public hygienists, medical statisticians, and others closely bound up with government bureaucracies long before Durkheim and others undertook the entrepreneurial task of establishing sociology as a separate scientific profession.[23]

The degrees of influence of the public demand on expert groups have varied greatly. But no group has been more affected by the public demand for expert knowledge than has psychiatry. Because they were medical doctors, they were socially categorized as scientists and were licensed and bound up with official action very early in their history. At the same time, because of the great fears associated with insanity, the public demand placed on them for scientific solutions has been immense. Even though the evidence indicates a lack of predictability, and cure rates are no better than by spontaneous remission, the psychiatrists have continually assumed the social category of scientists: they have met the intense demands by developing a high degree of expertise.

## The Expertists' Destruction of Free Will
## and Individual Responsibility

Public demand and expertise entrepreneurs have also helped produce another fundamental change in our society: they have helped destroy the social belief in individual freedom and individual responsibility.[24]

Throughout most of his history, Western man has firmly believed in some form of individual freedom (free will) and individual responsibility. In the last hundred years this belief has changed drastically. Today man is often seen as the product of his physical, genetic, and social situation.

The reasons for this change are many. Certainly man's dependence on a mass society over which he has little control has been one cause. In the nineteenth century, experts on man and society became convinced that the *order* in man's actions proves the lack of free will. For example, de Guerry, Quetelet, Wagner, and Durkheim all felt forced toward a deterministic position by the order in official statistics on suicide, crime, and so on, since they believed free will would produce disordered results. (Actually, traditional free will theory sees man as having free will within the limits set by God through the creation of an ordered moral universe and an ordered conscience. Free choices based on an ordered conscience and made in an ordered universe would produce ordered outcomes of action.)[25] They then produced as-if knowledge to legitimatize this belief. Today this rejection of free will is a background assumption of almost all social science education.

The destruction of belief in free will has increasingly destroyed the belief in individual responsibility. This externalistic conception of man has grown rapidly.[26] If man's actions are caused by his external situations, and by what is inside him producing choices, then it is the situation we must study and change if we want changes in his actions.

## The Rise of Expert Administrative Justice
## and Government

The combination of public belief in expert knowledge of man and society, an increasing belief in the external (or sociologistic)[27] causation of action, and the increasing public demand for expert solutions to socially defined social problems is rapidly producing other, more specific changes in the social meanings of man and society.

Among the more important changes, I believe, are those taking place in the social meanings of justice and in our practices in the realms of criminal legislation, adjudication, and corrections. One important recent example is found in *The President's Crime Commission Report* and the succeeding criminal legislation. There is no mention in the general report of individual responsibility,[28] in spite of the fact that the assumption of individual responsibility has always been considered a moral and scientific necessity of the deterrence system which the Report does accept.

It need hardly be pointed out that the Report urges a vast and rapid increase in expert knowledge about crime, in the utilization of such knowledge, and in government funds for the production and utilization of this knowledge. In view of the analysis thus far, we can predict that the well-funded research will produce "expert knowledge" and that further research will be funded and provided when this first batch proves ineffective in stopping crime, and so on.[29]

The experts are rapidly becoming the primary factors in determining the directions our system of justice will take in other ways as well. In order to compete with the influence of experts in psychiatry and social science, the police have created the "expert knowledge" of police science, which is just one example of the rush to expertise and to its related professionalise in a society in which expert knowledge is the ultimate determinant of power and symbol of prestige.[30] As their expertise grows, the police will have increasing influence in determining the laws and methods of enforcement.

Administrative justice, or justice administered by those believed to have expert knowledge of crimes and criminals, has been displacing our traditional form of justice for a long time. Psychiatric justice has been growing even more rapidly. Szasz, Goffman, Scheff, Schwartz, and many others have analyzed the details of psychiatric justice, the power that psychiatrists actually administer in decisions regarding guilt, imprisonment, and internment. In a few states addicts can now be psychiatrically committed for indeterminate periods—a truly radical innovation in our society. Now the rapidly growing, massively funded community psychiatry movement is reaching out beyond the legally committed; the expert knowledge of psychiatrists is now presumed to be so great that they can spot potential insanity and put an end to it before it spreads.[31]

The social science experts and expertists have now trained teachers and business executives, who are themselves becoming professional experts in education and business administration and in turn supporting the rapid rise of new expert groups—the counselors, personnel experts, social workers, scientific consulting firms, school psychologists, church sensitivity trainers, and so on.

These spin-off "expert" groups are rapidly becoming the spearhead of expertise-induced change in our society. Being in direct contact and increasingly affiliated with the academic experts, they look increasingly like experts to the necessarily ignorant public. Being in fields in which academic and other controls are still minimal, they attract expertise entrepreneurs. Being in direct contact with the public, they experience more the pressures of public demands for expert solutions.

These intermediary groups have created rationales for their being (meeting the needs for expert knowledge); adopted scientific vocabularies, methods, and theories to their purposes; begun to achieve professional (monopolistic) control of jobs in education and industry; and are becoming major interpreters of expert knowledge for the public. They have become the primary means by which business and government make use of the prestige of expert knowledge.[32]

Scientific consulting firms have already become especially important in this respect. Key members of these groups hold academic degrees and have often taught in the academic world. Yet they are completely dependent on contracts for their livelihood and, except in economics, these contracts are generally government financed. This is an ideal way for men in business and politics to buy the aura of expert knowledge for their purposes: they get the answers they want and they get them sanctified. The consulting firm leaders know or learn how to compromise to get the right answers while using the "valid scientific methods." We can predict a dramatic increase in intermediary expertise groups. They will be important agents of change, helping to control public responses and, thereby, helping the social planning of men of business and government to succeed. In fact, as I have previously argued in "The Relevance of Sociology," [33] the very nature of science, as socially defined, makes it difficult for the experts to control these intermediary expertise groups. Both the natural and social sciences have been increasingly defined in all societies as value-free and nonpolitical. Don Price has described this political neutralization of the social scientists.

> This suggests that the social sciences may now be following the earlier examples of the physical and the biological sciences not merely in trying to achieve greater precision and reliability in their methods, but

also in understanding that such precision is purchased by an abstraction, and an exclusion of concern for purposes and values, that make it impossible to deal simultaneously with all the aspects of any concrete problem. The maturity of a science may be measured not only by its power, but by its discrimination in knowing the limits of its power. And if this is so, the layman does not need to worry lest the social sciences, as they become more scientific, will be more likely to usurp political authority. On the contrary, they will stop short of trying to solve completely our major political problems not because they are unlike the natural sciences, but to the extent that they are like them. And the more they get to be like them, the more they will be of specific service to the policy maker, and the less they will pretend that their methods can measure all relevant aspects of any concrete problem and supply its final answer.[34]

What he has failed to see is that this political neutralization has not only the effect of allowing business and government to use the aura of science for their own purposes through the consulting relationship, but that it also allows them to make even more free use—even patently distorted use— of this aura to control the public by buying the expertise they need from the intermediary expertise groups.

## Controlling Expertise in the Technological Society

By helping to destroy the social belief in individual freedom and individual responsibility and by creating the forms of social science expertise, the social scientists have, quite inadvertently, helped create a situation in which technological tyranny becomes far more possible. Indeed, they have helped create both the means of such tyrannical controls, through the use of social (or behavioral) science expertise, and the social justification for such controls, since human beings without freedom not only can but should be controlled and manipulated by the experts "for their own good." They have even helped create an alienative sense of individual powerlessness that furthers acquiescence, the very kind of alienative force many of these same social scientists have most decried in modern society.

The fundamental theoretical issues involved in these considerations of individual freedom and individual power can only be resolved honestly and effectively by continual reinvestigation of the problems involved. Social scientists must recognize that in a technological society working under the aegis of science gives them a special responsibility for making such re-investigations of positions that have such radical implications for society. Today these fundamental problems are, in fact, being thoroughly reexamined by the growing number of existential thinkers who are challenging the absolutist assumptions underlying the traditional structural theories of man and society. By showing that the structural-functional theories falsely concluded that man has no freedom because they began with certain absolutist presuppositions and falsely accepted the official statistics of absolutist official organizations as true representations of social reality, these existential social thinkers are showing that man's social actions are free—necessarily free because no predetermined rules can meet the necessary uncertainties of everyday life—as well as constrained by the situations he faces.[35]

But there are many more apparent and immediate ways that the social scientists should control expertise, Most obviously, the social sciences must become more basically committed to studying the problems of greatest relevance to our society,[36] especially the problems of freedom and tyranny in a technological society. They, like the natural scientists, must become far more concerned with the social meanings of their own scientific activities and their effect on society: they must especially be concerned with studying the ways in which their own expert knowledge is used by expertise entrepreneurs to manipulate society.

At present, the greatest contribution social scientists can make to preserving and increasing individual freedom in the technological society seems to be that of serving as social ombudsmen: that is, they can perform the unique and crucial function of ferreting out the largely private (and privileged) information about the workings of official and (supposedly) expert groups which have so much power in a technological society. They can bring forcefully to public attention the likely effects of such activities and suggest the most realistic alternatives of public action. Obtaining and using such information does necessitate judicious personal involvement in the practical activities in order to observe the private activities, but it seems unlikely that this involvement will soon have as great an influence as the "revealing" information.[37]

## General Conclusions

Our society is increasingly based on expert, scientific knowledge. This knowledge and the technological society of which it is the foundation have already produced wondrous results, and there is realistic hope that we have seen only the barest beginning.

It is essential that we recognize the extraordinary scope and pervasiveness of the scientific revolution now taking place in the world. The knowledge we are gaining is already being used and will increasingly be employed to reorder the world in which we live. In particular, it provides us with the possibility of developing many kinds of machinery to take the place of human labor and skills. We are moving beyond the "industrial" revolution, which was based on the combination of the power of the machine with the skill of the human being. We have now entered a new revolutionary era in which the power of the machine is combined with the skill of the machine to form a productive system of, in effect, unlimited capacity.[38]

But the use of technology also poses fundamental threats to our society, and, especially over the long run, to our individual freedoms. Short-run dangers are even more apparent. Though cybernation and automation have not yet produced the mass unemployment that some prophesied in the 1950s, there is already a considerable stagnant, technologically induced unemployment among the poorly educated and, as a consequence, we face the danger of permanent poverty.[39] To eliminate and prevent such problems, we will have to radically revise some of our fundamental ideas about social policy and government, especially about the relations between work and income. We will, for example, have to redefine education as work and pay individuals to get it just as we pay them to work today; we will have to define (broadly) socially rewarding forms of leisure that are paid for; and we will have to redefine all forms of social welfare as social investments with real payoffs for all of us. But, most importantly, we will have to eliminate the social definitions of work and status, the market virtues of a society dominated by scarcity, as the primary goals of adult life if we are to achieve the renaissance of spirit, the liberation, made possible by science and technology. (See Robert Theobald's "Can We Survive Abundance?" in this volume, pp. 256–269.)

If we can make these basic changes, and I believe we are slowly and painfully beginning to do so, then we can hope to achieve a society in which individuals are freer to pursue their own self-fulfillment, as well as lesser goals, than today's self-styled radicals have dared to dream. (See Theobald, p. 267.)

But such hopes can be realized only if we can choose collectively to act wisely. If we refuse to recognize the challenges or to accept the necessary social changes, then we could well precipitate a self-reinforcing cycle of technologically induced poverty, rebellion, and political reaction which could in turn produce technological tyranny for us all.

In trying to avoid these dangers, further dangers arise. Indeed, on the surface of it, it would appear that I am proposing a homeopathic remedy for our ills: more of science and technology to control the dangers of science and technology. This is precisely what I am proposing, but with the idea that this new kind of scientific-technological knowledge will serve as a check against the dangers of the earlier kind. I believe this is an example of the process Gerald Holton has analyzed so well.

> The dire state of affairs is supposed to be remedied by an injection of a larger scientific and technological component into our culture, yet the recent advances in science and technology are themselves identified as the forces responsible for the state of affairs in the first place. These are the agencies that have been contributing to the enormous increase in the rate of innovation and social change, and that have helped to perfect new weapons that make the possibility of instantaneous destruction of Western civilization a real and continued threat. Thus, it would seem that we are asked to seek safety by delivering ourselves more fully to the very forces that appear to be responsible for the crisis.
>
> While we may intuitively feel that the choice is unpleasant, it is perhaps not necessarily so paradoxical as it seems. A number of social or physical systems offer models in which stability when disrupted by the introduction of a new factor, can be re-established at some level only by increasing the role of the new factor even further. Examples that come readily to mind are the introduction of literacy or industrialization or political emancipation into a traditional primitive society.[40]

But we must also be on guard against the dangers of social science expertise created by this addition. The technological society accords the highest prestige and rewards for expert knowledge, and it has made us all socially ignorant, largely incapable of knowing directly the truth of claims to expert knowledge. This situation, combined with our entrepreneurial ingenuity, has produced a dawning Age of Expertise, an age in which the rhetoric of science is used to bridge the gap between the possibilities of expert knowledge and the demands of necessarily ignorant publics.

When combined with the destruction of social belief in free will and individual responsibility, expert control of public needs becomes possible and legitimized. When expertise is added to go beyond the actual possibilities of expert knowledge, when the symbolic forms of science can readily be bought through the intermediary groups, the traditional wielders of power—businessmen and government officials—have an important new means of managing public responses and, thereby, making their own plans for a technological society work.

There will, of course, be countervailing forces, and these will grow. The ignorant public will become more distrustful and will discount expert knowledge as they do advertising. Demands for proof by results will increase. The various types of closely related experts will aid these developments by criticizing each other's claims. The academics may make it harder for the intermediaries. They may even become more moderate in their own use of the rhetoric of science—in their use of the as-if knowledge of most official statistics, in their extravagant claims to precision, and in their use of the metaphorical jargon of mathematics and computers. The social scientists may even question the wisdom of abrogating something so basic to our society as individual causation and responsibility, especially in view of the meager evidence. By looking beyond their rhetoric, by seeing how very little they can in fact predict (beyond the limits of common sense), and by seeing how variable and irrational everyday life is, they may become less assertive. The social scientists can provide a crucial check on such expertise and expertise powers by making them and the social sciences in general a focal point of concern for their studies and analyses. Such built-in self-criticism can help prevent the realization of the grave dangers of expert and expertise manipulation, but only if it is combined with the ancient democratic virtue—eternal vigilance of an educated public.

Still, the combination of forces supporting the growth of technological tyranny is very powerful. Manipulation through propaganda, especially when vastly augmented by the power of experts and expertists, could stay several jumps ahead of the countervailing forces. It is possible that such manipulation will prove benign, even if necessarily excluding the greatest personal freedoms of self-knowledge and self-control. While I believe all present signs point in the opposite direction, I make no claims to scientific precision for such an analysis. Any such analysis can at best cast only a dim light on the labyrinthian complexities and ineluctable uncertainties facing us. We still must act largely in darkness, do our best, and hope.

# NOTES

1. Samuelsson has challenged both the validity of and the conclusions from these associations. See Kurt Samuelsson, *Religion and Economic Action* (New York: Harper, 1964).
2. Max Weber, *The Protestant Ethic and the Spirit of Capitalism*, Talcott Parsons (tr.) (New York: Scribner's, 1954).
3. Robert K. Merton, "Science, Technology, and Society in Seventeenth Century England," *Osiris*, IV (1938), pt. 2.

4. See Samuelsson, *op. cit.;* and Lewis S. Feuer, *The Scientific Intellectual* (New York: Basic Books, 1963).

5. Richard Foster Jones, *Ancients and Moderns* (Los Angeles: University of California Press, 1965), p. xi.
   John Wilkinson (tr.), "Translator's Introduction," in Jacques Ellul, *The Technological Society* (New York: Random House, 1964), pp. xi–xii.

6. As an excellent example of this see Max Born as quoted in Gerald Holton (ed.), *Science and Culture* (Boston: Beacon Press, 1965), p. xxiii.

7. Don K. Price, "The Established Dissenters," in Holton, *op. cit.*, p. 139. See Jack D. Douglas, "The Rhetoric of Science and The Origins of Statistical Social Thought," in E. A. Tiryakian (ed.), *The Phenomena of Sociology* (New York: Appleton-Century-Crofts, 1969).

8. On the absolutism of science, see Jack D. Douglas, "The Impact of the Social Sciences," in Jack D. Douglas (ed.), *The Impact of Sociology* (New York: Appleton-Century-Crofts, 1970).

9. See Douglas, "The Rhetoric of Science," *op. cit.*

10. Galbraith's definition of technology is probably the most widely used: "Technology means the systematic application of scientific or other organized knowledge to practical tasks." (*The New Industrial State* [Boston: Houghton Mifflin, 1967], p. 12.)

11. Galbraith, *op. cit.*, pp. 6–7.

12. Galbraith, *op. cit.*, pp. 341–342.

13. See Herbert Marcuse, "Repressive Tolerance," in R. P. Wolff *et al.*, *A Critique of Pure Tolerance* (Boston: Beacon Press, 1965).

14. F. Machlup, *The Production and Distribution of Knowledge in the United States* (Princeton, N.J.: Princeton University Press, 1962).

15. See Galbraith on committees, *op. cit.*, especially pp. 11–35.

16. See Thomas Kuhn, *The Structure of Scientific Revolutions* (Chicago: University of Chicago Press, 1962).

17. See Robert Boguslaw, *The New Utopians* (Englewood Cliffs, N.J.: Prentice-Hall, 1965).

18. The expertise entrepreneurs are of many types, ranging from idealists seeking to solve all man's problems to the self-seeking charlatans who create and manage illusions but do not submit to them.

19. The revelations of behind the scenes practices in the Apollo projects and the studies of industrial engineering *expertise* make it apparent that expertise is very generally found in natural science and engineering disciplines. However, there are almost certainly important differences in degrees of expertise.

20. The fine work of Sophia Robison showing the great biases in official statistics on delinquency was published in 1936. It has recently been rediscovered.

21. See Aaron Cicourel, *Method and Measurement in Sociology* (New York: Free Press, 1964).

22. See Boguslaw, *op. cit.*

23. See Douglas, "The Rhetoric of Science," in Tiryakian, *op. cit.*

24. One of the only good discussions of this matter can be found in David Matza's *Delinquency and Drift* (New York: Wiley, 1964). I disagree with his idea that the assumption is waning among the social scientists. It has simply become a background assumption, talked about only for purposes of instruction.

25. Calvin, Augustine, and most other great theologians went further by eliminating all *uncontrolled* choice. As Augustine argued, after the fall man had only relative freedom to choose between evils (*libertad*), not absolute freedom (*libertas*). See *Enchiridion*. But they did not destroy the basis for belief in free will and, thence, individual responsibility.

26. For a discussion of the "externalized conception" of man see Jack D. Douglas, *The Social Meanings of Suicide* (Princeton, N.J.: Princeton University Press, 1967), pt. IV.

27. I believe that external, social factors are increasingly seen by the general public as the primary causes of action. The biological, genetic explanations became disfavored in the thirties and forties in some good part because the Nazis arrived at some obvious, "reasonable" conclusions from them which we disliked. The genetic-psychology (childhood) theories have now largely run their course. The sociologistic and economistic theories are coming into increasing favor: welfare workers, government officials, and so on, are turning increasingly to sociologists, economists, anthropologists, and others for expert knowledge. I believe these cycles in fads are largely the result of exposing the expert knowledge as rhetoric: that is, as the experts are more in public view and get a chance to show how well they can handle affairs, their "expert knowledge" is increasingly seen as so much rhetoric. They don't solve the problems. So another group of experts sharing the same general orientation is favored and the process is repeated. In the long run I believe the so-called behavioral scientists may well win out over all the rest because they combine all the special perspectives of the general orientation (thereby spreading the risk of exposure) and because they use a "hot rhetoric." The term "behavioral science" is already a hot word in publishing and academic administration. In a few decades these expertise entrepreneurs may dominate the older disciplines in global departments.

28. For a discussion of this see Jack D. Douglas, "The Relevance of Sociology," in Jack D. Douglas, *The Relevance of Sociology* (New York: Appleton-Century-Crofts, 1970).

29. See Jack D. Douglas, "Crime and Justice in American Society," in Jack D. Douglas, *Crime and Justice in America* (New York: Bobbs-Merrill, 1970).

30. All groups who want to compete for power and prestige must become *professional experts*. Sanitation workers become sanitary engineers and librarians become library scientists. Thus academic degrees, as symbols of expert knowledge, have become the basic requirement for employment, regardless of what knowledge the job really requires.

If the academic world maintains control of real expert knowledge and of the symbols of expert knowledge, it will become the major center of potential power in our society. How much of this potential power will be realized is hard to say. But surely business and government organizations will compete to control the expert knowledge and symbols as they see their power threatened. (General Motors University and IBM Tech are likely to become increasingly more important).

31. See L. Schatzman and A. Strauss, "A Sociology of Psychiatry," and Ronald Leifer, "Community Psychiatry and Social Power," in *Social Problems,* 14 (1966), 3–15, 16–23.

32. This whole process has been analyzed in Douglas, "The Relevance of Sociology," *op. cit.*

33. *Ibid.*

34. Price, "The Established Dissenters," *op. cit.*, p. 133.

35. See Jack D. Douglas (ed.), *Existential Sociology* (New York: Appleton-Century-Crofts, 1972).

36. See Douglas, "The Relevance of Sociology," *op. cit.*

37. See Douglas, "The Relevance of Sociology," *op. cit.*

38. Robert Theobald, *Free Men and Free Markets* (New York: Potter, 1963), p. 17.

39. See Ben B. Seligman, *Permanent Poverty* (New York: Quadrangle, 1968).

40. Holton, *op. cit.*, p. x.

PART II

## The Secret Tyranny in

## the Technological Society

# The New Forms of Control

## HERBERT MARCUSE

No critic of modern society has been more outspoken about the dangers of technology and science to our basic human rights than Herbert Marcuse. No critic of science and technology has been more influential than Marcuse, and probably no work has been more widely read and more influential in the growing debate over science and technology than Marcuse's book *One-Dimensional Man,* from which this selection is taken.

Marcuse's basic argument is that individual freedoms are being rapidly suppressed in all areas of our life because of the demands of technological-industrial production. Moreover, he argues that this technological tyranny has become almost invisible to most members of our industrial civilization because the propaganda of the mass media is so tremendously successful in hiding this tyranny from us and in making us believe that we are actually free men.

*Reprinted from Herbert Marcuse,* One-Dimensional Man, *by permission of the Beacon Press and Routledge & Kegan Paul, Ltd. Copyright © 1964 by Herbert Marcuse.*

Marcuse is extremely pessimistic about the possibilities of changing this course of development. He argues that, paradoxical as it may seem, the very success of our industrial civilization makes both freedom and effective opposition to tyranny increasingly impossible.

In our society today, technological controls and the growing technological tyranny are presented as the embodiment of reason, and therefore all opposition is seen as irrational and unrealistic. This is especially true, as we have seen in Chapter 1, when technological control is presented in the guise of expert knowledge.

Marcuse argues that the radical empiricism of modern scientific thought, which he believes has replaced all other criteria of knowledge, defines all forms of knowing in such a way that one cannot be critical of the status quo. The basic forms of knowledge make it irrational and absurd to think in terms of anything other than what already exists. This system of thought and its social system absorb all criticisms and make all opposition into a support for itself. This is basically what he means by a one-dimensional society or a one-dimensional man.


A comfortable, smooth, reasonable, democratic unfreedom prevails in advanced industrial civilization, a token of technical progress. Indeed, what could be more rational than the suppression of individuality in the mechanization of socially necessary but painful performances; the concentration of individual enterprises in more effective, more productive corporations; the regulation of free competition among unequally equipped economic subjects; the curtailment of prerogatives and national sovereignties which impede the international organization of resources. That this technological order also involves a political and intellectual coordination may be a regrettable and yet promising development.

The rights and liberties which were such vital factors in the origins and earlier stages of industrial society yield to a higher stage of this society: they are losing their traditional rationale and content. Freedom of thought, speech, and conscience were—just as free enterprise, which they served to promote and protect—essentially *critical* ideas, designed to replace an obsolescent material and intellectual culture by a more productive and rational one. Once institutionalized, these rights and liberties shared the fate of the society of which they had become an integral part. The achievement cancels the premises.

To the degree to which freedom from want, the concrete substance of all freedom, is becoming a real possibility, the liberties which pertain to a state of lower productivity are losing their former content. Independence of thought, autonomy, and the right to political opposition are being deprived of their basic critical function in a society which seems increasingly capable of satisfying the needs of the individuals through the way in which it is organized. Such a society may justly demand acceptance of its principles and institutions, and reduce the opposition to the discussion and promotion of alternative policies *within* the status quo. In this respect, it seems to make little difference whether the increasing satisfaction of needs is accomplished by an authoritarian or a non-authoritarian system. Under the conditions of a rising standard of living, non-conformity with the system itself appears to be socially useless, and the more so when it entails tangible economic and political disadvantages and threatens the smooth operation of the whole. Indeed, at least in so far as the necessities of life are involved, there seems to be no reason why the production and distribution of goods and services should proceed through the competitive concurrence of individual liberties.

Freedom of enterprise was from the beginning not altogether a blessing. As the liberty to work or to starve, it spelled toil, insecurity, and fear for the vast majority of the population. If the individual were no longer compelled to prove himself on the market, as a free economic subject, the disappearance of this kind of freedom would be one of the greatest achievements of civilization. The technological processes of mechanization and standardization might release individual energy into a yet uncharted realm of freedom beyond necessity. The very structure of human existence would be altered; the individual would be liberated from the work world's imposing upon him alien needs and alien possibilities. The individual would be free to exert autonomy over a life that would be his own. If the productive apparatus could be organized and directed toward the satisfaction of the vital needs, its control might well be centralized; such control would not prevent individual autonomy, but render it possible.

This is a goal within the capabilities of advanced industrial civilization, the "end" of technological rationality. In actual fact, however, the contrary trend operates: the apparatus imposes its economic and political requirements for defense and expansion on labor time and free time, on the material and intellectual culture. By virtue of the way it has organized its technological base, contemporary industrial society tends to be totalitarian. For "totalitarian" is not only a terroristic political coordination of society, but also a nonterroristic economic-technical coordination which operates through the manipulation of needs by vested interests. It thus precludes the emergence of an effective opposition against the whole. Not only a specific form of government or party rule makes for totalitarianism, but also a specific system of production and distribution which may well be compatible with a "pluralism" of parties, newspapers, "countervailing powers," etc.[1]

Today political power asserts itself through its power over the machine process and over the technical organization of the apparatus. The government of advanced and advancing industrial societies can maintain and secure itself only when it succeeds in mobilizing, organizing, and exploiting the technical, scientific, and mechanical productivity available to industrial civilization. And this productivity mobilizes society as a whole, above and beyond any particular individual or group interests. The brute fact that the machine's physical (only physical?) power surpasses that of the individual, and of any particular group of individuals, makes the machine the most effective political instrument in any society whose basic organization is that of the machine process. But the political trend may be reversed; essentially the power of the machine is only the stored-up and projected power of man. To the extent to which the work world is conceived of as a machine and mechanized accordingly, it becomes the *potential* basis of a new freedom for man.

Contemporary industrial civilization demonstrates that it has reached the stage at which "the free society" can no longer be adequately defined in the traditional terms of economic, political, and intellectual liberties, not because these liberties have become insignificant, but because they are too significant to be confined within the traditional forms. New modes of realization are needed, corresponding to the new capabilities of society.

Such new modes can be indicated only in negative terms because they would amount to the negation of the prevailing modes. Thus economic freedom would mean freedom *from* the economy—from being controlled by economic forces and relationships; freedom from the daily struggle for existence, from earning a living. Political freedom would mean liberation of the individuals *from* politics over which they have no effective control. Similarly, intellectual freedom would mean the restoration of individual thought now absorbed by mass communication and indoctrination, abolition of "public opinion" together with its makers. The unrealistic sound of these propositions is indicative, not of their utopian character, but of the strength of the forces which prevent their realization. The most effective and enduring form of warfare against liberation is the implanting of material and intellectual needs that perpetuate obsolete forms of the struggle for existence.

The intensity, the satisfaction and even the character of human needs, beyond the biological level, have always been preconditioned. Whether or not the possibility of doing or leaving, enjoying or destroying, possessing or rejecting something is seized as a *need* depends on whether or not it can be seen as desirable and necessary for the prevailing societal institutions and interests. In this sense, human needs are historical needs and, to the extent to which the society demands the repressive development of the individual, his needs themselves and their claim for satisfaction are subject to overriding critical standards.

We may distinguish both true and false needs. "False" are those which are superimposed upon the individual by particular social interests in his repression: the needs which perpetuate toil, aggressiveness, misery, and injustice. Their satisfaction might be most gratifying to the individual, but this happiness is not a condition which has to be maintained and protected if it serves to arrest the development of the ability (his own and others) to recognize the disease of the whole and grasp the chances of curing the disease. The result then is euphorian unhappiness. Most of the prevailing needs to relax, to have fun, to behave and consume in accordance with the advertisements, to love and hate what others love and hate, belong to this category of false needs.

Such needs have a societal content and function which are determined by external powers over which the individual has no control; the development and satisfaction of these needs is heteronomous. No matter how much such needs may have become the individual's own, reproduced and fortified by the conditions of his existence; no matter how much he identifies himself with them and finds himself in their satisfaction, they continue to be what they were from the beginning—products of a society whose dominant interest demands repression.

The prevalence of repressive needs is an accomplished fact, accepted in ignorance and defeat, but a fact that must be undone in the interest of the happy individual as well as all those whose misery is the price of his satisfaction. The only needs that have an unqualified claim for satisfaction are the vital ones—nourishment, clothing, lodging at the attainable level of culture. The satisfaction of these needs is the prerequisite for the realization of *all* needs, of the unsublimated as well as the sublimated ones.

For any consciousness and conscience, for any experience which does not accept the prevailing societal interest as the supreme law of thought and behavior, the established universe of needs and satisfactions is a fact to be questioned—questioned in terms of truth and falsehood. These terms are historical throughout, and their objectivity is historical. The judgment of needs and their satisfaction, under the given conditions, involves standards of *priority*—standards which refer to the optimal development of the individual, of all individuals, under the optimal utilization of the material and intellectual resources available to man. The resources are calculable. "Truth" and "falsehood" of needs designate objective conditions to the extent to which the universal satisfaction of vital needs and, beyond it, the progressive alleviation of toil and poverty, are universally valid standards. But as historical standards, they do not only vary according to area and stage of development, they also can be defined only in (greater or lesser) *contradiction* to the prevailing ones. What tribunal can possibly claim the authority of decision?

In the last analysis, the question of what are true and false needs must be answered by the individuals themselves, but only in the last analysis; that is, if and when they are free to give their own answer. As long as they are kept incapable of being autonomous, as long as they are indoctrinated and manipulated (down to their very instincts), their answer to this question cannot be taken as their own. By the same token, however, no tribunal can justly arrogate to itself the right to decide which needs should be developed and satisfied. Any such tribunal is reprehensible, although our revulsion does not do away with the question: how can the people who have been the object of effective and productive domination by themselves create the conditions of freedom? [2]

The more rational, productive, technical, and total the repressive administration of society becomes, the more unimaginable the means and ways by which the administered individuals might break their servitude and seize their own liberation. To be sure, to impose Reason upon an entire society is a paradoxical and scandalous idea—although one might dispute the righteousness of a society which ridicules this idea while making its own population into objects of total administration. All liberation depends on the consciousness of servitude, and the emergence of this consciousness is always hampered by the predominance of needs and satisfactions which, to a great extent, have become the individual's own. The process always replaces one system of preconditioning by another; the optimal goal is the replacement of false needs by true ones, the abandonment of repressive satisfaction.

The distinguishing feature of advanced industrial society is its effective suffocation of those needs which demand liberation—liberation also from that which is tolerable and rewarding and comfortable—while it sustains and absolves the destructive power and repressive function of the affluent society. Here, the social controls exact the overwhelming need for the production and consumption of waste; the need for stupefying work where it is no longer a real necessity; the need for modes of relaxation which soothe and prolong this stupefaction; the need for maintaining such deceptive liberties as free competition at administered prices, a free press which censors itself, free choice between brands and gadgets.

Under the rule of a repressive whole, liberty can be made into a powerful instrument of domination. The range of choice open to the individual is not the decisive factor in determining the degree of human freedom, but *what* can be chosen and what *is* chosen by the individual. The criterion for free choice can never be an absolute one, but neither is it entirely relative. Free election of masters does not abolish the masters or the slaves. Free choice among a wide variety of goods and services does not signify freedom if these goods and services sustain social controls over a life of toil and fear—that is, if they sustain alienation. And the spontaneous reproduction of superimposed needs by the individual does not establish autonomy; it only testifies to the efficacy of the controls.

Our insistence on the depth and efficacy of these controls is open to the objection that we overrate greatly the indoctrinating power of the "media," and that by themselves the people would feel and satisfy the needs which are now imposed upon them. The objection misses the point. The preconditioning does not start with the mass production of radio and television and with the centralization of their control. The people enter this stage as preconditioned receptacles of long standing; the decisive difference is in the flattening out of the contrast (or conflict) between the given and the possible, between the satisfied and the unsatisfied needs. Here, the so-called equalization of class distinctions reveals its ideological function. If the worker and his boss enjoy the same television program and visit the same resort places, if the typist is as attractively made up as the daughter of her employer, if the Negro owns a Cadillac, if they all read the same newspaper, then this assimilation indicates not the disappearance of classes, but the extent to which the needs and satisfactions that serve the preservation of the Establishment are shared by the underlying population.

Indeed, in the most highly developed areas of contemporary society, the transplantation of social into individual needs is so effective that the difference between them seems to be purely theoretical. Can one really distinguish between the mass media as instruments of information and entertainment, and as agents of manipulation and indoctrination? Between the automobile as nuisance and as convenience? Between the horrors and the comforts of functional architecture? Between the work for national defense and the work for corporate gain? Between the private pleasure and the commercial and political utility involved in increasing the birth rate?

We are again confronted with one of the most vexing aspects of advanced industrial civilization: the rational character of its irrationality. Its productivity and efficiency, its capacity to increase and spread comforts, to turn waste into need, and destruction into construction, the extent to which this civilization transforms the object world into an extension of man's mind and body makes the very notion of alienation questionable. The people recognize themselves in their commodities; they find their soul in their automobile, hi-fi set, split-level home, kitchen equipment. The very mechanism which ties the individual to his society has changed, and social control is anchored in the new needs which it has produced.

The prevailing forms of social control are technological in a new sense. To be sure, the technical structure and efficacy of the productive and destructive apparatus has been a major instrumentality for subjecting the population to the established social division of labor throughout the modern period. Moreover, such integration has always been accompanied by more obvious forms of compulsion: loss of livelihood, the administration of justice, the police, the armed forces. It still is. But in the contemporary period, the technological controls appear to be the very embodiment of Reason for the benefit of all social groups and interests—to such an extent that all contradiction seems irrational and all counteraction impossible.

No wonder then that, in the most advanced areas of this civilization, the social controls have been introjected to the point where even individual protest is affected at its roots. The intellectual and emotional refusal "to go along" appears neurotic and impotent. This is the socio-psychological aspect of the political event that marks the contemporary period: the passing of the historical forces which, at the preceding stage of industrial society, seemed to represent the possibility of new forms of existence.

But the term "introjection" perhaps no longer describes the way in which the individual by himself reproduces and perpetuates the external controls exercised by his society. Introjection suggests a variety of relatively spontaneous processes by which a Self (Ego) transposes the "outer" into the "inner." Thus introjection implies the existence of an inner dimension distinguished from and even antagonistic to the external exigencies— an individual consciousness and an individual unconscious *apart from* public opinion and behavior.[3] The idea of "inner freedom" here has its reality: it designates the private space in which man may become and remain "himself."

Today this private space has been invaded and whittled down by technological reality. Mass production and mass distribution claim the *entire* individual, and industrial psychology has long since ceased to be confined to the factory. The manifold processes of introjection seem to be ossified in almost mechanical reactions. The result is, not adjustment but *mimesis:* an immediate identification of the individual with *his* society and, through it, with the society as a whole.

This immediate, automatic identification (which may have been characteristic of primitive forms of association) reappears in high industrial civilization; its new "immediacy," however, is the product of a sophisticated, scientific management and organization. In this process, the "inner" dimension of the mind in which opposition to the status quo can take root is whittled down. The loss of this dimension, in which the power of negative thinking—the critical power of Reason—is at home, is the ideological counterpart to the very material process in which advanced industrial society silences and reconciles the opposition. The impact of progress turns Reason into submission to the facts of life, and to the dynamic capability of producing more and bigger facts of the same sort of life. The efficiency of the system blunts the individuals' recognition that it contains no facts which do not communicate the repressive power of the whole. If the individuals find themselves in the things which shape their life, they do so, not by giving, but by accepting the law of things—not the law of physics but the law of their society.

I have just suggested that the concept of alienation seems to become questionable when the individuals identify themselves with the existence which is imposed upon them and have in it their own development and satisfaction. This identification is not illusion but reality. However, the reality constitutes a more progressive stage of alienation. The latter has become entirely objective; the subject which is alienated is swallowed up by its alienated existence. There is only one dimension, and it is everywhere and in all forms. The achievements of progress defy ideological indictment as well as justification; before their tribunal, the "false consciousness" of their rationality becomes the true consciousness.

This absorption of ideology into reality does not, however, signify the "end of ideology." On the contrary, in a specific sense advanced industrial culture is *more* ideological than its predecessor, inasmuch as today the ideology is in the process of production itself.[4] In a provocative form, this proposition reveals the political aspects of the prevailing technological rationality. The productive apparatus and the goods and services which it produces "sell" or impose the social system as a whole. The means of mass transportation and communication, the commodities of lodging, food, and clothing, the irresistible output of the entertainment and information industry carry with them prescribed attitudes and habits, certain intellectual and emotional reactions which bind the consumers more or less pleasantly to the producers and, through the latter, to the whole. The products indoctrinate and manipulate; they promote a false consciousness which is immune against its falsehood. And as these beneficial products become available to more individuals in more social classes, the indoctrination they carry ceases to be publicity; it becomes a way of life. It is a good way of life—much better than before—and as a good way of life, it militates against qualitative change. Thus emerges a pattern of *one-dimensional thought and behavior* in which ideas, aspirations, and objectives that, by their content, transcend the established universe of discourse and action are either repelled or reduced to terms of this universe. They are redefined by the rationality of the given system and of its quantitative extension.

The trend may be related to a development in scientific method: operationalism in the physical, behaviorism in the social sciences. The common feature is a total empiricism in the treatment of concepts; their meaning is restricted to the representation of particular operations and behavior. The operational point of view is well illustrated by P. W. Bridgman's analysis of the concept of length:

> We evidently know what we mean by length if we can tell what the length of any and every object is, and for the physicist nothing more is required. To find the length of an object, we have to perform certain physical operations. The concept of length is therefore fixed when the opera-

tions by which length is measured are fixed: that is, the concept of length involves as much and nothing more than the set of operations by which length is determined. In general, we mean by any concept nothing more than a set of operations; *the concept is synonymous with the corresponding set of operations.*[5]

Bridgman has seen the wide implications of this mode of thought for the society at large:

To adopt the operational point of view involves much more than a mere restriction of the sense in which we understand "concept," but means a far-reaching change in all our habits of thought, in that we shall no longer permit ourselves to use as tools in our thinking concepts of which we cannot give an adequate account in terms of operations.[6]

Bridgman's prediction has come true. The new mode of thought is today the predominant tendency in philosophy, psychology, sociology, and other fields. Many of the most seriously troublesome concepts are being "eliminated" by showing that no adequate account of them in terms of operations or behavior can be given. The radical empiricist onslaught thus provides the methodological justification for the debunking of the mind by the intellectuals—a positivism which, in its denial of the transcending elements of Reason, forms the academic counterpart of the socially required behavior.

Outside the academic establishment, the "far-reaching change in all our habits of thought" is more serious. It serves to coordinate ideas and goals with those exacted by the prevailing system, to enclose them in the system, and to repel those which are irreconcilable with the system. The reign of such a one-dimensional reality does not mean that materialism rules, and that the spiritual, metaphysical, and bohemian occupations are petering out. On the contrary, there is a great deal of "Worship together this week," "Why not try God," Zen, existentialism, and beat ways of life, etc. But such modes of protest and transcendence are no longer contradictory to the status quo and no longer negative. They are rather the ceremonial part of practical behaviorism, its harmless negation, and are quickly digested by the status quo as part of its healthy diet.

One-dimensional thought is systematically promoted by the makers of politics and their purveyors of mass information. Their universe of discourse is populated by self-validating hypotheses which, incessantly and monopolistically repeated, become hypnotic definitions or dictations. For example, "free" are the institutions which operate (and are operated on) in the countries of the Free World; other transcending modes of freedom are by definition either anarchism, communism, or propaganda. "Socialistic" are all encroachments on private enterprises not undertaken by private enterprise itself (or by government contracts), such as universal and comprehensive health insurance, or the protection of nature from all too sweeping commercialization, or the establishment of public services which may hurt private profit. This totalitarian logic of accomplished facts has its Eastern counterpart. There, freedom is the way of life instituted by a communist regime, and all other transcending modes of freedom are either capitalistic, or revisionist, or leftist sectarianism. In both camps, non-operational ideas are non-behavioral and subversive. The movement of thought is stopped at barriers which appear as the limits of Reason itself.

Such limitation of thought is certainly not new. Ascending modern rationalism, in its speculative as well as empirical form, shows a striking contrast between extreme critical radicalism in scientific and philosophic method on the one hand, and an uncritical quietism in the attitude toward established and functioning social institutions. Thus Descartes' *ego cogitans* was to leave the "great public bodies" untouched, and Hobbes held that "the present ought always to be preferred, maintained, and accounted best." Kant agreed with Locke in justifying revolution *if and when* it has succeeded in organizing the whole and in preventing subversion.

However, these accommodating concepts of Reason were always contradicted by the evident misery and injustice of the "great public bodies" and the effective, more or less conscious rebellion against them. Societal conditions existed which provoked and permitted real dissociation from the established state of affairs; a private as well as political dimension was present in which dissociation could develop into effective opposition, testing its strength and the validity of its objectives.

With the gradual closing of this dimension by the society, the self-limitation of thought assumes a larger significance. The interrelation between scientific-philosophical and societal processes, between theoretical and practical Reason, asserts itself "behind the back" of the scientists and philosophers. The society bars a whole type of oppositional operations and behavior; consequently, the concepts pertaining to them are rendered illusory or meaningless. Historical transcendence appears as metaphysical transcendence, not acceptable to science and scientific thought. The operational and behavioral point of view, practiced as a "habit of thought" at large, becomes the view of the established universe of discourse and action, needs and aspirations. The "cunning of Reason" works, as it so often did, in the interest of the powers that be. The insistence on operational and behavioral concepts turns against the efforts to free thought and behavior *from* the given reality and *for* the suppressed alternatives. Theoretical and practical Reason, academic and social behaviorism meet on common ground: that of an advanced society which makes scientific and technical progress into an instrument of domination.

"Progress" is not a neutral term; it moves toward specific ends, and these ends are defined by the possibilities of ameliorating the human condition. Advanced industrial society is approaching the stage where continued progress would demand the radical subversion of the prevailing direction and organization of progress. This stage would be reached when material production (including the necessary services) becomes automated to the extent that all vital needs can be satisfied while necessary labor time is reduced to marginal time. From this point on, technical progress would transcend the realm of necessity, where it served as the instrument of domination and exploitation which thereby limited its rationality; technology would become subject to the free play of faculties in the struggle for the pacification of nature and of society.

Such a state is envisioned in Marx's notion of the "abolition of labor." The term "pacification of existence" seems better suited to designate the historical alternative of a world which—through an international conflict which transforms and suspends the contradictions within the established societies—advances on the brink of a global war. "Pacification of existence" means the development of man's struggle with man and with nature, under conditions where the competing needs, desires, and aspirations are no longer organized by vested interests in domination and scarcity—an organization which perpetuates the destructive forms of this struggle.

Today's fight against this historical alternative finds a firm mass basis in the underlying population, and finds its ideology in the rigid orientation of thought and behavior to the given universe of facts. Validated by the accomplishments of science and technology, justified by its growing productivity, the status quo defies all transcendence. Faced with the possibility of pacification on the grounds of its technical and intellectual achievements, the mature industrial society closes itself against this alternative. Operationalism, in theory and practice, becomes the theory and practice of *containment*. Underneath its obvious dynamics, this society is a thoroughly static system of life: self-propelling in its oppressive productivity and in its beneficial coordination. Containment of technical progress goes hand in hand with its growth in the established direction. In spite of the political fetters imposed by the status quo, the more technology appears capable of creating the conditions for pacification, the more are the minds and bodies of man organized against this alternative.

The most advanced areas of industrial society exhibit throughout these two features: a trend toward consummation of technological rationality, and intensive efforts to contain this trend within the established institutions. Here is the internal contradiction of this civilization: the irrational element in its rationality. It is the token of its achievements. The industrial society which makes technology and science its own is organized for the ever-more-effective domination of man and nature, for the ever-more-effective utilization of its resources. It becomes irrational when the success of these efforts opens new dimensions of human realization. Organization for peace is different from organization for war; the institutions which served the struggle for existence cannot serve the pacification of existence. Life as an end is qualitatively different from life as a means.

Such a qualitatively new mode of existence can never be envisaged as the mere by-product of economic and political changes, as the more or less spontaneous effect of the new institutions which constitute the necessary prerequisite. Qualitative change also involves a change in the *technical* basis on which this society rests—one which sustains the economic and political institutions through which the "second nature" of man as an aggressive object of administration is stabilized. The techniques of industrialization are political techniques; as such, they prejudge the possibilities of Reason and Freedom.

To be sure, labor must precede the reduction of labor, and industrialization must precede the development of human needs and satisfactions. But as all freedom depends on the conquest of alien necessity, the realization of freedom depends on the *techniques* of this conquest. The highest productivity of labor can be used for the perpetuation of labor, and the most efficient industrialization can serve the restriction and manipulation of needs.

When this point is reached, domination—in the guise of affluence and liberty—extends to all spheres of private and public existence, integrates all authentic opposition, absorbs all alternatives. Technological rationality reveals its political character as it becomes the great vehicle of better domination, creating a truly totalitarian universe in which society and nature, mind and body are kept in a state of permanent mobilization for the defense of this universe.

# NOTES

1. See Herbert Marcuse, *One-Dimensional Man* (Boston: Beacon Press, 1967), p. 50.
2. *Ibid.*, p. 40.
3. The change in the function of the family here plays a decisive role: its "socializing" functions are increasingly taken over by outside groups and media. See Herbert Marcuse, *Eros and Civilization* (Boston: Beacon Press, 1955), pp. 96 ff.
4. Theodor W. Adorno, *Prismen, Kulturkritik und Gesellschaft* (Frankfurt: Suhrkamp, 1955), pp. 24 f.
5. P. W. Bridgman, *The Logic of Modern Physics* (New York: Macmillan, 1928), p. 5. The operational doctrine has since been refined and qualified. Bridgman himself has extended the concept of "operation" to include the "paper-and-pencil" operations of the theorist (in Philipp J. Frank, *The Validation of Scientific Theories* [Boston: Beacon Press, 1954], Chap. II). The main impetus remains the same: it is "'desirable" that the paper-and-pencil operations "be capable of eventual contact, although perhaps indirectly, with instrumental operations."
6. P. W. Bridgman, *The Logic of Modern Physics, loc. cit.*, p. 31.

# Jacques Ellul as the Philosopher
# of the Technological Society

## JOHN WILKINSON

**P**robably the most profound critique of modern
technology and its relationship to modern society is Jacques
Ellul's *The Technological Society*. Ellul's critique has
greatly influenced many other works in this area. Since
it involves a far more careful consideration of a mass of
empirical data on modern society than do works such as
Marcuse's, it must be given careful consideration by anyone
seriously concerned with the dangers of the technological
tyranny.

Ellul believes that technology is no longer simply a
means by which we achieve our ends in modern society, but
rather that technology has become an end in itself, an end
which dominates all other ends. Technology has become
the god of modern man, especially the god of modern
Americans, whom he sees as the most conformist people in
the modern world. This general introduction to the

technological society, written by John Wilkinson, who translated Ellul's book into English, is the best introduction to Ellul's argument. It is also one of the best introductions to the whole theory of the technological tyranny.

Ernest Jünger once wrote that technology is the real metaphysics of the twentieth century. The irreversible collectivist tendencies of technology, whether it calls itself democratic or authoritarian, were already apparent to him, at the end of World War I. It is this society, in all its forms, which Jacques Ellul, of the Faculty of Law of Bordeaux, seeks to analyze.

Professor Ellul, unlike most of the other surviving leaders of the French Resistance, still functions as a voice of conscience for a France which seems to feel itself in danger of being overwhelmed from literally every point of the compass by the materialistic values of the cold war—consumer society. Greater influence is enjoyed by others such as Malraux and Sartre; but Malraux is in the service of the welfare state (albeit one with Gallic flourishes) and Sartre is growing rich by dispensing absinthe morality in the cellars of the Left Bank. "I sometimes wonder," says Ellul in a related connection, "about the revolutionary value of acts accompanied by such a merry jingle of the cash register."

Ellul's principal work appeared under the title *La Technique* and the subtitle *L'enjeu du siècle*. The subtitle, which means literally "the stake of the century," is a characteristically dark and difficult Ellulian phrase which may or may not refer to a kind of "Pascal wager" put on technology by twentieth-century man. The *Technique* of the title, however, lends itself more easily to interpretation, although, characteristically, it too is used in a sense it does not usually enjoy. *Technique,* the reader discovers more or less quickly, must be distinguished from the several *techniques* which are its elements. It is more even than a generalized mechanical technique; it is, in fact, nothing less than the organized ensemble of *all* individual techniques which have been used to secure any end whatsoever. Harold Lasswell's definition comes closest to Ellul's conception: "The ensemble of practices by which one uses available resources to achieve values." This definition has the merit of emphasizing the *scope* of technique; but Ellul's further account makes it clear that it does not go far enough, since technique has become indifferent to all the traditional human ends and values by becoming an end-in-itself. Our erstwhile means have all become an end, an end, furthermore, which has nothing human in it and to which we must accommodate ourselves as best we may. We cannot even any longer pretend to act as though the ends justified the means, which would still be recognizably human, if not particularly virtuous. Technique, as the universal and autonomous technical fact, is revealed as the technological society itself in which man is but a single tightly integrated and articulated component. *The Technological Society* is a description of the way in which an autonomous technology is in process of taking over the traditional values of every society without exception, subverting and suppressing these values to produce at last a monolithic world culture in which all nontechnological difference and variety is mere appearance.

The technical malaise so deeply felt in non-Communist Europe at the imminent takeover has brought forth in recent years an astonishingly large number of literary, philosophic, and sociological analyses of the technical phenomenon. One of the great merits of Ellul's book arises from the fact that he alone has pushed such analysis to the limit in all spheres of human activity and in the totality of their interrelatedness. It may be added that what some authors feel to be the book's demerits arise from the same source; they maintain that society more often than not refuses to be pushed to that *reductio ad absurdum* which is the inevitable end point of every thoroughgoing analysis. The books of such authors generally end on a note of optimism. A final chapter always asks: "What is to be done?" Unfortunately, their answers to the question are either inefficacious myths which confront reality with slogans, or only too efficacious technical solutions to technical problems which end only in subjecting man the more thoroughly to technology. The former are exemplified by most modern religions, philosophical systems, and political doctrines; the latter by schemes for mass education or mass cultivation of leisure, which, in Ellul's analysis, are themselves highly impersonal and technicized structures having much more in common with the assembly line than with what mankind has traditionally designated by these names.

The technological malaise seems to have been much less acutely felt in the United States. Individuals such as Aldous Huxley, Paul Tillich, and Erich Fromm, who have raised their voices in protest, are of European origin and received their education in Europe. Technolaters such as Professors B. F. Skinner of Harvard and most other American professors represent the familiar type of the American intellectual caught in an ecstatic technical vertigo and seldom proceeding beyond certain vague meditations on isolated problem areas such as the "population explosion," if indeed he considers the real problems posed by technology at all. Ellul holds the Americans to be the most conformist people in the world, but in fairness it must be objected that, in his own analysis, the Soviets seem better to deserve this dubious honor since they have made even politics into a technique. The Americans, apart from technicizing the electoral process, have left at least the sphere of politics to the operations of amateurish bunglers and have thereby preserved a modicum of humanity. It may be added that France, too, has been taken into the technological orbit with a speed which must have astonished Ellul. De Gaulle's plans for his new France contemplate the complete technicization of French society in nine years instead of the quarter century of grace which Ellul predicts in his book.

Since the religious object is that which is uncritically worshipped, technology tends more and more to become the new god. This is true for all modern societies, but especially so for Communist societies, since Marxism, in Ellul's analysis of it, *consciously* identifies the material infrastructure, upon which the social superstructure is raised, with technology.[1] The expression of technological malaise in the Soviet Union or in Red China, where technolatry has become the new Establishment, would be blasphemy in the strictest sense of the word.

In composition and style, Ellul's book is certain to be an enigma, and even a scandal, to many. It is not sociology, political economy, history, or any other academic discipline, at least as these terms are usually understood. It will not even appear to be philosophy to a generation whose philosophic preoccupations are almost exclusively analytic. Ellul himself is in doubt about the value of the designation *philosopher*. But, if we think back to the *dialectical philosophies of the whole* of thinkers such as Plato and Hegel, Ellul's book *is* philosophy. If an American specialist, say, in economics, with his "terribly linear" logic and his apparently unshakable conviction that his arbitrarily delimited systems can and should be studied in isolation from all others, were to flip open Ellul's book to those sections which treat of matters economic, it is conceivable that he would be repelled by what he found. But if this same specialist could somehow or other implausibly be persuaded to persevere in the attempt to see with Ellul economics in the light of the whole of modern technical culture, it is likewise conceivable that he would gain important insights, not perhaps into the fine-structure of academic economic problems, but in the border region where his subject abuts on other disciplines, in that area where basic discoveries in economics (and everything else) are always made by gifted amateurs, who *faute de mieux* must be called philosophers.

Ellul's admittedly difficult style is not to be referred to that *style heurté* affected by so many postwar French existentialists. An element of this is doubtless present, but it would be much more accurate to say that, in an essentially dramatic work such as the present book must be deemed to be, the transitions and turns of thought must have a character entirely different from those to be encountered in the ultra-respectable academic texts which have taken over from mathematics certain linear and deductive modes of presentation; modes, which, whatever their pedagogic value may be, serve, even in mathematics, only to obscure the way in which truth comes into being. To its dramatic presentation of what are, after all, well-known facts, Ellul's book owes its high persuasive quality.

This dramatic character would have been clearly evident if the book had been written as a dialogue. Indeed, a reader could easily cast it into this form by representing to himself the various thinkers who are introduced by name as the dramatis personae, and by treating the nameless "On the one hands" and "On the other hands" in the same way. In this way the "successive recantations" of some positions and the development of others in the light of a guiding concept of the whole become clear, and the book's essential affinity to a Platonic dialogue like the *Republic* is evident. (Nowhere is this successive recantation more evident than in the first chapter's search for definitions.) Even clearer is the similarity of the book to Hegel's *Phänomenologie des Geistes,* the last work of Western philosophy with which, in the translator's opinion, the present work bears comparison. *The Technological Society* is not a "phenomenology of mind" but rather a "phenomenology of the technical state of mind." Like Hegel's book, it is intensely histrionic; and like it, it shows, *without offering causal mechanisms,* how its subject in its lowest stage (technique as machine technique) develops dialectically through the various higher stages to become at last the fully evolved phenomenon (the technical phenomenon identical with the technical society). Again, as with Hegel, what the philosopher J. Loewenberg has called the "histrionic irony" of statement must drive the literal-minded reader mad.

The Danish historian of philosophy, Harald Hoeffding, says of Hegel's *Phenomenology:*

> The course of development described in this unique work is at once that of the individual and of the race; it gives at the same time a psy-

chology and a history of culture—and in the exposition the two are so interwoven that it is often impossible to tell which of the two is intended.

With the stipulation that Ellul is treating of culture in the sense of the technological society, Hoeffding's penetrating remark holds as well for Ellul's book.

In such a work it is impossible to separate method from content. Yet, in another sense, and especially for a translator, it is imperative to do so. Although, after the time of Descartes, French savants in general were preoccupied with clarifying problems of method, it has been almost impossible *in the twentieth century* to extort from French writers on sociology and economics an adequate account of their procedures. Some of them have doubtless been oversensitive to Poincaré's famous jibe concerning the sciences "with the most methods and the fewest results." In Ellul's case, however, disinclination to discuss methodology specifically is almost certainly due in large part to his pervasive distrust of anything at all resembling a fixed doctrine. Nevertheless, throughout the book are scattered a large number of references to method, and it is possible and necessary to reconstruct from them a satisfactory account of the author's methodology.

Ellul first "situates" the "facts" of experience in a general context, and then proceeds to "focus" them. This figure of speech, drawn from, or at least appropriate to, descriptive astronomy, appears over and over again in connection with each supervening stage of complexity of the subject matter. The final result of the procedure is to bring to a common focal point rays proceeding from very different spheres. The reader should be warned that it is only possible to approximate in English the mixed metaphors and the studied imprecisions of each new beginning of the process, which are gradually refined to yield *at the focus* a precise terminology. The translator was always uncomfortably aware of too little precision, or too much, in his choice of English words. The reader seriously interested in these nuances has no recourse but to consult the original. The translator can do little more for him than to call his attention to the problem. Anyone familiar with similar "dialectic moments" in the works of Hegel or of Max Weber will understand at once what is meant.

Ellul repeats again and again that he is concerned not to make value judgments but to report things as they are. One might be tempted to smile at such statements in view of the intensely personal and even impassioned quality of a work in which one is never for a moment unaware where the author's own sympathies lie. Nonetheless, on balance, it seems clear that he has not allowed his own value judgments to intrude in any illegitimate way on questions of fact. "Fact" is very important to Ellul, but only as experienced in the context of the whole. Facts as they figure in uninterpreted statistical analyses of a given domain, or as they may be revealed by opinion polls and in newspapers, are anathema to him; and he permits himself many diatribes against this kind of "abstract," disembodied fact which is so dear to the hearts of Americans, at least as Ellul imagines them to be. With this proviso, Ellul can echo the dictum of Hegel's *Phenomenology* that the only imaginable point of departure of philosophy is experience.

The insistence on rendering a purely phenomenological account of fact, without causal explanation of the interrelation of the subordinate facts, may seem distasteful to some readers. Since Aristotle it has been a common conception of science that we have knowledge only when we know the Why. Admittedly, whenever causal knowledge *is* available, it is indeed valuable. But it ought not to be forgotten that such knowledge is increasingly hard to come by, and, in fact, hardly makes its appearance at all in modern physics, say, where one must, for the most part, be content with purely functional (that is, phenomenological) equations, which dispense with any appeal to mechanism but which are nonetheless adequate for prediction and explanation, and which have the enormous additional advantage of containing no hidden concepts unconfrontable by experience. The important questions concerning the technological society rarely turn for Ellul on how or why things came to be so, but rather on whether his description of them is a true one.

Ellul's methodology is fundamentally dominated by the principle which has come to be called Engel's law, that is, the law asserting the passage of quantity into quality. To give a commonplace example, the city, after it reaches a certain threshold of population, is supposed to pass over into a qualitatively different type of urban organization. Unfortunately, both the popular and the usual philosophical accounts of Engel's law are incomplete, to use no worse word.

*First,* it is incorrect to speak at all of a "threshold" of quantity which, having been transcended, gives rise to a change of quality and to a new set of laws and explanatory principles. In dialectical logic, *every* change of quantity *is* simultaneously a change of quality; and the discernment of a "threshold" quantity is partly a psychological fact of awareness, and partly an illicit attempt to try to import back into a dialectical logic some of the unequivocalness of the ordinary either/or logic. Now, Ellul's explanation of the technical takeover is based fundamentally on the fact that the material (that is, technical) substratum of human existence, which was traditionally not allowed to be a legitimate end of human action, has become so "enormous," so "immense," that men are no longer able to cope with it as means, so that it has become an end-in-itself, to which men must adapt themselves. But, with a better understanding of the illusory nature of the "threshold quantity," we are able to turn aside the objections which are always raised by those who rightly but extraneously urge that historical societies have *always* had to struggle with the possibility of a material takeover and that the present state of affairs is therefore not something new. The answer, of course, is that the objection is irrelevant. Ellul could not mean to assert that men in the past have not had to contend with material means which threatened to exceed their capacity to make good use of them, but that men in the past were not confronted with technical means of production and organization which in their sheer numerical proliferation and velocity unavoidably surpassed man's relatively unchanging biological and spiritual capacities to exploit them as means to human ends.

*Second,* Engel's law must *never* be taken to imply a one-way transition of quantity into quality. In dialectical logic the transformation of quality into quantity is a necessary concomitant of the reversible transformation of quantity into quality. It is, in fact, *the essence of technique to compel the qualitative to become quantitative,* and in this way to force every stage of human activity and man himself to submit to its mathematical calculations. Ellul gives examples of this at every level. Thus, technique forces all sociological phenomena to submit to the clock, for Ellul the most characteristic of all modern technical instruments. The substitution of the *tempus mortuum* of the mechanical clock for the biological and psychological time "natural" to man is in itself sufficient to suppress all the traditional rhythms of human life in favor of the mechanical. Again, genuine human communities are suppressed by the technological society to form collectivities of "mass men" incapable of obeying any other law than the statistical "law of large numbers." All the technical devices of education, propaganda, amusement, sport, and religion are mobilized to persuade the human being to be satisfied with his condition of mechanical, mindless "mass man," and ruthlessly to exterminate the deviant and the idiosyncratic.

The reduction of everything to quantity is partly a cause, and partly an effect, of the modern omnipresence of computing machines and cybernated factories.

It should not be imagined, however, that the universal concentration camp which Ellul thinks is coming into being in all technical societies without exception will be felt as harsh or restrictive by its inmates. Hitler's concentration camps of hobnailed boots were symptoms of a deficient political technique. The denizen of the technological state of the future will have everything his heart ever desired, except, of course, his freedom. Admittedly, modern man, forced by technique to become in reality and without residue the imaginary producer-consumer of the classical economists, shows disconcertingly little regard for his lost freedom; but, according to Ellul, there are ominous signs that human spontaneity, which in the rational and ordered technical society has no expression except madness, is only too capable of outbreaks of irrational suicidal destructiveness.

The escape valves of modern literature and art, which technique has contrived, may or may not turn out to be adequate to the harmless release of the pent-up "ecstatic" energies of the human being. Technique, which can in principle only oppose technical and quantitative solutions to technical problems, must, in such a case, seek out other technical safety valves. It could, for example, convince men that they were happy and contented by means of drugs, even though they were visibly suffering from the worst kind of spiritual and material privation. It is obvious that *all such ultimate technical measures* must cause the last meager "idealistic" motifs of the whole technical enterprise to disappear. Ellul does not specifically say so, but it seems that he must hold that the technological society, like everything else, bears within itself the seeds of its own destruction.

It must not be imagined that the autonomous technique envisioned by Ellul is a kind of "technological determinism," to use a phrase of Veblen. It may sometimes seem so, but only because *all* human institutions, like the motions of all physical bodies, have a certain permanence, or vis inertiae, which makes it highly probable that the near future of statistical aggregations will see them continue more or less in the path of the immediate past. Things *could* have eventuated in the technological society otherwise than as they have.

Technique, to Ellul, is a "blind" force, but one which unfortunately seems to be more perspicacious than the best discernible human intelligences. There *are* other ways out, Ellul maintains, but nobody wants any part of them.

Ellul's insistence that the technical phenomenon is not a determinism is not weakened by the enumeration (in the second chapter) of five conditions which are said to be "necessary and sufficient" for its outburst in the recent past, since the sufficient conditions for the conditions (for example, the causes of the population explosion) are not ascertainable.

The inertia of the technical phenomenon guarantees not only the continued refinement and production of relatively beneficial articles such as flush toilets and wonder drugs, but also the emergence of those unpredictable secondary effects which are always the result of ecological meddling and which today are of such magnitude and acceleration that they can scarcely be reconciled with even semistable equilibrium conditions of society. Nuclear explosions and population explosions capture the public's imagination; but I have argued that Ellul's analysis demands that *all* indices of modern technological culture are exploding, too, and are potentially just as dangerous to the continued well-being of society, if by well-being we understand social equilibrium.

Reference to the vis inertiae of technique should not obscure the fact that technique has become the only fully spontaneous activity of the modern world. Art and science are mentioned as other human activities by Ellul. But art, though it is concrete, is subjective; and science, though objective in its description of reality, is abstract. Only technique is at once both concrete and objective in that it creates the reality it describes. Ellul *must* conclude that from among the data of science technique *legislates* those which it deems most efficient and rejects the rest. Economic and social "model builders," those assiduous technocratic apes, may seek to soften the violence of this description by pointing out that *all* sciences "specify a universe of discourse." It remains unfortunately true, however, that such "specification" proceeds by way of elimination of the human.

Ellul is no machinoclast like the partisans of the weak-minded Ludd seeking to wreck the stocking frames. He has no doctrinal delusions at all, a fortiori none like those of Rousseau and certain of his disciples, who imagined that man would be happy in a state of nature.

In view of the fact that Ellul continually apostrophizes technique as "unnatural" (except when he calls it the "new nature"), it might be thought surprising that he has no fixed conception of nature or of the natural. The best answer seems to be that he considers "natural" (in the good sense) *any* environment able to satisfy man's material needs, *if* it leaves him free to use it as means to achieve his individual, internally generated ends. The necessary and sufficient condition for this state of affairs is that man's means should be (qualitatively and quantitatively) "at the level" of man's capacities. Under these dubiously realizable circumstances, Ellul apparently thinks of techniques as so many blessings.

Since men are unwilling to acknowledge their demotion to the status of joyous robots, and since they demand justification for their individual and collective acts as never before in history, it is easy to understand why the modern intellectuals (and their forcing-house, the university) have become veritable machines for the invention of new myths and the propagation of old ones. It would be easy to compile a list of all the things which Ellul must deem "myth." Such a list would quite simply contain *all* philosophical, historical, religious, and political doctrines known to man, except insofar as such doctrines have technological components. The Western democracies, for example, are out after money and the Eastern Communists are out after power; otherwise they share an identical view of life, and the epiphenomenal variant ideologies which accompany identical acts can only be described as a cruel hoax.

It is disconcerting in the extreme to contemplate the possibility that cherished democratic institutions have become empty forms which have no visible connection with the acts of democratic nations, except perhaps to render these acts technically less efficient than they otherwise need have been. But the fact that they have no connection is, paradoxically, a powerful reason for their survival. Ellul evidently contemplates a long future in which sclerotic rival ideologies will carry on their sham polemics.

Ellul, in agreement with much of Greek philosophy, seems to think that the distinction usually drawn between thought and action is a pernicious one. To him, to *bear witness to the fact* of the technological society is the most revolutionary of all possible acts. His personal reason for doing so is that he is a Christian, a fact which is spelled out in his book *La Présence.* His concept of the duty of a Christian, who stands uniquely (is "present") at the point of intersection of this material world and the eternal world to come, is not to concoct ambiguous ethical schemes or programs of social action, but to testify to the truth of both worlds and thereby to affirm his freedom through the revolutionary nature of his religion.

It is clear that many people who will accept Ellul's diagnosis of the technical disease will not accept his Christian therapy. The issue is nevertheless joined: if massive technological intervention is the only imaginable means to turn aside technology from its headlong career, how may we be sure that this intervention will be something other than just some new technical scheme, which, more likely than not, will be catastrophic?

# NOTE

1. Ellul once again showed much prescience. Marxist publications of the last few years have come to speak of the "technical-material infrastructure" instead of the "material infrastructure."

# A Look at the Future

JACQUES ELLUL

**T**his final chapter of Ellul's *The Technological Society*
is one of the most pessimistic and most dismal critiques of
modern society to be found. Ellul believes that modern
man has striven mightily to escape ancient necessities by
creating technology. But in so doing he has created a new
necessity, one more oppressive than the ancient one. He
also believes that technology has alienated man from his
ancient natural environment and has created an artificial
environment in which man's natural inclinations are no
longer at home.

Ellul's picture of modern man is one of sterility and a
hopeless, endless irrelevance. He sees the ultimate triumph
of technology in the increasing tendency of technological
man to replace men with machines.

Ellul has in many instances chosen to attack the more
naive scientific optimists, but he is undoubtedly right in

*Reprinted from Jacques Ellul,* The Technological Society, *by permission of Alfred A. Knopf, Inc. Copyright © 1964 by Alfred A. Knopf, Inc.*

arguing that many of those who foresee technological utopia as necessarily growing out of our present situation are totally credulous. He is certainly right in arguing that many of the utopian goals they have described would in fact constitute a terrible tyranny.

Ellul's critique is bitter and all encompassing; it is a hopeless critique. He sees no way out, no exit. He proposes no solution.

We have completed our examination of the monolithic technical world that is coming to be. It is vanity to pretend it can be checked or guided. Indeed, the human race is beginning confusedly to understand at last that it is living in a new and unfamiliar universe. The new order was meant to be a buffer between man and nature. Unfortunately, it has evolved autonomously in such a way that man has lost all contact with his natural framework and has to do only with the organized technical intermediary which sustains relations both with the world of life and with the world of brute matter. Enclosed within his artificial creation, man finds that there is "no exit"; that he cannot pierce the shell of technology to find again the ancient milieu to which he was adapted for hundreds of thousands of years.

The new milieu has its own specific laws which are not the laws of organic or inorganic matter. Man is still ignorant of these laws. It nevertheless begins to appear with crushing finality that a new necessity is taking over from the old. It is easy to boast of victory over ancient oppression, but what if victory has been gained at the price of an even greater subjection to the forces of the artificial necessity of the technical society which has come to dominate our lives?

In our cities there is no more day or night or heat or cold. But there is overpopulation, thraldom to press and television, total absence of purpose. All men are constrained by means external to them to ends equally external. The further the technical mechanism develops which allows us to escape natural necessity, the more we are subjected to artificial technical necessities. (I have analyzed human victory over hunger in this vein.) The artificial necessity of technique is not less harsh and implacable for being much less obviously menacing than natural necessity. When the Communists claim that they place the development of the technical society in a historical framework that automatically leads to freedom through the medium of the dialectical process; when Humanists such as Bergson, or Catholics such as Mounier, assert that man must regain control over the technical "means" by an additional quantity of soul, all of them alike show both their ignorance of the technical phenomenon and an impenitent idealism that unfortunately bears no relation to truth or reality.

Alongside these parades of mere verbalisms, there has been a real effort, on the part of the technicians themselves, to control the future of technical evolution. The principle here is the old one we have so often encountered:

"A technical problem demands a technical solution." At present, there are two kinds of new techniques which the technicians propose as solutions.

The first solution hinges on the creation of new technical instruments able to mediate between man and his new technical milieu. Robert Jungk, for example, in connection with the fact that man is not completely adaptable to the demands of the technical age, writes that "it is impossible to create interstellar man out of the existing prime matter; auxiliary technical instruments and apparatus must compensate for his insufficiencies." The best and most striking example of such subsidiary instruments is furnished by the complex of so-called "thinking machines," which certainly belong to a very different category of techniques than those that have been applied up to now. But the whole ensemble of means designed to permit human mastery of what were means and have now become milieu are techniques of the second degree, and nothing more. Pierre de Latil, in his *La Pensée artificielle,* gives an excellent characterization of some of these machines of the second degree:

"In the machine, the notion of finality makes its appearance, a notion sometimes attributed in living beings to some intelligence inherent in the species, innate to life itself. Finality is artificially built into the machine and regulates it, an effect requiring that some factor be modified or reinforced so that the effect itself does not disturb the equilibrium . . . Errors are corrected without human analysis, or knowledge, without even being suspected. The error itself corrects the error. A deviation from the prescribed track itself enables the automatic pilot to rectify the deviation . . . For the machine, as for animals, error is fruitful; it conditions the correct path."

The second solution revolves about the effort to discover (or rediscover) a new end for human society in the technical age. The aims of technology, which were clear enough a century and a half ago, have gradually disappeared from view. Humanity seems to have forgotten the wherefore of all its travail, as though its goals had been translated into an abstraction or had become implicit; or as though its ends rested in an unforeseeable future of undetermined date, as in the case of Communist society. Everything today seems to happen as though ends disappear, as a result of the magnitude of the very means at our disposal.

Comprehending that the proliferation of means brings about the disappearance of the ends, we have become preoccupied with rediscovering a purpose or a goal. Some optimists of good will assert that they have rediscovered a Humanism to which the technical movement is subordinated. The orientation of this Humanism may be Communist or non-Communist, but it hardly makes any difference. In both cases it is merely a pious hope with no chance whatsoever of influencing technical evolution. The further we advance, the more the purpose of our techniques fades out of sight. Even things which not long ago seemed to be immediate objectives—rising living standards, hygiene, comfort—no longer seem to have that character, possibly because man finds the endless adaptation to new circumstances disagreeable. In many cases, indeed, a higher technique obliges him to sacrifice comfort and hygienic amenities to the evolving technology which possesses a monopoly of the instruments necessary to satisfy them. Extreme examples are furnished by the scientists isolated at Los Alamos in the middle of the desert because of the danger of their experiments; or by the would-be astronauts who are forced to live in the discomfort of experimental camps in the manner so graphically described by Jungk.

But the optimistic technician is not a man to lose heart. If ends and goals are required, he will find them in a finality which can be imposed on technical evolution precisely because this finality can be technically established and calculated. It seems clear that there must be some common measure between the means and the ends subordinated to it. The required solution, then, must be a technical inquiry into ends, and this alone can bring about a systematization of ends and means. The problem becomes that of analyzing individual and social requirements technically, of establishing, numerically and mechanistically, the constancy of human needs. It follows that a complete knowledge of ends is requisite for mastery of means. But, as Jacques Aventur has demonstrated, such knowledge can only be technical knowledge. Alas, the panacea of merely theoretical humanism is as vain as any other.[1]

"Man, in his biological reality, must remain the sole possible reference point for classifying needs," writes Aventur. Aventur's dictum must be extended to include man's psychology and sociology, since these have also been reduced to mathematical calculation. Technology cannot put up with intuitions and "literature." It must necessarily don mathematical vestments. Everything in human life that does not lend itself to mathematical treatment must be excluded—because it is not a possible end for technique— and left to the sphere of dreams.

Who is too blind to seē that a profound mutation is being advocated here? A new dismembering and a complete reconstitution of the human being so that he can at last become the objective (and also the total object) of techniques. Excluding all but the mathematical element, he is indeed a fit end for the means he has constructed. He is also completely despoiled of everything that traditionally constituted his essence. Man becomes a pure appearance, a kaleidoscope of external shapes, an abstraction in a milieu that is frighteningly concrete—an abstraction armed with all the sovereign signs of Jupiter the Thunderer.

## A Look at the Year 2000

In 1960 the weekly *l'Express* of Paris published a series of extracts from texts by American and Russian scientists concerning society in the year 2000. As long as such visions were purely a literary concern of science-fiction writers and sensational journalists, it was possible to smile at them.[2] Now we have like works from Nobel Prize winners, members of the Academy of Sciences of Moscow, and other scientific notables whose qualifications are beyond dispute. The visions of these gentlemen put science fiction in the shade. By the year 2000, voyages to the moon will be commonplace; so will inhabited artificial satellites. All food will be completely synthetic. The world's population will have increased fourfold but will have been stabilized. Sea water and ordinary rocks will yield all the necessary metals. Disease, as well as famine, will have been eliminated; and there will be universal hygienic inspection and control. The problems of energy production will have been completely resolved. Serious scientists, it must be repeated, are the source of these predictions, which hitherto were found only in philosophic utopias.

The most remarkable predictions concern the transformation of educational methods and the problem of human reproduction. Knowledge will be accumulated in "electronic banks" and transmitted directly to the human nervous system by means of coded electronic messages. There will no longer be any need of reading or learning mountains of useless information; everything will be received and registered according to the needs of the moment. There will be no need of attention or effort. What is needed will pass directly from the machine to the brain without going through consciousness.

In the domain of genetics, natural reproduction will be forbidden. A stable population will be necessary, and it will consist of the highest human types. Artificial insemination will be employed. This, according to Muller, will "permit the introduction into a carrier uterus of an ovum fertilized *in vitro,* ovum and sperm . . . having been taken from persons representing the masculine ideal and the feminine ideal, respectively. The reproductive cells in question will preferably be those of persons dead long enough that a true perspective of their lives and works, free of all personal prejudice, can be seen. Such cells will be taken from cell banks and will represent the most precious genetic heritage of humanity . . . The method will have to be applied universally. If the people of a single country were to apply it intelligently and intensively . . . they would quickly attain a practically invincible level of superiority . . ." Here is a future Huxley never dreamed of.

Perhaps, instead of marveling or being shocked, we ought to reflect a little. A question no one ever asks when confronted with the scientific wonders of the future concerns the interim period. Consider, for example, the problems of automation, which will become acute in a very short time. How, socially, politically, morally, and humanly, shall we contrive to get there? How are the prodigious economic problems, for example, of unemployment, to be solved? And, in Muller's more distant utopia, how shall we force humanity to refrain from begetting children naturally? How shall we force them to submit to constant and rigorous hygienic controls? How shall man be persuaded to accept a radical transformation of his traditional modes of nutrition? How and where shall we relocate a billion and a half persons who today make their livings from agriculture and who, in the promised ultrarapid conversion of the next forty years, will become completely useless as cultivators of the soil? How shall we distribute such numbers of people equably over the surface of the earth, particularly if the promised fourfold increase in population materializes? How will we handle the control and occupation of outer space in order to provide a stable *modus vivendi?* How shall national boundaries be made to disappear? (One of the last two would be a necessity.) There are many other "hows," but they are conveniently left unformulated. When we reflect on the serious although relatively minor problems that were provoked by the industrial exploitation of coal and electricity, when we reflect that after a hundred and fifty years these problems are still not satisfactorily resolved, we are entitled to ask whether there are any solutions to the infinitely more complex "hows" of the next forty years. In fact, there is one and only one means to their solution, a world-wide totalitarian dictatorship which will allow technique its full scope and at the same time resolve the concomitant difficulties. It is not difficult to understand why the scientists and worshippers of technology prefer not to dwell on this solution, but rather to leap nimbly across the dull and uninteresting intermediary period and land squarely in the golden age. We might indeed ask ourselves if we will succeed in getting through the transition period at all, or if the blood and the suffering required are not perhaps too high a price to pay for this golden age.

If we take a hard, unromantic look at the golden age itself, we are struck with the incredible naïveté of these scientists. They say, for example, that they will be able to shape and reshape at will human emotions, desires, and thoughts and arrive scientifically at certain efficient, pre-established collective decisions. They claim they will be in a position to develop certain collective desires, to constitute certain homogeneous social units out of aggregates of individuals, to forbid men to raise their children, and even to persuade them to renounce having any. At the same time, they speak of assuring the triumph of freedom and of the necessity of avoiding dictatorship at any price.[3] They seem incapable of grasping the contradiction involved, or of understanding that what they are proposing, even after the intermediary period, is in fact the harshest of dictatorships. In comparison, Hitler's was a trifling affair. That it is to be a dictatorship of test tubes rather than of hobnailed boots will not make it any less a dictatorship.

When our savants characterize their golden age in any but scientific terms, they emit a quantity of down-at-the-heel platitudes that would gladden the heart of the pettiest politician. Let's take a few samples. "To render human nature nobler, more beautiful, and more harmonious." What on earth can this mean? What criteria, what content, do they propose? Not many, I fear, would be able to reply. "To assure the triumph of peace, liberty, and reason." Fine words with no substance behind them. "To eliminate cultural lag." What culture? And would the culture they have in mind be able to subsist in this harsh social organization? "To conquer outer space." For what purpose? The conquest of space seems to be an end in itself, which dispenses with any need for reflection.

We are forced to conclude that our scientists are incapable of any but the emptiest platitudes when they stray from their specialties. It makes one think back on the collection of mediocrities accumulated by Einstein when he spoke of God, the state, peace, and the meaning of life. It is clear that Einstein, extraordinary mathematical genius that he was, was no Pascal; he knew nothing of political or human reality, or, in fact, anything at all outside his mathematical reach. The banality of Einstein's remarks in matters outside his specialty is as astonishing as his genius within it. It seems as though the specialized application of all one's faculties in a particular area inhibits the consideration of things in general. Even J. Robert Oppenheimer, who seems receptive to a general culture, is not outside this judgment. His political and social declarations, for example, scarcely go beyond the level of those of the man in the street. And the opinions of the scientists quoted by *l'Express* are not even on the level of Einstein or Oppenheimer. Their pomposities, in fact, do not rise to the level of the average. They are vague generalities inherited from the nineteenth century, and the fact that they represent the furthest limits of thought of our scientific worthies must be symptomatic of arrested development or of a mental block. Particularly disquieting is the gap between the enormous power they wield and their critical ability, which must be estimated as null. To wield power well entails a certain faculty of criticism, discrimination, judgment, and option. It is impossible to have confidence in men who apparently lack these faculties. Yet it is apparently our fate to be facing a "golden age" in the power of sorcerers who are totally blind to the meaning of the human adventure. When they speak of preserving the seed of outstanding men, whom, pray, do they mean to be the judges. It is clear, alas, that they propose to sit in judgment themselves. It is hardly likely that they will deem a Rimbaud or a Nietszche worthy of posterity. When they announce that they will conserve the genetic mutations which appear to them most favorable, and that they propose to modify the very germ cells in order to produce such and such traits; and when we consider the mediocrity of the scientists themselves outside the confines of their specialties, we can only shudder at the thought of what they will esteem most "favorable."

None of our wise men ever pose the question of the end of all their marvels. The "wherefore" is resolutely passed by. The response which would occur to our contemporaries is: for the sake of happiness. Unfortunately, there is no longer any question of that. One of our best-known specialists in diseases of the nervous system writes: "We will be able to modify man's emotions, desires and thoughts, as we have already done in a rudimentary way with tranquillizers." It will be possible, says our specialist to produce a conviction or an impression of happiness without any real basis for it. Our man of the golden age, therefore, will be capable of "happiness" amid the worst privations. Why, then, promise us extraordinary comforts, hygiene, knowledge, and nourishment if, by simply manipulating our nervous systems, we can be happy without them? The last meager motive we could possibly ascribe to the technical adventure thus vanishes into thin air through the very existence of technique itself.

But what good is it to pose questions of motives? of Why? All that must be the work of some miserable intellectual who balks at technical progress. The attitude of the scientists, at any rate, is clear. Technique exists because it is technique. The golden age will be because it will be. Any other answer is superfluous.

# N O T E S

1. It must be clear that the ends sought cannot be determined by moral science. The dubiousness of ethical judgments, and the differences between systems, make moral science unfit for establishing these ends. But, above all, its subjectivity is a fatal blemish. It depends essentially on the refinement of the individual moral conscience. An average morality is ceaselessly confronted with excessive demands with which it cannot comply. Technical modalities cannot tolerate subjectivity.
2. Some excellent works, such as Robert Jungk's *Le Futur a déjà commencé*, were included in this classification.
3. The material here and below is cited from actual texts.

# The Industrial System and the Cold War

## JOHN KENNETH GALBRAITH

In his book *The New Industrial State,* from which this selection is taken, Galbraith argues that in the technological society all major industrial production involves such long-run planning and such massive investment that the industrialists must find some way of controlling public response. In American society, this requirement of maintaining a growing aggregate demand is met by maintaining a high level of military expenditure which is more easily justified to the public than expenditures more directly related to the public welfare. He believes this is a basic reason for the existence of the Cold War, and that the very nature of the modern technologically based industrial system is conducive to the perpetuation of international military conflict, which in turn poses an ever present danger of total destruction to human civilization.

Modern technology lies behind the threat of eminent destruction to us all.

Galbraith, however, is in no way as pessimistic as Ellul or Marcuse. Galbraith believes that men can in fact control their own destinies if they will only make the effort. As he has made clear in other parts of *The New Industrial State,* he especially believes that in the technological society the scientists and academic intellectuals necessarily come to have a great deal of power, and they may prove to be the one power capable of reversing the trend toward military control and nuclear destruction.

Every man, woman, and child lives under a nuclear sword of Damocles hanging by the slenderest of threads, capable of being cut at any moment by accident or miscalculation or by madness.

JOHN F. KENNEDY, while President

Almost everyone who wins a positive score in an intelligence test recognizes that the selling of goods—the management of demand for particular products—requires well-considered mendacity. Most goods perform commonplace functions—they suppress hunger, serve alcohol or nicotine addiction, move people gradually through heavy traffic, move waste products more rapidly through the intestinal tract or assist in removing filth. Little or nothing of importance can truthfully be said about the way a product performs these routine functions. Flat lies as to their performance are generally impermissible. But a surrogate for the truth, in which minor or even imaginary qualities confer great benefits, is essential.

It is hard to compromise on the advantages of rigorous candor but it may be, as a practical matter, that this contrivance does little direct damage. As noted, only in a comparatively affluent country are people open to persuasion on how they spend their money. Being affluent, it does not greatly matter how they spend it. Meretricious argument, if it influences unimportant decision, is evidently undamaging. And, more important, the case is recognized, subjectively, as being meretricious. That is because modern man is exposed to a large volume of information of varying degrees of unreliability. In response he establishes a system of discounts which he applies to various sources almost without thought. Information from a friend or neighbor, in the absence of a specific reputation for falsehood, is assumed to be reliable. Similarly that from a teacher or a scientist on his subject, and that from a physician, prognoses of the effects of overeating, alcohol and tobacco and diagnoses of cancer apart. Historians, as distinct from official historians and autobiographers, are assumed to tell the truth. So are most journalists. For pundits and preachers on the probability of doom there is a very heavy discount, as there is for politicians discussing moral integrity, peace and disarmament. The discount becomes nearly total for all forms of advertising. The merest child watching television dismisses the health and status-giving claims of a breakfast cereal as "a commercial." Conceivably, for nonlethal products, the government should not presume to insist on truth in advertising. People might assume success and then fail to apply the automatic discount which is their present more comprehensive protection.

Failure to win belief does not impair the effectiveness of the management of demand for consumer products. Management involves the creation of a compelling image of the product in the mind of the consumer. To this he responds more or less automatically under circumstances where the purchase does not merit a great deal of thought. For building this image, palpable fantasy may be more valuable than circumstantial evidence.

## 2

Fantasy and image-building also play an important role in the relationship between the industrial system and the state. By contriving an appropriate image of the position, prospects, problems or dangers of the state the industrial system can insure a reaction favorable to its needs. If the image is one of a country lagging in technological development in a world where that is a prime test of national success, it can insure investment in scientific research and technological development. If the image is of a nation beset by enemies, there will be responding investment in weapons. If it is one of a state in which liberty is threatened by controls, there will be resistance to regulation of various kinds.

However, the process of building these images is a good deal less obvious than that by which the demands of the consumer are created. In consequence, belief is a good deal deeper. A measure of amiable cynicism is associated with the management of demand for cigarettes or soap; not all involved will imagine that their use provides a formula for a long, happy or infinitely inoffensive life. More often, perhaps, there is professional pride in a measure of workmanlike bamboozlement. Only the oratory of the advertising industry is firmly grounded in sincerity. But the images of the state, in contrast, are taken very seriously. The men who contrive, or in the more frequent case perpetuate them, do so with the utmost seriousness. They persuade themselves. They see the result not as the image of reality but as the reality. To suggest that it is imagery is to be irresponsible, eccentric or, conceivably, subversive. As a result, though in public affairs as well as in private affairs, and for the same reasons, we are subject to contrivance that serves the industrial system, it takes a far greater effort of mind to see imagery as imagery and contrivance as contrivance in the field of public affairs. But since, for that reason, the normal discounts do not operate, it is much more important that they be identified.

### 3

The industrial system requires, we have seen, a large public sector for the stabilization of aggregate demand. And the system's planning, we have seen, reaches its highest state of development in conjunction with modern military procurement. The latter is supported by large sums of money. These are easily obtained by a process that is routine; it would require far more effort by a President to reduce military spending by twenty per cent than to increase it by a like amount. To hold at a given level or, better, to allow modest increases from year to year, is the easiest of all.[1] It is necessary, however, that there be an image of the world which justifies or rationalizes the military expenditures that the arrangement requires.

For nearly twenty years, as this is written, the requisite image has been that of the Cold War. That this image owes its existence only to the needs of the industrial system is not suggested for a second. The revolutionary and national aspirations of the Soviets, and more recently of the Chinese, and the compulsive vigor of their assertion, were the undoubted historical source. But history must be separated from result. (We may also ignore for the moment the purposes the Cold War serves in the Communist countries.)

In its more simplistic outline in the last twenty years, the relation of the Cold War to the needs of the industrial system has been remarkably close. It is a relentless, implacable, permanent, but ultimately benign, struggle with the world Communist movement as led by the Soviet Union. It is occasioned by the difference in economic systems from which, primarily, are derived differences in individual liberty.[2] The latter contrast is stark and unshackled. The highly organized and planned system of the Soviets requires the subordination of the individual to the goals of the state. He is constrained in his expression to a spectrum of acceptable belief. No such constraint by organization or planning is required by the western system of free enterprise.

Both systems must be evangelistic. Communism, tactical concessions to coexistence notwithstanding, is committed to ultimate and universal dominance. But no man who believes in liberty can accept a world that is forever half slave and half free.

The incompatibility of the systems, and the associated evangelism, lead directly to military competition. The Soviets would impose their system by force if they could; a strong deterrent prevents this and sustains faith in the ultimate and necessary triumph of liberty. In the main, this competition is technological—its decisive feature is the competitive development of weapons and weapons systems and related defenses.

This competition is not unlimited; it proceeds within generous but real limits of cost. But although it is deemed somewhat reckless to say so, the competition is ultimately benign. That is because, if the competition is energetically pursued, it tends to a stalemate—neither side can destroy the other without suffering unacceptable damage itself. And, both being rational, the showdown is avoided. Disarmament is regarded as a serious threat to a balanced prospect for reciprocal destruction. For, since ambitions are unrelenting and good faith lacking, there is danger of being tricked by negotiations into concessions which would allow the other side to destroy with impunity. The competition is held to be safer, so, although it is discussed, few associated with these matters take seriously the possibility of disarmament. Rather, the discussion is an act of obeisance. It makes clear that the arms competition is being undertaken in lieu of successful disarmament instead of for its own sake.

All features of this competition are closely congruent with need. Since the aspirations of the Communists are implacable, there is no danger that momentary accommodation or easing of tension will lead to a reduction in outlays. It can only be tactical or a trick. The ruling passion will always be "how to get on with their world revolution." [3] In an orthodox conflict the arrival of peace abruptly removes the support for further outlays. A war without fighting neatly obviates the danger that fighting will stop. By its nature a technological competition is never resolved. Safety depends on keeping innovations at a high level—although not at the highest possible level, for there are some things that are simply too expensive. Obsolescence in a technological competition is a nearly perfect substitute for battlefield attrition. Formal agreement to arrest the competition is excluded by the belief that it is more dangerous than the competition. Once war involved the conscription of a large mass of low-wage participants on whom the dangers and discomforts of the battlefield fell with particular weight. In consequence it encountered, although by no means universally, the opposition of the working masses. The Cold War arouses no such antipathy. Nor has the modern union energy to spare for what would seem to be a purely intellectual reaction against immediate interest. So the unions, too, find the Cold War image generally agreeable.

Even a calculation that the competition may, at some point, lead to total destruction of all life is not a definitive objection. Liberty, not material well-being, is involved. This is an ultimate value that cannot be compromised in the face of any threat. "I am confident that the vast majority of the American people would passionately reject . . . ignominious defeatism and, instead, proclaim: 'Rather dead than Red!' " [4] Thus the competition is protected from even the most adverse estimates of its outcome.

The power of the Cold War image in the United States has not been constant. In the decade of the fifties it reached something of a zenith. The then Secretary of State, John Foster Dulles, saw its acceptance not only as an exercise in social belief but as a test of religious ardor and moral stamina. Nor was acceptance entirely voluntary. Congressional committees, other public investigatory bodies, personnel security boards and private magistrates in the motion picture and communications industries reasoned that if the struggle for liberty were so important it should be obligatory. Dissent or even insufficient zeal could lead to loss of employment, other economic sanction or social ostracism. These circumstances were highly favorable to the weapons competition. It proceeded with vigor and even abandon. Numerous weapons systems, some emerging from the services and some from firms individually identified with a service, were put into simultaneous and overlapping development. To the competition with the Soviets was added the further zest of competition between the sponsoring services. Identification and adaptation were facilitated by drawing officials of the Defense Department for short terms of duty—the average during much of the decade was less than a year—from the industrial technostructure. Secretaries of Defense, during this period, refrained from interfering with subordinate decision-making and, indeed, were principally functional in their public relations. That the weapons competition, and the image of international relations on which it depended, originated partly in the industrial system was recognized with remarkable explicitness by President Eisenhower. He noted just before leaving office that the "conjunction of an immense military establishment and a large arms industry" was something new in the American experience and urged that the nation "guard against the acquisition of unwarranted influence, whether sought or unsought, by the military industrial complex. The potential for the disastrous rise of misplaced power exists and will persist . . . we should take nothing for granted."

## 4

The problem is what not to take for granted—and how. The industrial system helps win belief for the image of implacable conflict (with associated features) that justifies its need. Belief being won, the arms competition seems normal, natural and inevitable as do the actions based upon it. Dissent seems eccentric and irresponsible. Herein is the power of a system that depends on persuasion rather than on compelled support.

Yet, on examination, much of what is believed turns out to be fanciful. The reality in the case of the United States and the Soviet Union is of two large industrial nations. Both, it has been amply shown, can achieve success by their very similar economic tests of success at the same time. Theirs is anything but implacable conflict, anything but a zero sum game as it is actually being played.

There is a large and unquestioned difference in the two systems in the role of politicians, writers, artists and scientists. None may minimize the difference made by the First Amendment. But it is less clear that the contrast in the systems of economic management is so great. Both systems are subject to the imperatives of industrialization. This for both means planning. And while each uses different techniques for dealing with the individual who contracts out of the planning, planning in all cases means setting aside the market mechanism in favor of the control of prices and individual economic behavior. Both countries, quite clearly, solicit belief for what serves the goals of the industrial mechanism. Instead of contrast leading to implacable conflict, a more evident economic tendency is convergence.

The notion that the arms competition is ultimately benign likewise has small foundation. There is no inconsiderable chance of accident. There is always a chance that some day some true believer will react to the liturgy of conflict and provoke the ultimate conflict.

That the risks of agreed disarmament are greater than those of a continuing and unresolved weapons competition is also unproven. It is not clear why agreements can be negotiated in good faith with the Communists on all subjects except disarmament. To eliminate civilized life for all time in response to a short-run calculation that liberty might otherwise be endangered is also irrational. And those who would make such a decision are themselves strongly subordinate to a system of belief. They are not free men.

It is extremely important in itself to know that our imagery is, in part, derived from the needs of the industrial system. This leads to introspection and scrutiny that would not, otherwise, be forthcoming. For the same reason it helps us to know that part of our view of the world and of its politics originates not in our minds but in the needs of the industrial system.

But two other steps are also necessary. One is to insure that skeptical scrutiny of official belief is an important political function. The other is to meet the technological and planning needs of the industrial system by ways that are less mortal than the weapons competition.


# 5


In the past, imagery favorable to the entrepreneur was assured of close scrutiny because of the opposed pecuniary interest of the trade unions. If the entrepreneur sought to impose on the society in which enterprise was promoted by a tax system which fell resoundingly on the poor, the unions could be counted upon to come up with a countering doctrine. There is no hope that they will serve a similar function in relation to the images of foreign policy. For, apart from their general enfeeblement, their needs on these matters are far too closely aligned with those of the technostructure.

The principal hope for such scrutiny, in conjunction with the political power to make it effective, lies with the educational and scientific estate. In the past, this community has been ambiguous as regards the imagery of the industrial system. In economics, on such matters as the control of the firm by the market or the origin of wants with the sovereign individual, its tendency, we have seen, has been to underwrite the needed beliefs of the industrial system. On larger questions of foreign policy, this tendency has been less clear. In the early years of the Cold War, there was a fairly full acceptance of its tenets. And for very good reason. Stalinist oppression, later to be affirmed by the Soviets themselves, was no contrivance. It was highly objective. So was the overt attack in Korea. In their wake university specialists in Cold War strategy, and the associated arms competition, proliferated. Doctrines of deterrence, war games, coalition architecture and economic warfare became fashionable subjects for university re- search, reflection and instruction. At the highest levels of sophistication, scholars calculated the acceptable levels of loss in the event of nuclear war and weighed the comparative disadvantages of 40 or 80 million casu- alties. University centers for the study of international relations, which had once concerned themselves with peace, became preoccupied with the Cold War. Close relations were maintained with the services; a small aristocracy of scholars did periodic duty with RAND. Scientists and en- gineers had similar association with the services or defense firms. It was easy to imagine that the educational and scientific estate would come to have much the same relation, by identification and adaptation, to the state in these matters as the technostructure itself. Any hope of a different view of the imagery by which all alike were sustained would be lost.

On the whole, it has not happened. The larger educational and scientific estate has not been strongly receptive to the Cold War imagery. Its mood has on the whole been one of growing skepticism. And the Cold War spe- cialists within the scholarly community have become an increasingly alien- ated group. The price of an intimate and committed association with official war planning has often been some slight suspicion of scholarly rectitude.

There are a number of reasons for this. The scientists have been pecul- iarly situated to see the dangers of the weapons competition including the possibilities of conflict by accident. It was they, not the university special- ists on international relations or the professional diplomats, who instituted the steps leading to the partial test ban. They have similarly led on other discussions with the Soviets[5] on weapons control and disarmament. There has been general and growing suspicion of the doctrine of implacable con- flict based on a bilateral confrontation of good and evil. The educational and scientific estate has also been open to evidence on the growing plural- ism of the Communist world with its adverse effect on the doctrine of monolithic and hostile conspiracy. There would appear to have been a similar response to liberalizing trends in the Communist world with the accompanying implication that the appropriate policy is not one of conflict but of patience. Finally, the educational and scientific estate has been open to the view that Communist protestations in behalf of a policy of peaceful coexistence may not be a trick but could reflect a disinterest in nuclear annihilation.

In the present decade there has been a recurrent conflict between the university community and the intellectuals on the one hand and the State Department and foreign policy establishment on the other. The image of a unified conspiracy as manifested in the Cold War imagery requires an automatic reaction to any Communist initiative. Otherwise, after exploiting one opportunity, it will be encouraged to proceed to the next. This has been deeply questioned by the educational and scientific estate. It is, on the whole, an encouraging development.

As the educational and scientific estate grows in numbers and self-confidence; and as it comes to realize that foreign policy is based on an imagery that derives in part from the needs of the industrial system; and as it realizes further that this tendency is organic; and as it sees that the only corrective is its own scrutiny and involvement and that this involvement is not a matter of choice but an obligation imposed by its position in the economic and political structure, we can reasonably expect it to be more effective. Nothing in our time is more important.

## 6

In the field of international relations, especially since the onset of the Cold War, high public officials have invariably been more diligent in instructing other governments than their own. Though often cautious and deferential in their relations with the Congress, Secretaries of State have been bold and forthright in informing the Soviets of their error. The late John Foster Dulles rarely missed an opportunity to advise the Russians on the merits of liberty and the rule of law and the sanctity of freedom of speech. He was more reserved as regards Senator Joseph McCarthy although the latter, on frequent occasions, attacked freedom of expression and due process and did not omit to concern himself with Mr. Dulles's own Department. Mr. Dean Rusk, a circumspect man in dealing with domestic critics, especially those who might charge undue liberalism in relations with China, has shown contrasting boldness in telling the Communist powers of their shortcomings. Indeed, it may be laid down as a rule of foreign relations that the lower the probability that advice will be taken, the more firmly it will be proffered. Our officials are more circumspect in advising the Congress of its error than in admonishing the British. They are much more cautious in telling the British what to do than the French. They are least inhibited in instructing the Soviets and the Chinese, and it is rare that the leaders of either of the latter two countries will encounter a State Department speech which fails to inform them of their faults and point the way to improvement. The tendency of Soviet and Chinese leaders in instructing the United States is the same. The action in response to this advice is slight but does not discourage it.

No progress can be made in reducing the commitment to the Cold War without concurrent action of the Soviet Union.[6] On this it is well to be completely clear. Still there is merit in departing from the rules and addressing advice in this matter to the United States. It is the country that one can advise with effect as distinct from immunity. It is also richer than the Soviet Union, has greater scientific and technological resources and tends, in consequence, to be the pace-setter in the weapons competition. If we understand that we are subject to the imagery of the industrial system in these matters, and seek to act in accordance not with the image but with the reality of our situation, then it may be possible to make a bargain with the Soviets. It may also prove impossible. We do not know for sure to what images the Soviets are subject. We may wisely assume that, as in other matters, there are parallel tendencies here and that the weapons competition has an organic role in Soviet society. Yet it remains that the Cold War has elements of a self-fulfilling prophecy for it has cultivated the reciprocal mistrust which it assumes. Only if we understand our situation is there a chance that matters will improve.

It is also extremely important that we be aware of what, given the needs of the industrial system, can be made to happen most easily. Escape from the weapons competition, with its attendant dangers, should follow the path of least rather than of maximum resistance. In the past we have proposed Calvinist solutions and made no progress. We shall do better with Catholic solutions which, if less deeply satisfying to the Calvinist soul, could serve to keep it longer in this world.

# 7

In the conventional view, as earlier noted, we could escape our commitment to the weapons competition without insuperable economic difficulty. We would need to offset the decline in arms expenditure by increasing other public outlays or by cutting taxes or by both, and we would need to help those affected retrain, re-educate and relocate themselves. These would be formidable but feasible undertakings. And without minimizing the required action, the orthodox discussion of disarmament almost invariably concludes by saying how welcome would be this challenging task. This pious expression of hope is also partly liturgical. Given the remarkable destructiveness of modern weapons, it is necessary to assure ourselves that we are not dependent on their production. Any other view of the economy is unsettling.[7] Additionally, the ancient Marxian contention, still reflected in some modern Soviet propaganda, holds that a capitalist economy suffers from an inherently limited market. Arms expenditure, like imperialism, is one of the necessary correctives. No circumspect scholar wishes to have it said that he has served, wittingly or unwittingly, the purposes of Communist propaganda. Indeed, one of the more cautious tenets of Cold War behavior was that no scholar should do so. So grave was this conflict that embarrassing truth should be constrained for *raison d'état*.

There is, in fact, nothing to the Marxian contention. The market is not limited as Marx held; the management of aggregate demand, a possibility which he did not foresee, can be served by different types of public spending. And it has now been amply shown that, by such management, the size of the market can be increased as employment or other considerations require.[8] Arms expenditures have no unique value for increasing aggregate demand.

But the orthodox statement of the problem of disarmament, as the present analysis also amply shows, is deficient in two other respects. One cannot replace the spending for armaments with private outlays for consumption and investment, such as would be encouraged by a massive reduction in taxes. The regulation of aggregate demand requires that the public sector of the economy be large. It must be so if personal income and corporation taxes are to be large enough to have their indispensable stabilizing effect.

And while all expenditures, whether for arms or old age pensions or air pollution, add to demand, not all play the same role in underwriting technology. Military spending, we have seen, is highly serviceable in this regard. It also pays for innovation that may be useful for civilian production.[9] Risks that would otherwise be unacceptable can be assumed in the civilian economy if they are protected by the much more nearly riskless weapons economy. General Dynamics was helped to survive its disastrous misadventure on jet air transports earlier mentioned,[10] and the Studebaker

Corporation was able to survive the loss of its automobile business[11] because of a large (and in the case of Studebaker) expanding participation in military procurement. These advantages of the weapons competition to the industrial system could not easily be sacrificed by the industrial system. A simple increase in consumer spending resulting from tax reduction or in public spending for housing or pensions would be no substitute. A drastic reduction in weapons competition following a general release from the commitment to the Cold War would be sharply in conflict with the needs of the industrial system.[12]

But these needs do not have to be met by weapons. Anything that is roughly equivalent in scale and technical complexity will serve. Thus, could the image of the conflict with the Soviet Union be shifted from weapons competition to more general scientific and engineering competition, this would be equally satisfactory provided always that the costs are sufficiently great.

## 8

It is the nature of competition that the rewards of winning need not be examined. To excel, or to hope to excel, is sufficient to justify the contest, and this is equally the case for football, chess, sexual prowess, money-making or scientific achievement. A scientific and engineering competition in any field is thus quite as capable of enlisting the serious energies of man as a weapons competition. And akin to an athletic competition, while it is capable of generating a substantial amount of reciprocal ill will, it could be much more benign as to pollution of atmosphere, possibility of accident, and ultimate outcome than a weapons competition.

It is also clear that we have already come some distance along this path in our relations with the Soviet Union. The competition in space exploration is largely—although not totally—devoid of military implication. It has shown that it can arouse the competitive passions of both countries. It is devoid of danger of accident except to the passengers. And, as compared with earlier competition in transoceanic aviation, this is small. In relation to the needs of the industrial system, the space competition is nearly ideal. It requires very high spending on complex and sophisticated technology. It underwrites the same highly developed planning as does the weapons competition and, hence, is an admirable substitute for it.

The imagery of the industrial system strongly supports the space race.

It is held to be of the utmost importance to the international prestige of the United States that its vehicles be first to the moon, the other parts of the solar system and the less convenient reaches of the universe.

There has been some tendency to question the validity of this imagery. Why is it uniquely important that the United States be first to Saturn? Is it likely that the imperial prospect will be especially rewarding? Is not the area of cultivable land likely to be small? Are there not better uses for the resources so employed? There is no rational answer to these questions as there is none to a query as to why negotiated disarmament is inherently more dangerous than a continuance of the weapons competition. Truth in both instances is subordinate to need and the needed belief. But this does not affect the value of the space competition in meeting the needs of the industrial system in a comparatively harmless instead of in an extremely dangerous competition. A similar case can be made for competitive underwriting of the widest area of general scientific research; in high speed land and air communications; in exploring the ocean floor and the regions below the earth's crust; in altering climate for better or worse; and much more.

The industrial system has not become identified with the weapons competition by preference or because it is inherently bloody. Rather, this has been the area where the largest amount of money to support planning was available with the fewest questions asked. And since armies and cannon have always been in the public sector, government underwriting in this area had the fewest overtones of socialism. But the space race shows that underwriting outside the area of weaponry is equally acceptable.

The path to salvation for the two great industrial systems is now clear. Whether it will be followed is less certain. There must be agreement on arresting and eliminating the competition in lethal technology. On this, survival of both the industrial and the nonindustrial populations of the world plausibly depends. It is of prime importance to this effort that it be realized how much of past action has been based not on reality but on imagery and the sources of the latter. Nor may it be supposed that this imagery is confined to one side. Discussion of disarmament must now result in action. It can no longer serve, as now, as the surrogate for action.

But agreement will be much less painful if competition continues and is encouraged and widened in nonlethal spheres. This competition is not a luxury; it serves an organic need of the industrial system as now constituted. And it does not culminate in explosions of immeasurable effect.

# NOTES

1. ". . . an established tradition . . . holds that a bill to spend billions of dollars for the machinery of war must be rushed through the House and the Senate in a matter of hours, while a treaty to advance the cause of peace, or a program to help the undeveloped nations . . . guarantee the rights of all our citizens, or . . . to advance the interests of the poor must be scrutinized and debated and amended and thrashed over for weeks and perhaps months." Senator Gaylord Nelson, U. S. Senate, February, 1964. Quoted by Julius Duscha, *Arms, Money and Politics* (New York: Ives Washburn, 1965), p. 2.

2. "The Soviet leadership is irrevocably committed to the achievement of the ultimate Communist objective, which is annihilation of the capitalist system and establishment of Communist dictatorship over all the nations of the world. . . . Any pacts and agreements with the Soviets can be expected to be as meaningless and one-sided in the future as they have been in the past. . . . The Soviets endeavor to attain their ends without getting involved in a nuclear war, even if they were certain of winning it." Thomas S. Power, General, USAF Ret., *Design for Survival* (New York: Coward, 1964), pp. 43–44.

3. Secretary of State Dean Rusk, "Address before American Political Science Association," Washington, D.C., September, 1965.

4. Power, *op. cit.,* p. 69.

5. Soviet scientists, perhaps similarly motivated, seem to have assumed similar leadership.

6. In the mystique of the Cold War, the Chinese are playing an increasingly important role and their behavior is highly favorable to the image of enduring conflict. However, it is not yet practical to argue that China is scientifically and technologically a serious competitor to the United States in the weapons competition.

7. For a very good but generally orthodox view of the task, see *Report of the Committee on the Economic Impact of Defense Disarmament*, July, 1965. This report does urge, very sensibly, that the government replace defense expenditures with increased support for scientific and technological development.

8. The point is now conceded at least by the younger generation of Soviet economists.

9. Although it is increasingly the view of scientists and engineers that the civilian applications of military research and development are rather limited. "Of the total [present research and development] effort, overwhelmingly oriented to defense, relatively little is directed toward the creation of new consumer products, or to improve machines to make

the products, or to improve processes to make the machines." Secretary of Commerce Luther Hodges. Quoted by Don K. Price in *The Scientific Estate* (Cambridge: Harvard University Press, 1965), p. 40.

10. Richard Austin Smith, *Corporations in Crisis* (New York: Doubleday, 1963), pp. 63 *et seq.*

11. The effect of military orders in saving the company is described by Duscha, *op. cit.*, p. 16.

12. The latter, we may be reminded once more, would not react with open advocacy of the Cold War. But in conjunction with the services, the industrial system is the source of attitudes and estimates on disarmament action and its effects. The relevant estimates would show the impact on technical development, on parallel Soviet development, probable evasion, eventual Soviet reaction and, in sum, on national security. These estimates will be the working materials of those who make policy on disarmament as well as of the White House, Bureau of the Budget and the Congress. Far more effectively than any open advocacy, they will reflect the needs of the industrial system.

# The Scientific Intellectual

## L E W I S   S.   F E U E R

In this essay Feuer strikingly depicts the crisis of
conscience of the modern scientist. For several centuries
scientists maintained that science necessarily leads to
greater happiness for human beings. Progress was the
watchword and the one belief shared by all scientists and
all friends of science. But the present generation of
scientists has created nuclear weapons and, thereby, the
capacity to destroy human life. The result of this discovery
of sin has been one of profound shock for many scientists
and of deep concern to all of them.

While Feuer believes that the managerial technicism of
many modern scientists poses a grave danger to human
welfare, especially the danger of a technological tyranny,
he believes that scientists retain a residue of the ancient
commitment to the values of human freedom and human
welfare. The recent rapid growth of scientific concern over
the dangers of science and technology in modern society

*Reprinted from Lewis S. Feuer,* The Scientific Intellectual, *by permission of Basic Books, Inc.* © *1963 by Basic Books, Inc. Publishers,
New York.*

would seem to bear out this more optimistic view of the scientists and technologists.


The ethic of the scientific revolution, as we have seen, was that of an optimistic, expansive view of human life. It was filled with the conviction that science would enhance human happiness. It had confidence in the human estate and in the aims and possibilities of human knowledge. It proposed to alleviate drudgery, and to transform work from an eternal curse to a human joy. It aspired, in its reading of the book of nature, to abrogate the tired dictum of Ecclesiastes, "Knowledge increaseth sorrow." Above all, the scientific revolutionists felt themselves part of an international community of scientific intellectuals who were pointing a way beyond the religious and national creeds which divided mankind.[1] Thus, the American Philosophical Society in 1780 assumed that its members could, despite their country's war with England, communicate freely with English scientists. Its charter declared "that it shall and may be lawful for the said Society by their proper officers, at all times, whether in peace or war, to correspond with learned Societies, as well as individual learned men, of any nation or country. . . ."

The scientific revolutionists had a firm faith in the triumph of human rationality. They knew that scientific advances made possible new modes of destructive warfare, but they believed that the advent of peace would thereby be hastened—for certainly, they thought, people would prefer peace rather than mutual self-destruction. Shortly after the first balloons were flown in 1783, Benjamin Franklin wrote optimistically that now that "five thousand balloons, capable of raising two men each" could be constructed as cheaply as five warships, the age of wars was over. For what princes would wish to undertake the huge expenditure for defense against such an attack? Scientific advance would thus convince "Sovereigns of the Folly of wars." When Franklin was asked what use this new invention would be, he replied, "What good is a new-born baby?" [2] The image of birth was a familiar metaphor among the scientific revolutionists.

During our generation, however, science has become the bearer of a death wish. A scientific counterrevolution has been taking place. When J. Robert Oppenheimer, on July 16, 1945, saw at Alamagordo, New Mexico, the first explosion of an atomic bomb, he recalled the lines of the Bhagavad-Gita, "I am become death—the shatterer of worlds." Two years later, Oppenheimer said, "The physicists have known sin; and this is a knowledge which they cannot lose."

No scientist in the seventeenth century would have dreamed of saying "I am become death." For the scientific revolutionists regarded themselves as harbingers of life. They came to undo the age-old damage to men's minds, to liberate them with the light of knowledge from the dark mythology of original sin. Today a thanatistic conception of knowledge is operative in the scientific unconscious; to know an object is to destroy it. The "new philosophy" of the seventeenth-century scientists was virtually done to death by the committee of scientists which recommended the use of the atomic bomb on the Japanese mainland in 1945. Since then, an ethic of original sin, translated into the languages of decision-making, power-seeking, and electronic computation, has pervaded scientific circles. The scientist is no longer the scientific revolutionist but the laboratory managerialist. The scientists are becoming just one more of society's interest groups, lobbying for their greater share in the national income, and for the perquisites of power and prestige. Scientists, enlisted in nuclear warfare, have become hostile to the hedonist-libertarian ethic, and have nearly severed the cosmopolitan bond of the scientific community.

Among the various groups which had a voice in the decision to use the atomic bomb, the official leaders of science were the least humane. The military chiefs, oddly enough, showed the greatest human compassion. Admiral Leahy declared that to drop the atomic bomb on the Japanese was to adopt "an ethical standard common to the barbarians of the Dark Ages. . . . I was not taught to make war in that fashion. . . ." General Eisenhower hoped we would not "take the lead in introducing into war something as horrible and destructive." General Marshall had compunctions about the bomb's use. On the other hand, the statesmen from left to right, without exception, were singularly oblivious of the moral issues involved. President Truman, in some ways the most Lincolnesque figure to have occupied the White House in the last century, the unsuccessful store-keeper with a common man's touch, read the memorandum of April 25, 1945, from his Secretary of War, Henry L. Stimson: "Within four months we shall in all probability have completed the most terrible weapon ever known in human history. . . . The world in its present state of moral advancement compared with its technical development would be eventually at the mercy of such a weapon. In other words, modern civilization might be completely destroyed." The President, relying on the counsel of his

Secretary and the Scientific Advisory Panel, disregarded the moral issues, and looked upon the question solely as a "military decision." He never coped with the fact that a novel type of warfare was being declared ethically admissible, never thought of the fact that he was contributing to a collapse of the already fractured moral standards of the world. He scarcely pondered the new guilt and anxiety that he was bequeathing to the next generation. His fellow-statesmen were of the same mind. Prime Minister Churchill of Great Britain made similar calculations leading to an identical conclusion, and the leader of the Labour Opposition, Clement Attlee, concurred. Joseph Stalin, on behalf of the Soviet Union, wished the Americans "good use" of the bomb against the Japanese. The patrician Secretary of War, Stimson, sensitive to the arts, decided to spare the city of Kyoto, renowned for its shrines. People were more expendable; the bomb was to be used against Hiroshima, a dual target, a "military installation" surrounded by civilian houses, "most susceptible to damage." "The face of war is the face of death," he later said.[3] As for the Scientific Advisory Panel, composed of four most eminent scientists—Enrico Fermi, Ernest O. Lawrence, J. Robert Oppenheimer, and Arthur H. Compton— it advised and agreed on this final decision. A grotesque compulsion seemed to preside over the deliberations as to the use of the bomb. Japanese arms were beaten, the first peace overtures from the enemy had been received, their navy was destroyed, their economy shattered. The experiment, however, had to be made. Einstein, the godfather of the atomic project, a man with the classical ethics of the scientific revolution, was "completely powerless," as he later said, "to prevent the fateful decision." [4]

Civilization swung a full hundred and eighty degrees from the century of Galileo, Descartes, and the Royal Society to the era of our own Scientific Advisory Panel. For once, the scientists could say they had the accord of public opinion; a poll in the United States, Canada, Britain, and France showed that overwhelming majorities in 1945 approved the atomic bombing of Hiroshima. But herein was the tragedy of the scientific intellectuals. They were no longer the guardians of the "new philosophy," the prophets of a new hope. They were technicians with the prejudices of ordinary men carried away with pride by their new technological accomplishment. A process of what Norbert Wiener has called "the increasing entropy" of the scientific intellect and ethic was under way.

The four great men of the Scientific Advisory Panel believed that there could have been no other decision. Arthur Compton felt that a "firm negative stand" on his part "might still prevent an atomic attack on Japan," but that military considerations made the attack essential. Enrico Fermi had no faith in political progress, and was for the full use of scientific resources: "Whatever Nature has in store for mankind, unpleasant as it may be, men must accept, for ignorance is never better than knowledge." Some of his colleagues at Los Alamos, conscience-stricken, tried to organize on behalf of some scheme of world peace. Fermi would have no part in such activities.[5] What would Bishop Sprat have written, in a new *History of the Scientific Society,* of the virtuosi who felt humanity must press on with nuclear experiment even if it destroyed itself in the process?

During those last fateful weeks, some scientists tried somehow to prevent the use of the atomic bomb. James Franck tried to persuade the administration that the bomb's use was morally reprehensible and that a test demonstration on a barren island before Japanese observers would be effective in bringing about the Japanese surrender. The powerful Scientific Advisory Panel, however, argued that such a test was not practicable; they were for nothing short of the bomb's full military use against a Japanese city. Leo Szilard in desperation prepared a petition, signed by sixty-seven scientists, which said plainly that the bomb's use would be an international crime which would set the precedent for an era of destruction. "Almost without exception," says Szilard in retrospect, "all the creative physicists had misgivings about the use of the bomb." [6] Yet his petition in 1945 elicited a counter-petition among scientists advocating atomic warfare against Japan: "If we can save even a handful of American lives, then let us use this weapon—now!" [7]

According to Norbert Wiener, the managerial scientists were influenced by two types of motives in advocating the bomb's use. In the first place, they had spent billions of dollars, and wished to be able to justify these huge expenditures before any later Congressional interrogation. In this eventuality, "the position of the high administrators of nuclear research would be much stronger if they could make a legitimate or plausible claim that this research had served a major purpose in terminating the war." Second, writes Wiener, there were

> . . . the desires of the gadgeteer to see the wheels go round. Moreover, the whole idea of push-button warfare has an enormous temptation for those who are confident of their power of invention and have a deep distrust of human beings. . . . It is unfortunate in more than one way that the war and the subsequent uneasy peace have brought them to the front. [Although the] working scientists felt very little personal power and had very little desire for it, there was a group of ad-

ministrative gadget workers who were quite sensible of the fact that they now had a new ace in the hole in the struggle for power.[8]

In Nazi Germany, of course, the bureaucratization and sadistification of science had meanwhile proceeded to the most advanced levels. Werner Heisenberg, a genius in theoretical physics with the political philosophy of a Nazi storm trooper, "considered the Nazis' efforts to make Germany powerful of more importance than their excesses." Toward the end of the war, he said, "How fine would it have been if we had won this war." He opposed Nazi stupidities only when they hurt German science, and he talked with Himmler to persuade him that Einstein's theory of relativity, essential in practical work, should not be proscribed because of Einstein's Jewishness. But he also appreciated the Nazis for their presumable readiness to give money "if the plans one has are large enough." Fortunately, Heisenberg never thought of using plutonium for a bomb, and his design for a uranium pile was inferior. When the American bomb was exploded at Hiroshima, the deepest dejection and chagrin came over the interned German physicists, not from humanitarian motives, but because they had failed to invent the bomb for Adolf Hitler. Walther Gerlach, the distinguished physicist, "was the most violently upset of all. He acted like a defeated general. He, the 'Reichsmarshal' for nuclear physics, had not succeeded in his assignment." [9] A hysteria came over the Nazi scientists from which they later emerged with suitable rationalizations. They remained assertive "Aryans." They complained that American Negro troops were among their guards. They were the genteel scientific wing of the moral degeneracy which performed lethal experiments on prisoners and annihilated several million human beings.

The new idol, Experiment, seemed to demand the largest possible magnitude of destruction. An American physicist winced when a Japanese radiologist congratulated him during the first week of the occupation: "I did the experiments years ago, but only on a few rats. But you Americans—you are wonderful. You have made the human experiment!" The benefactors of humanity were transmuted into its malefactors.

The career of the brilliant physicist Edward Teller was perhaps symbolic of the erosion of the classical ethic of science. Brooding in 1940 whether it was right or wrong for science to serve war, convinced in 1945 that the bombing of Hiroshima was a mistake, opposed in 1946 to secrecy in scientific research, he still declared in 1947 that atomic war might "endanger the survival of man," and held to the hope that "a successful, powerful, and patient world government" would secure the co-operation of the Soviet Union in the long run.[10] As the gloom, however, of the so-called Cold War deepened between the United States and the Soviet Union, as the paranoid Stalin put his impress of suspicion and mistrust on the nations' dealings, scientific intellectuals shed their residues of political idealism and became technicians of massive destruction. Edward Teller became the spokesman for the development of magnodestructive hydrogen bombs as well as for their continued testing. When Bertrand Russell proposed to Einstein in 1955 that they bring together an international group of scholars and scientists who would warn all nations of the perils created by atomic weapons, Einstein wrote ruefully that, in America, "the most renowned scientists, who occupy official positions of influence, will hardly be inclined to commit themselves to such an 'adventure.' " [11]

A new species of young scientist is said to be arising in America. He has no use for the hopes of the "new philosophy" of the seventeenth century. He has no philosophy; a few scraps of managerial ideology suffice for him.

> We are raising a generation of young men [writes Norbert Wiener], "who will not look at any scientific project which does not have millions of dollars invested in it. . . . We are for the first time finding a scientific career well paid and attractive to a large number of our best young go-getters. The trouble is that scientific work of the first quality is seldom done by the go-getters, and that the dilution of the intellectual milieu makes it progressively harder for the individual worker with any ideas to get a hearing. . . . The degradation of the position of the scientist as an independent worker and thinker to that of a morally irresponsible stooge in a science-factory has proceeded even more rapidly and devastatingly than I had expected.[12]

The new scientists entering into the positions of national influence, writes the editor of the *Bulletin of the Atomic Scientists,* will be "less intellectual, less different in their interests, social habits and attitudes from people in other walks of life." [13]

When Hitlerism came upon Germany, Einstein said, "The representatives of the scientific world have failed in their duty to defend intellectual values because they have completely lost their passionate love of them. . . . This is the only reason why vicious individuals of inferior intellect have been able to seize power. . . ." [14] The social forces of the atomic age tended similarly to corrupt the ethics of the scientific revolution.

The youth of the United States is now full of admiration for science; scientific careers have become highly desired. But, as the sociologists and pollsters say, the "image" of the scientist has been profoundly transformed. Once he was conceived very much as Sinclair Lewis conceived Arrowsmith—a selfless, disinterested seeker after truth, a benefactor of humanity. Now the sociologists find a new ingredient in the way American youth pictures the scientist; there is an admixture of brutality and sadism in his character. High-school students in the United States feel that the goals of science are not only humanitarian but also "destructive (dissecting, destroying enemies, making explosives that threaten the home, the country, or all mankind)." The scientist is also regarded as very likely engaged in pursuit of his individual gain ("making money, gaining fame and glory").[15] He is no longer, however, the embodiment of the free spirit: "If he works for a big company . . . he is just a cog in a wheel"; if for the government, he is bound to keep secrets, and is under constant surveillance. Einstein, a surviving voice from the classical revolution of 1905, warned at this time that the independence of the scientist was being threatened from within; "the shrewd methods of intellectual and psychic influence brought to bear upon the scientist will prevent the development of genuinely independent personalities. Intellectual individualism and the thirst for scientific knowledge," continued Einstein, "emerged simultaneously in history and have remained inseparable." Now, however, "the man of science has retrogressed to such an extent that he accepts as inevitable the slavery inflicted upon him by national states. He even degrades himself to such an extent that he obediently lends his talents to help perfect the means destined for the general destruction of mankind." Four years later, in 1954, Einstein amazed his fellow-Americans by saying that if he were a young man, deciding again how to make his living, "I would not try to become a scientist or scholar or teacher. I would rather choose to be a plumber or a peddler. . . ."[16]

Science fiction is, from one standpoint, a reflection of the fears and anxieties with which the imaginative reading public regards science and scientists. The tone of science fiction has tended to become increasingly "finimundialist." What is finimundialism? It is a frame of mind which is obsessed with the thought that the world is coming to an end, that atomic radiation, the collapse of the solar system, interplanetary war, the advent of a comet, heat death, or uncontrollable epidemic will soon terminate all human existence. The scientists of the seventeenth century, by contrast, transmitted to literary intellectuals their own attitude of "natiomundialism." Their new world in birth was to be not only braver but—more important—freer and happier. Cyrano de Bergerac wrote his *Voyage to the*

*Moon* in a vein of Epicurean cheerfulness. Cyrano, the empiricist follower of Gassendi, the libertine student of Campanella and Descartes, took pleasure in ridiculing through the eyes of the Moon's inhabitants the wars of earthly princes. With impish Cartesian doubt, he turned things topsy-turvy to awaken his fellow-planetarians from the torpor of their customs. There, where the Moon was not a Moon but a World, he depicted a realm which practiced free love, where "a woman may bring her action against a man for refusing her," and where parents gave obedience to their children. During the nineteenth century, Jules Verne, its most famous synthesizer of science and romance, remained all his life a confirmed optimist, secure in his Catholic faith yet firm in his belief in the triumph of human sanity. The science-fiction writer of today, however, tells of the end of the world —the final chapter written by the sinfulness of man raised to its highest power by the available tools of science. H. G. Wells, greatest of the science-fiction writers, began life as a pupil of Thomas Henry Huxley, strong in his teacher's faith of evolutionary progress. When he died a few months after Hiroshima, he was a total finimundialist: "This world is at the end of its tether. The end of everything we call life is close at hand and cannot be evaded. . . . The writer is convinced that there is no way out or round or through the impasse. It is the end." [17] Contemporary philosophy meanwhile has likewise become filled with this theme of self-destruction. Bertrand Russell, foremost of philosophers, wrote with prescience three decades ago of the new standpoint which would prevail among scientists; power-knowledge would supersede the science which was once born of love of things and persons; underlying emotions of hatred and aggression would come to pervade science, which would be eaten away by its own self-corrosive skepticism.[18]

There is a vitality, however, in the tradition of the scientific intellectuals of the seventeenth century that will survive the hegemony of the managerial technician. For their aspiration coincided with the universal nature of man in his deepest consciousness, and as such still partakes of a deathless quality. The anxieties that irrationalize men are not rooted in the nature of things; they are phenomena of time and place. The rule of the managerial technicians is not itself a technological necessity; it depends largely on the condition of unstable equilibrium in which the perpetual fear of atomic war prevails. The human spirit itself remains discontent with the perversion of its noblest aims to the service of destruction. With only a modicum of good fortune, the "new philosophy" may once more be renewed, and in altered circumstances be able to assert itself once again.

# NOTES

1. The Charter of the Royal Society in 1662 granted it the privilege "to enjoy mutual intelligence and knowledge with all and all manner of strangers and foreigners." *The Record of the Royal Society of London* (3rd ed., London, 1912), pp. 67–8. Thomas Birch, *The History of the Royal Society of London* (London, 1756–1757), Vol. I, pp. 406–7.

2. I. Bernard Cohen, "Benjamin Franklin and Aeronautics," *Journal of the Franklin Institute,* 232 (1941), 103–4, 112.

3. Henry L. Stimson, "The Decision to Use the Atomic Bomb," *Harper's,* 194 (February, 1947), 100.

4. *Einstein on Peace,* ed. Otto Nathan and Heinz Norden (New York, 1960), p. 589.

5. Laura Fermi, *Atoms in the Family* (Chicago, 1945), pp. 244–6. Arthur Compton, *Atomic Quest: A Personal Narrative* (New York, 1956), p. 247.

6. *U.S. News and World Report,* XLIX (August 15, 1960), 68, 64. Cf. Farrington Daniels and Arthur H. Compton, "A Poll of Scientists at Chicago," *Bulletin of the Atomic Scientists,* IV (February, 1948), 44. Michael Amrine, *The Great Decision: The Secret History of the Atomic Bomb* (New York, 1951), pp. 146–7.

7. Arthur H. Compton, *Atomic Quest,* pp. 241–2.

8. Norbert Wiener, *I Am a Mathematician* (New York, 1956), pp. 304–7.

9. Samuel A. Goudsmit, *Alsos* (New York, 1947), pp. 114–18, 120, 135, 168.

10. Philip Morrison, "The Laboratory Demobilizes," *Bulletin of the Atomic Scientists,* II (November, 1946), 5. Laura Fermi, *op. cit.,* p. 220. *U.S. News and World Report,* XLIX (August 15, 1960), 75. Edward Teller, "A Suggested Amendment to the Acheson Report," *Bulletin of the Atomic Scientists,* I (June 1, 1946), 5; "Atomic Scientists Have Two Responsibilities," III (December, 1947), 356; "How Dangerous Are Atomic Weapons?," III (February, 1947), 36.

11. *Einstein on Peace,* p. 631.

12. Norbert Wiener, "A Rebellious Scientist After Two Years," *Bulletin of the Atomic Scientists,* IV (November, 1948), 338–9. Earl W. Lindveit, *Scientists in Government* (Washington, 1960), p. 1.

13. Eugene Rabinowitch, "History's Challenge to Scientists," *Bulletin of the Atomic Scientists,* XII (1956), 239.

14. *Einstein on Peace,* p. 220. Cf. Max Born, "Physics and Politics," *Bulletin of the Atomic Scientists,* XVI (1960), 199.

15. Margaret Mead and Rhoda Metraux, "Images of the Scientist Among High-School Students," *Science,* 126 (August 30, 1957), 386–7.

16. *Einstein on Peace,* pp. 535–6, 613.

17. Cyrano de Bergerac, *A Voyage to the Moon,* trans. A. Lovell (New York, ed. of 1899), pp. xv, 137, 143, 152. Marguerite Allotte de la Füye, *Jules Verne,* trans. Erik de Mauny (New York, 1956), pp. 49–50, 213. H. G. Wells, *Mind at End of Its Tether* (New York, 1946), pp. 1–4.

18. Bertrand Russell, *The Scientific Outlook* (New York, 1931), pp. 94, 100.

# PART III

# The Tyranny of Propaganda

# in the Technological Society

# From News Gathering to News Making:
# A Flood of Pseudo-Events

DANIEL  J.  BOORSTIN

**P**ropaganda and the relation between propaganda
and the technological-industrial system are of crucial
importance in modern society, and they are certainly of
crucial importance in the basic criticisms of our increasingly
technological society. As we have already seen in these
selections from Marcuse, Ellul, and Galbraith, those critics
of modern society who believe we are rapidly developing
a technological tyranny believe that this tyranny is made
possible by the existence of mass propaganda communicated
through the mass media. It is through the propaganda
of the mass media that the technocrats, who are the rulers
of the technological society, manage the beliefs and
responses of the public in order to meet the needs of the
technological system. At least, this is what the critics
of the technological society are arguing. Through
propaganda the technocrats are supposedly able to create

*Reprinted from Daniel J. Boorstin,* The Image, *by permission of
Atheneum Publishers and Weidenfeld & Nicolson. Copyright © 1961
by Daniel J. Boorstin.*

false consciousness among the masses. The masses are not able to see that what they themselves believe in, what they themselves support politically, is contrary to their own best interests, to their own freedom, and to their own economic welfare.

One of the most important works on mass media and propaganda in modern American society is Daniel Boorstin's *The Image*. This work was published long before the works of Marshall McLuhan, and constitutes a more balanced and reasoned argument concerning the relations between the media and the messages.

Boorstin argues that the nature of the media has become an important determinant of the nature of messages used by individuals to arrive at decisions about social action. But Boorstin is not primarily concerned with the physical nature of the media. McLuhan is concerned with the physical media, and he believes that somehow the meanings of messages created in our minds are controlled by the physical nature of the media. Boorstin believes that *the social organization of the media* becomes a primary determinant of the messages constructed and communicated to the public. Boorstin's argument is far more subtle and probably far nearer the truth.

Boorstin argues that the media have become not merely communicators of messages, but creators of messages. In this selection from his work he shows us some of the ways in which this is done and some of the reasons why it is done.

ADMIRING FRIEND:
*"My, that's a beautiful baby you have there!"*
MOTHER:
*"Oh, that's nothing—you should see his photograph!"*

The simplest of our extravagant expectations concerns the amount of novelty in the world. There was a time when the reader of an unexciting newspaper would remark, "How dull is the world today!" Nowadays he says,

"What a dull newspaper!" When the first American newspaper, Benjamin Harris' *Publick Occurrences Both Forreign and Domestick,* appeared in Boston on September 25, 1690, it promised to furnish news regularly once a month. But, the editor explained, it might appear oftener "if any Glut of Occurrences happen." The responsibility for making news was entirely God's—or the Devil's. The newsman's task was only to give "an Account of such considerable things as have arrived unto our Notice."

Although the theology behind this way of looking at events soon dissolved, this view of the news lasted longer. "The skilled and faithful journalist," James Parton observed in 1866, "recording with exactness and power the thing that has come to pass, is Providence addressing men." The story is told of a Southern Baptist clergyman before the Civil War who used to say, when a newspaper was brought in the room, "Be kind enough to let me have it a few minutes, till I see how the Supreme Being is governing the world." Charles A. Dana, one of the great American editors of the nineteenth century, once defended his extensive reporting of crime in the New York *Sun* by saying, "I have always felt that whatever the Divine Providence permitted to occur I was not too proud to report."

Of course, this is now a very old-fashioned way of thinking. Our current point of view is better expressed in the definition by Arthur MacEwen, whom William Randolph Hearst made his first editor of the San Francisco *Examiner:* "News is anything that makes a reader say, 'Gee whiz!' " Or, put more soberly, "News is whatever a good editor chooses to print."

We need not be theologians to see that we have shifted responsibility for making the world interesting from God to the newspaperman. We used to believe there were only so many "events" in the world. If there were not many intriguing or startling occurrences, it was no fault of the reporter. He could not be expected to report what did not exist.

Within the last hundred years, however, and especially in the twentieth century, all this has changed. We expect the papers to be full of news. If there is no news visible to the naked eye, or to the average citizen, we still expect it to be there for the enterprising newsman. The successful reporter is one who can find a story, even if there is no earthquake or assassination or civil war. If he cannot find a story, then he must make one —by the questions he asks of public figures, by the surprising human interest he unfolds from some commonplace event, or by "the news behind the news." If all this fails, then he must give us a "think piece"—an embroidering of well-known facts, or a speculation about startling things to come.

This change in our attitude toward "news" is not merely a basic fact about the history of American newspapers. It is a symptom of a revolutionary change in our attitude toward what happens in the world, how much of it is new, and surprising, and important. Toward how life can be enlivened, toward our power and the power of those who inform and educate and guide us, to provide synthetic happenings to make up for the lack of spontaneous events. Demanding more than the world can give us, we require that something be fabricated to make up for the world's deficiency. This is only one example of our demand for illusions.

Many historical forces help explain how we have come to our present immoderate hopes. But there can be no doubt about what we now expect, nor that it is immoderate. Every American knows the anticipation with which he picks up his morning newspaper at breakfast or opens his evening paper before dinner, or listens to the newscasts every hour on the hour as he drives across country, or watches his favorite commentator on television interpret the events of the day. Many enterprising Americans are now at work to help us satisfy these expectations. Many might be put out of work if we should suddenly moderate our expectations. But it is we who keep them in business and demand that they fill our consciousness with novelties, that they play God for us.

# I

The new kind of synthetic novelty which has flooded our experience I will call "pseudo-events." The common prefix "pseudo" comes from the Greek word meaning false, or intended to deceive. Before I recall the historical forces which have made these pseudo-events possible, have increased the supply of them and the demand for them, I will give a commonplace example.

The owners of a hotel, in an illustration offered by Edward L. Bernays in his pioneer *Crystallizing Public Opinion* (1923), consult a public relations counsel. They ask how to increase their hotel's prestige and so improve their business. In less sophisticated times, the answer might have been to hire a new chef, to improve the plumbing, to paint the rooms, or to install a crystal chandelier in the lobby. The public relations counsel's technique is more indirect. He proposes that the management stage a celebration of the hotel's thirtieth anniversary. A committee is formed, including a prominent banker, a leading society matron, a well-known lawyer, an influential preacher, and an "event" is planned (say a banquet) to call attention to the distinguished service the hotel has been rendering the community. The celebration is held, photographs are taken, the occasion is widely reported, and the object is accomplished. Now this occasion is a pseudo-event, and will illustrate all the essential features of pseudo-events.

This celebration, we can see at the outset, is somewhat—but not entirely—misleading. Presumably the public relations counsel would not have been able to form his committee of prominent citizens if the hotel had not actually been rendering service to the community. On the other hand, if the hotel's services had been all that important, instigation by public relations counsel might not have been necessary. Once the celebration has been held, the celebration itself becomes evidence that the hotel really is a distinguished institution. The occasion actually gives the hotel the prestige to which it is pretending.

It is obvious, too, that the value of such a celebration to the owners depends on its being photographed and reported in newspapers, magazines, newsreels, on radio, and over television. It is the report that gives the event its force in the minds of potential customers. The power to make a reportable event is thus the power to make experience. One is reminded of Napoleon's apocryphal reply to his general, who objected that circumstances were unfavorable to a proposed campaign: "Bah, I make circumstances!" The modern public relations counsel—and he is, of course, only one of many twentieth-century creators of pseudo-events—has come close to fulfilling Napoleon's idle boast. "The counsel on public relations," Mr. Bernays explains, "not only knows what news value is, but knowing it, he is in a position to *make news happen*. He is a creator of events."

The intriguing feature of the modern situation, however, comes precisely from the fact that the modern news makers are not God. The news they make happen, the events they create, are somehow not quite real. There remains a tantalizing difference between man-made and God-made events.

A pseudo-event, then, is a happening that possesses the following characteristics:

(1) It is not spontaneous, but comes about because someone has planned, planted, or incited it. Typically, it is not a train wreck or an earthquake, but an interview.

(2) It is planted primarily (not always exclusively) for the immediate purpose of being reported or reproduced. Therefore, its occurrence is arranged for the convenience of the reporting or reproducing

media. Its success is measured by how widely it is reported. Time relations in it are commonly fictitious or factitious; the announcement is given out in advance "for future release" and written as if the event had occurred in the past. The question, "Is it real?" is less important than, "Is it newsworthy?"

(3) Its relation to the underlying reality of the situation is ambiguous. Its interest arises largely from this very ambiguity. Concerning a pseudo-event the question, "What does it mean?" has a new dimension. While the news interest in a train wreck is in *what* happened and in the real consequences, the interest in an interview is always, in a sense, in *whether* it really happened and in what might have been the motives. Did the statement really mean what it said? Without some of this ambiguity a pseudo-event cannot be very interesting.

(4) Usually it is intended to be a self-fulfilling prophecy. The hotel's thirtieth-anniversary celebration, by saying that the hotel is a distinguished institution, actually makes it one.

.    .    .

## IV

In many subtle ways, the rise of pseudo-events has mixed up our roles as actors and as audience—or, the philosophers would say, as "object" and as "subject." Now we can oscillate between the two roles. "The movies are the only business," Will Rogers once remarked, "where you can go out front and applaud yourself." Nowadays one need not be a professional actor to have this satisfaction. We can appear in the mob scene and then go home and see ourselves on the television screen. No wonder we become confused about what is spontaneous, about what is really going on out there!

New forms of pseudo-events, especially in the world of politics, thus offer a new kind of bewilderment to both politician and newsman. The politician . . . himself in a sense composes the story; the journalist . . . himself generates the event. The citizen can hardly be expected to assess the reality when the participants themselves are so often unsure who is doing the deed and who is making the report of it. Who is the history, and who is the historian?

An admirable example of this new intertwinement of subject and object, of the history and the historian, of the actor and the reporter, is the so-called news "leak." By now the leak has become an important and well-established institution in American politics. It is, in fact, one of the main vehicles for communicating important information from officials to the public.

A clue to the new unreality of the citizen's world is the perverse new meaning now given to the word "leak." To leak, according to the dictionary, is to "let a fluid substance out or in accidentally: as, the ship leaks." But nowadays a news leak is one of the most elaborately planned ways of emitting information. It is, of course, a way in which a government official, with some clearly defined purpose (a leak, even more than a direct announcement, is apt to have some definite devious purpose behind it) makes an announcement, asks a question, or puts a suggestion. It might more accurately be called a *"sub rosa* announcement," an "indirect statement," or "cloaked news."

The news leak is a pseudo-event par excellence. In its origin and growth, the leak illustrates another axiom of the world of pseudo-events: pseudo-events produce more pseudo-events. I will say more on this later.

With the elaboration of news-gathering facilities in Washington—of regular, planned press conferences, of prepared statements for future release, and of countless other practices—the news protocol has hardened. Both government officials and reporters have felt the need for more flexible and more ambiguous modes of communication between them. The Presidential press conference itself actually began as a kind of leak. President Theodore Roosevelt for some time allowed Lincoln Steffens to interview him as he was being shaved. Other Presidents gave favored correspondents an interview from time to time or dropped hints to friendly journalists. Similarly, the present institution of the news leak began in the irregular practice of a government official's helping a particular correspondent by confidentially giving him information not yet generally released. But today the leak is almost as well organized and as rigidly ruled by protocol as a formal press conference. Being fuller of ambiguity, with a welcome atmosphere of confidence and intrigue, it is more appealing to all concerned. The institutionalized leak puts a greater burden of contrivance and pretense on both government officials and reporters.

In Washington these days, and elsewhere on a smaller scale, the custom has grown up among important members of the government of arranging to dine with select representatives of the news corps. Such dinners are usually preceded by drinks, and beforehand there is a certain amount of restrained conviviality. Everyone knows the rules: the occasion is private, and any information given out afterwards must be communicated according to rule and in the technically proper vocabulary. After dinner the undersecretary, the general, or the admiral allows himself to be questioned. He may recount "facts" behind past news, state plans, or declare policy. The reporters have confidence, if not in the ingenuousness of the official, at least in their colleagues' respect of the protocol. Everybody understands the degree of attribution permissible for every statement made: what, if anything, can be directly quoted, what is "background," what is "deep background," what must be ascribed to "a spokesman," to "an informed source," to speculation, to rumor, or to remote possibility.

Such occasions and the reports flowing from them are loaded with ambiguity. The reporter himself often is not clear whether he is being told a simple fact, a newly settled policy, an administrative hope, or whether perhaps untruths are being deliberately diffused to allay public fears that the true facts are really true. The government official himself (who is sometimes no more than a spokesman) may not be clear. The reporter's task is to find a way of weaving these threads of unreality into a fabric that the reader will not recognize as entirely unreal. Some people have criticized the institutionalized leak as a form of domestic counter-intelligence inappropriate in a republic. It has become more and more important and is the source today of many of the most influential reports of current politics.

One example will be enough. On March 26, 1955, *The New York Times* carried a three-column headline on the front page: "U.S. Expects Chinese Reds to Attack Isles in April; Weighs All-Out Defense." Three days later a contradictory headline in the same place read: "Eisenhower Sees No War Now Over Chinese Isles." Under each of these headlines appeared a lengthy story. Neither story named any person as a source of the ostensible facts. The then-undisclosed story (months later recorded by Douglass Cater) was this. In the first instance, Admiral Robert B. Carney, Chief of Naval Operations, had an off-the-record "background" dinner for a few reporters. There the Admiral gave reporters what they (and their readers) took to be facts. Since the story was "not for attribution," reporters were not free to mention some very relevant facts—such as that this was the opinion only of Admiral Carney, that this was the same Admiral Carney who had long been saying that war in Asia was inevitable, and that many in Washington (even in the Joint Chiefs of Staff) did not agree with him. Under the ground rules the first story could appear in the papers only by being given an impersonal authority, an atmosphere of official unanimity which it did not merit. The second, and contradictory, statement was in fact made not by the President himself, but by the President's press secretary, James Hagerty, who, having been alarmed by what he saw in the papers, quickly called a second "background" meeting to deny the stories that had sprouted from the first. What, if anything, did it all mean? Was there any real news here at all—except that there was disagreement between Admiral Carney and James Hagerty? Yet this was the fact newsmen were not free to print.

Pseudo-events spawn other pseudo-events in geometric progression. This is partly because every kind of pseudo-event (being planned) tends to become ritualized, with a protocol and a rigidity all its own. As each type of pseudo-event acquires this rigidity, pressures arise to produce other, derivative, forms of pseudo-event which are more fluid, more tantalizing, and more interestingly ambiguous. Thus, as the press conference (itself a pseudo-event) became formalized, there grew up the institutionalized leak. As the leak becomes formalized still other devices will appear. Of course the shrewd politician or the enterprising newsman knows this and knows how to take advantage of it. Seldom for outright deception; more often simply to make more "news," to provide more "information," or to "improve communication."

For example, a background off-the-record press conference, if it is actually a mere trial balloon or a diplomatic device (as it sometimes was for Secretary of State John Foster Dulles), becomes the basis of official "denials" and "disavowals," of speculation and interpretation by columnists and commentators, and of special interviews on and off television with Senators, Representatives, and other public officials. Any statement or non-statement by anyone in the public eye can become the basis of counter-statements or refusals to comment by others. All these compound the ambiguity of the occasion which first brought them into being.

Nowadays the test of a Washington reporter is seldom his skill at precise dramatic reporting, but more often his adeptness at dark intimation. If he wishes to keep his news channels open he must accumulate a vocabulary and develop a style to conceal his sources and obscure the relation of a supposed event or statement to the underlying facts of life, at the same time seeming to offer hard facts. Much of his stock in trade is his own and other people's speculation about the reality of what he reports. He lives in a penumbra between fact and fantasy. He helps create that very obscurity without which the supposed illumination of his reports would be unnecessary. A deft administrator these days must have similar skills. He must master "the technique of denying the truth without actually lying."

These pseudo-events which flood our consciousness must be distinguished from propaganda. The two do have some characteristics in common. But our peculiar problems come from the fact that pseudo-events are in some respects the opposite of the propaganda which rules totalitarian countries. Propaganda—as prescribed, say, by Hitler in *Mein Kampf*—is information intentionally biased. Its effect depends primarily on its emotional appeal. While a pseudo-event is an ambiguous truth, propaganda is an appealing falsehood. Pseudo-events thrive on our honest desire to be informed, to have "all the facts," and even to have more facts than there really are. But propaganda feeds on our willingness to be inflamed. Pseudo-events appeal to our duty to be educated, propaganda appeals to our desire to be aroused. While propaganda substitutes opinion for facts, pseudo-events are synthetic facts which move people indirectly, by providing the "factual" basis on which they are supposed to make up their minds. Propaganda moves them directly by explicitly making judgments for them.

In a totalitarian society, where people are flooded by purposeful lies, the real facts are of course misrepresented, but the representation itself is not ambiguous. The propaganda lie is asserted as if it were true. Its object is to lead people to believe that the truth is simpler, more intelligible, than it really is. "Now the purpose of propaganda," Hitler explained, "is not continually to produce interesting changes for a few blasé little masters, but to convince; that means, to convince the masses. The masses, however, with their inertia, always need a certain time before they are ready even to notice a thing, and they will lend their memories only to the thousandfold repetition of the most simple ideas." But in our society, pseudo-events make simple facts seem more subtle, more ambiguous, and more speculative than they really are. Propaganda oversimplifies experience, pseudo-events overcomplicate it.

At first it may seem strange that the rise of pseudo-events has coincided with the growth of the professional ethic which obliges newsmen to omit editorializing and personal judgments from their news accounts. But now it is in the making of pseudo-events that newsmen find ample scope for their individuality and creative imagination.

In a democratic society like ours—and more especially in a highly literate, wealthy, competitive, and technologically advanced society—the people can be flooded by pseudo-events. For us, freedom of speech and of the press and of broadcasting includes freedom to create pseudo-events. Competing politicians, competing newsmen, and competing news media contest in this creation. They vie with one another in offering attractive, "informative" accounts and images of the world. They are free to speculate on the facts, to bring new facts into being, to demand answers to their own contrived questions. Our "free market place of ideas" is a place where people are confronted by competing pseudo-events and are allowed to judge among them. When we speak of "informing" the people this is what we really mean.

## V

Until recently we have been justified in believing Abraham Lincoln's familiar maxim: "You may fool all the people some of the time; you can even fool some of the people all the time; but you can't fool all of the people all the time." This has been the foundation-belief of American democracy. Lincoln's appealing slogan rests on two elementary assumptions. First, that there is a clear and visible distinction between sham and reality, between the lies a demagogue would have us believe and the truths which are there all the time. Second, that the people tend to prefer reality to sham, that if offered a choice between a simple truth and a contrived image, they will prefer the truth.

Neither of these any longer fits the facts. Not because people are less intelligent or more dishonest. Rather because great unforeseen changes— the great forward strides of American civilization—have blurred the edges of reality. The pseudo-events which flood our consciousness are neither true nor false in the old familiar senses. The very same advances which have made them possible have also made the images—however planned, contrived, or distorted—more vivid, more attractive, more impressive, and more persuasive than reality itself.

We cannot say that we are being fooled. It is not entirely inaccurate to say that we are being "informed." This world of ambiguity is created by those who believe they are instructing us, by our best public servants, and with our own collaboration. Our problem is the harder to solve because it is created by people working honestly and industriously at respectable jobs. It is not created by demagogues or crooks, by conspiracy or evil purpose. The efficient mass production of pseudo-events—in all kinds of packages, in black-and-white, in technicolor, in words, and in a thousand other forms —is the work of the whole machinery of our society. It is the daily product of men of good will. The media must be fed! The people must be informed! Most pleas for "more information" are therefore misguided. So long as we define information as a knowledge of pseudo-events, "more information" will simply multiply the symptoms without curing the disease.

The American citizen thus lives in a world where fantasy is more real than reality, where the image has more dignity than its original. We hardly dare face our bewilderment, because our ambiguous experience is so pleasantly iridescent, and the solace of belief in contrived reality is so thoroughly real. We have become eager accessories to the great hoaxes of the age. These are the hoaxes we play on ourselves.

Pseudo-events from their very nature tend to be more interesting and more attractive than spontaneous events. Therefore in American public life today pseudo-events tend to drive all other kinds of events out of our consciousness, or at least to overshadow them. Earnest, well-informed citizens seldom notice that their experience of spontaneous events is buried by pseudo-events. Yet nowadays, the more industriously they work at "informing" themselves the more this tends to be true.

In his now-classic work, *Public Opinion,* Walter Lippmann in 1922 began by distinguishing between "the world outside and the pictures in our heads." He defined a "stereotype" as an oversimplified pattern that helps us find meaning in the world. As examples he gave the crude "stereotypes we carry about in our heads," of large and varied classes of people like "Germans," "South Europeans," "Negroes," "Harvard men," "agitators," etc. The stereotype, Lippmann explained, satisfies our needs and helps us defend our prejudices by seeming to give definiteness and consistency to our turbulent and disorderly daily experience. In one sense, of course, stereotypes—the excessively simple, but easily grasped images of racial, national, or religious groups—are only another example of pseudo-events. But, generally speaking, they are closer to propaganda. For they simplify rather than complicate. Stereotypes narrow and limit experience in an emotionally satisfying way; but pseudo-events embroider and dramatize experience in an interesting way. This itself makes pseudo-events far more seductive; intellectually they are more defensible, more intricate, and more intriguing. To discover how the stereotype is made—to unmask the sources of propaganda—is to make the stereotype less believable. Information about the staging of a pseudo-event simply adds to its fascination.

Lippmann's description of stereotypes was helpful in its day. But he wrote before pseudo-events had come in full flood. Photographic journalism was then still in its infancy. Wide World Photos had just been organized by *The New York Times* in 1919. The first wirephoto to attract wide attention was in 1924, when the American Telephone and Telegraph Company sent to *The New York Times* pictures of the Republican Convention in Cleveland which nominated Calvin Coolidge. Associated Press Picture Service was established in 1928. *Life,* the first wide-circulating weekly picture news magazine, appeared in 1936; within a year it had a circulation of 1,000,000, and within two years, 2,000,000. *Look* followed, in 1937. The newsreel, originated in France by Pathé, had been introduced to the United States only in 1910. When Lippmann wrote his book in 1922, radio was not yet reporting news to the consumer; television was of course unknown.

Recent improvements in vividness and speed, the enlargement and multiplying of news-reporting media, and the public's increasing news hunger now make Lippmann's brilliant analysis of the stereotype the legacy of a simpler age. For stereotypes made experience handy to grasp. But pseudo-events would make experience newly and satisfyingly elusive. In 1911 Will Irwin, writing in *Collier's,* described the new era's growing public demand for news as "a crying primal want of the mind, like hunger of the body." The mania for news was a symptom of expectations enlarged far beyond the capacity of the natural world to satisfy. It required a synthetic product. It stirred an irrational and undiscriminating hunger for fancier, more varied items. Stereotypes there had been and always would be; but they only dulled the palate for information. They were an opiate. Pseudo-events whetted the appetite; they aroused news hunger in the very act of satisfying it.

In the age of pseudo-events it is less the artificial simplification than the artificial complication of experience that confuses us. Whenever in the public mind a pseudo-event competes for attention with a spontaneous event in the same field, the pseudo-event will tend to dominate. What happens on television will overshadow what happens off television. Of course I am concerned here not with our private worlds but with our world of public affairs.

Here are some characteristics of pseudo-events which make them overshadow spontaneous events:

(1) Pseudo-events are more dramatic. A television debate between candidates can be planned to be more suspenseful (for example, by reserving questions which are then popped suddenly) than a casual encounter or consecutive formal speeches planned by each separately.

(2) Pseudo-events, being planned for dissemination, are easier to dis-

seminate and to make vivid. Participants are selected for their newsworthy and dramatic interest.

(3) Pseudo-events can be repeated at will, and thus their impression can be re-enforced.

(4) Pseudo-events cost money to create; hence somebody has an interest in disseminating, magnifying, advertising, and extolling them as events worth watching or worth believing. They are therefore advertised in advance, and rerun in order to get money's worth.

(5) Pseudo-events, being planned for intelligibility, are more intelligible and hence more reassuring. Even if we cannot discuss intelligently the qualifications of the candidates or the complicated issues, we can at least judge the effectiveness of a television performance. How comforting to have some political matter we can grasp!

(6) Pseudo-events are more sociable, more conversable, and more convenient to witness. Their occurrence is planned for our convenience. The Sunday newspaper appears when we have a lazy morning for it. Television programs appear when we are ready with our glass of beer. In the office the next morning, Jack Paar's (or any other star performer's) regular late-night show at the usual hour will overshadow in conversation a casual event that suddenly came up and had to find its way into the news.

(7) Knowledge of pseudo-events—of what has been reported, or what has been staged, and how—becomes the test of being "informed." News magazines provide us regularly with quiz questions concerning not what has happened but concerning "names in the news"— what has been reported in the news magazines. Pseudo-events begin to provide that "common discourse" which some of my old-fashioned friends have hoped to find in the Great Books.

(8) Finally, pseudo-events spawn other pseudo-events in geometric progression. They dominate our consciousness simply because there are more of them, and ever more.

By this new Gresham's law of American public life, counterfeit happenings tend to drive spontaneous happenings out of circulation. The rise in the power and prestige of the Presidency is due not only to the broadening powers of the office and the need for quick decisions, but also to the rise of centralized news gathering and broadcasting, and the increase of the Washington press corps. The President has an ever more ready, more frequent, and more centralized access to the world of pseudo-events. A similar explanation helps account for the rising prominence in recent years of the Congressional investigating committees. In many cases these committees have virtually no legislative impulse, and sometimes no intelligible legislative assignment. But they do have an almost unprecedented power, possessed now by no one else in the Federal government except the President, to make news. Newsmen support the committees because the committees feed the newsmen: they live together in happy symbiosis. The battle for power among Washington agencies becomes a contest to dominate the citizen's information of the government. This can most easily be done by fabricating pseudo-events.

A perfect example of how pseudo-events can dominate is the recent popularity of the quiz show format. Its original appeal came less from the fact that such shows were tests of intelligence (or of dissimulation) than from the fact that the situations were elaborately contrived—with isolation booths, armed bank guards, and all the rest—and they purported to inform the public.

The application of the quiz show format to the so-called "Great Debates" between Presidential candidates in the election of 1960 is only another example. These four campaign programs, pompously and self-righteously advertised by the broadcasting networks, were remarkably successful in reducing great national issues to trivial dimensions. With appropriate vulgarity, they might have been called the $400,000 Question (Prize: a $100,-000-a-year job for four years). They were a clinical example of the pseudo-event, of how it is made, why it appeals, and of its consequences for democracy in America.

In origin the Great Debates were confusedly collaborative between politicians and news makers. Public interest centered around the pseudo-event itself: the lighting, make-up, ground rules, whether notes would be allowed, etc. Far more interest was shown in the performance than in what was said. The pseudo-events spawned in turn by the Great Debates were numberless. People who had seen the shows read about them the more avidly, and listened eagerly for interpretations by news commentators. Representatives of both parties made "statements" on the probable effects of the debates. Numerous interviews and discussion programs were broadcast exploring their meaning. Opinion polls kept us informed on the nuances of our own and other people's reactions. Topics of speculation multiplied. Even the question whether there should be a fifth debate became for a while a lively "issue."

The drama of the situation was mostly specious, or at least had an extremely ambiguous relevance to the main (but forgotten) issue: which participant was better qualified for the Presidency. Of course, a man's ability, while standing under klieg lights, without notes, to answer in two and a half minutes a question kept secret until that moment, had only the most dubious relevance—if any at all—to his real qualifications to make deliberate Presidential decisions on long-standing public questions after being instructed by a corps of advisers. The great Presidents in our history (with the possible exception of F.D.R.) would have done miserably; but our most notorious demagogues would have shone. A number of exciting pseudo-events were created—for example, the Quemoy-Matsu issue. But that, too, was a good example of a pseudo-event: it was created to be reported, it concerned a then-quiescent problem, and it put into the most factitious and trivial terms the great and real issue of our relation to Communist China.

The television medium shapes this new kind of political quiz-show spectacular in many crucial ways. Theodore H. White has proven this with copious detail in his *The Making of the President: 1960* (1961). All the circumstances of this particular competition for votes were far more novel than the old word "debate" and the comparisons with the Lincoln-Douglas Debates suggested. Kennedy's great strength in the critical first debate, according to White, was that he was in fact not "debating" at all, but was seizing the opportunity to address the whole nation; while Nixon stuck close to the issues raised by his opponent, rebutting them one by one. Nixon, moreover, suffered a handicap that was serious only on television: he has a light, naturally transparent skin. On an ordinary camera that takes pictures by optical projection, this skin photographs well. But a television camera projects electronically, by an "image-orthicon tube" which has an x-ray effect. This camera penetrates Nixon's transparent skin and brings out (even just after a shave) the tiniest hair growing in the follicles beneath the surface. For the decisive first program Nixon wore a make-up called "Lazy Shave" which was ineffective under these conditions. He therefore looked haggard and heavy-bearded by contrast to Kennedy, who looked pert and clean-cut.

This greatest opportunity in American history to educate the voters by debating the large issues of the campaign failed. The main reason, as White points out, was the compulsions of the medium. "The nature of both TV and radio is that they abhor silence and 'dead time.' All TV and radio discussion programs are compelled to snap question and answer back and forth as if the contestants were adversaries in an intellectual tennis match. Although every experienced newspaperman and inquirer knows that the most thoughtful and responsive answers to any difficult question come after long pause, and that the longer the pause the more illuminating the thought that follows it, nonetheless the electronic media cannot bear to suffer a pause of more than five seconds; a pause of thirty seconds of dead time on air seems interminable. Thus, snapping their two-and-a-half-minute answers back and forth, both candidates could only react for the cameras and the people, they could not think." Whenever either candidate found himself touching a thought too large for two-minute exploration, he quickly retreated. Finally the television-watching voter was left to judge, not on issues explored by thoughtful men, but on the relative capacity of the two candidates to perform under television stress.

Pseudo-events thus lead to emphasis on pseudo-qualifications. Again the self-fulfilling prophecy. If we test Presidential candidates by their talents on TV quiz performances, we will, of course, choose presidents for precisely these qualifications. In a democracy, reality tends to conform to the pseudo-event. Nature imitates art.

We are frustrated by our very efforts publicly to unmask the pseudo-event. Whenever we describe the lighting, the make-up, the studio setting, the rehearsals, etc., we simply arouse more interest. One newsman's interpretation makes us more eager to hear another's. One commentator's speculation that the debates may have little significance makes us curious to hear whether another commentator disagrees.

Pseudo-events do, of course, increase our illusion of grasp on the world, what some have called the American illusion of omnipotence. Perhaps, we come to think, the world's problems can really be settled by "statements," by "Summit" meetings, by a competition of "prestige," by overshadowing images, and by political quiz shows.

Once we have tasted the charm of pseudo-events, we are tempted to believe they are the only important events. Our progress poisons the sources of our experience. And the poison tastes so sweet that it spoils our appetite for plain fact. Our seeming ability to satisfy our exaggerated expectations makes us forget that they are exaggerated.

# Political Propaganda
# and Sociological Propaganda

---

## J A C Q U E S  E L L U L

**P**robably the most profound work written on modern
propaganda is Jacques Ellul's *Propaganda*. Unfortunately,
sociologists and other social scientists have done
exceedingly little creative research or theorizing about
mass media and propaganda in the last twenty years.
This is precisely the period in which the mass media have
really become massive and in which television, above all,
has become an omnipresent force in our national and
international life. Ellul's work has redressed much of
this lack in analysis and promises to stimulate a whole
new generation of thought and research on propaganda
and its relation to the rest of our society.

One of the crucial ideas in Ellul's analysis is
his distinction between political propaganda and
sociological propaganda. Political propaganda is what we
normally think of when we use the word propaganda.
Sociological propaganda permeates our everyday lives; it

*Reprinted from Jacques Ellul,* Propaganda, *by permission of Alfred
A. Knopf, Inc. Copyright © 1965 by Alfred A. Knopf, Inc.*

comes at us from innumerable sources as we make our way through the world. As Ellul argues, it is sociological propaganda that has such a profound effect on individuals' thinking and action. Sociological propaganda is the real subliminal propaganda. It is not flashed on a screen momentarily but is there all the time, all around us. It is omnipresent and so much a part of us that it becomes the background of our everyday lives. It becomes implicit in our thinking and in our actions. It is taken for granted and is no longer available for critical thinking, until someone such as Ellul makes it available by describing and analyzing it. By sociological propaganda Ellul means very largely all those forms of support in our everyday lives for what is often called the American Way of Life or the French Way of Life. It is this way of life that individuals turn into an ideology. It becomes the base point against which everything else is judged. It comes to encapsulate the individual, to enclose him. It becomes a form of tyrannical thought.

First we must distinguish between political propaganda and sociological propaganda. We shall not dwell long on the former because it is the type called immediately to mind by the word propaganda itself. It involves techniques of influence employed by a government, a party, an administration, a pressure group, with a view to changing the behavior of the public. The choice of methods used is deliberate and calculated; the desired goals are clearly distinguished and quite precise, though generally limited. Most often the themes and the objectives are political, as for example with Hitler's or Stalin's propaganda. This is the type of propaganda that can be most clearly distinguished from advertising: the latter has economic ends, the former political ends. Political propaganda can be either strategic or tactical. The former establishes the general line, the array of arguments, the staggering of the campaigns; the latter seeks to obtain immediate results within that framework (such as wartime pamphlets and loudspeakers to obtain the immediate surrender of the enemy).

But this does not cover all propaganda, which also encompasses phenomena much more vast and less certain: the group of manifestations by which any society seeks to integrate the maximum number of individuals into itself, to unify its members' behavior according to a pattern, to spread its style of life abroad, and thus to impose itself on other groups. We call this phenomenon "sociological" propaganda, to show, first of all, that the entire group, consciously or not, expresses itself in this fashion; and to indicate, secondly, that its influence aims much more at an entire style of life than at opinions or even one particular course of behavior.[1]

Of course, within the compass of sociological propaganda itself one or more political propagandas can be expressed. The propaganda of Christianity in the middle ages is an example of this type of sociological propaganda; Benjamin Constant meant just this when he said of France, in 1793: "The entire nation was a vast propaganda operation." And in present times certainly the most accomplished models of this type are American and Chinese propaganda. Although we do not include here the more or less effective campaigns and methods employed by governments, but rather the over-all phenomenon, we find that sociological propaganda combines extremely diverse forms within itself. At this level, advertising as the spreading of a certain style of life can be said to be included in such propaganda, and in the United States this is also true of public relations, human relations, human engineering, the motion pictures, and so on. It is characteristic of a nation living by sociological propaganda that all these influences converge toward the same point, whereas in a society such as France in 1960, they are divergent in their objectives and their intentions.

Sociological propaganda is a phenomenon much more difficult to grasp than political propaganda, and is rarely discussed. *Basically it is the penetration of an ideology by means of its sociological context.* This phenomenon is the reverse of what we have been studying up to now. Propaganda as it is traditionally known implies an attempt to spread an ideology through the mass media of communication in order to lead the public to accept some political or economic structure or to participate in some action. That is the one element common to all the propaganda we have studied. Ideology is disseminated for the purpose of making various political acts acceptable to the people.

But in sociological propaganda the movement is reversed. The existing economic, political, and sociological factors progressively allow an ideology to penetrate individuals or masses. Through the medium of economic and political structures a certain ideology is established, which leads to the active participation of the masses and the adaptation of individuals. The important thing is to make the individual participate actively and to adapt him as much as possible to a specific sociological context.

Such propaganda is essentially diffuse. It is rarely conveyed by catch-words or expressed intentions. Instead it is based on a general climate, an atmosphere that influences people imperceptibly without having the appearance of propaganda; it gets to man through his customs, through his most unconscious habits. It creates new habits in him; it is a sort of persuasion from within. As a result, man adopts new criteria of judgment and choice, adopts them spontaneously, as if he had chosen them himself. But all these criteria are in conformity with the environment and are essentially of a collective nature. Sociological propaganda produces a progressive adaptation to a certain order of things, a certain concept of human relations, which unconsciously molds individuals and makes them conform to society.

Sociological propaganda springs up spontaneously; it is not the result of deliberate propaganda action. No propagandists deliberately use this method, though many practice it unwittingly, and tend in this direction without realizing it. For example, when an American producer makes a film, he has certain definite ideas he wants to express, which are not intended to be propaganda. Rather, the propaganda element is in the American way of life with which he is permeated and which he expresses in his film without realizing it. We see here the force of expansion of a vigorous society, which is totalitarian in the sense of the integration of the individual, and which leads to involuntary behavior.

Sociological propaganda expresses itself in many different ways—in advertising, in the movies (commercial and non-political films), in technology in general, in education, in the *Reader's Digest;* and in social service, case work, and settlement houses. All these influences are in basic accord with each other and lead spontaneously in the same direction; one hesitates to call all this propaganda. Such influences, which mold behavior, seem a far cry from Hitler's great propaganda setup. Unintentional (at least in the first stage), non-political, organized along spontaneous patterns and rhythms, the activities we have lumped together (from a concept that might be judged arbitrary or artificial) are not considered propaganda by either sociologists or the average public.

And yet with deeper and more objective analysis, what does one find? These influences are expressed through the same media as propaganda. They are *really directed* by those who make propaganda. To me this fact seems essential. A government, for example, will have its own public relations, and will also make propaganda. Most of the activities described in this chapter have identical purposes. Besides, these influences follow the same stereotypes and prejudices as propaganda; they stir the same feelings and act on the individual in the same fashion. These are the similarities, which bring these two aspects of propaganda closer together, more than the differences, noted earlier, separate them.

But there is more. Such activities are propaganda to the extent that the combination of advertising, public relations, social welfare, and so on produces a certain general conception of society, a particular way of life. We have not grouped these activities together arbitrarily—they express the same basic notions and interact to make man adopt this particular way of life. From then on, the individual in the clutches of such sociological propaganda believes that those who live this way are on the side of the angels, and those who don't are bad; those who have this conception of society are right, and those who have another conception are in error. Consequently, just as with ordinary propaganda, it is a matter of propagating behavior and myths both good and bad. Furthermore, such propaganda becomes increasingly effective when those subjected to it accept its doctrines on what is *good or bad* (for example, the American Way of Life). There, a whole society actually expresses itself through this propaganda by advertising its kind of life.

By doing that, a society engages in propaganda on the deepest level. Sociologists have recognized that, above all, propaganda must change a person's environment. Krech and Crutchfield insist on this fact, and show that a simple modification of the psychological context can bring about changes of attitude without ever directly attacking particular attitudes or opinions. Similarly, MacDougall says: "One must avoid attacking any trend frontally. It is better to concentrate one's efforts on the creation of psychological conditions so that the desired result seems to come from them naturally." The modification of the psychological climate brings about still other consequences that one cannot obtain directly. This is what Ogle calls "suggestibility"; the degree of suggestibility depends on a man's environment and psychological climate. And that is precisely what modifies the activities mentioned above. It is what makes them propaganda, for their aim is simply to instill in the public an attitude that will prepare the ground for the main propaganda to follow.

Sociological propaganda must act gently. It conditions; it introduces a truth, an ethic in various benign forms, which, although sporadic, end by creating a fully established personality structure. It acts slowly, by penetration, and is most effective in a relatively stable and active society, or in the tensions between an expanding society and one that is disintegrating (or in an expanding group within a disintegrating society). Under these conditions it is sufficient in itself; it is not merely a preliminary sub-propaganda. But sociological propaganda is inadequate in a moment of crisis. Nor is it able to move the masses to action in exceptional circumstances. Therefore, it must sometimes be strengthened by the classic kind of propaganda, which leads to action.

At such times sociological propaganda will appear to be the medium that has prepared the ground for direct propaganda; it becomes identified with sub-propaganda. Nothing is easier than to graft a direct propaganda onto a setting prepared by sociological propaganda; besides, sociological propaganda may itself be transformed into direct propaganda. Then, by a series of intermediate stages, we not only see one turn into the other, but also a smooth transition from what was merely a spontaneous affirmation of a way of life to the deliberate affirmation of a truth. This process has been described in an article by Edward L. Bernays: this so-called "engineering approach" is tied to a combination of professional research methods through which one gets people to adopt and actively support certain ideas or programs as soon as they become aware of them. This applies also to political matters; and since 1936 the National Association of Manufacturers has attempted to fight the development of leftist trends with such methods. In 1938 the N.A.M. spent a half-million dollars to support the type of capitalism it represents. This sum was increased to three million in 1945 and to five million in 1946; this propaganda paved the way for the Taft-Hartley Law. It was a matter of "selling" the American economic system. Here we are truly in the domain of propaganda; and we see the multiple methods employed to influence opinion, as well as the strong tie between sociological and direct propaganda.

Sociological propaganda, involuntary at first, becomes more and more deliberate, and ends up by exercising influence. One example is the code drawn up by the Motion Picture Association, which requires films to promote "the highest types of social life," "the proper conception of society," "the proper standards of life," and to avoid "any ridicule of the law (natural or human) or sympathy for those who violate the law." Another is J. Arthur Rank's explanation of the purpose of his films: "When does an export article become more than an export article? When it is a British film. When the magnificent productions of Ealing Studios appear in the world, they represent something better than just a step forward toward a higher level of export. . . ." Such films are then propaganda for the British way of life.

The first element of awareness in the context of sociological propaganda is extremely simple, and from it everything else derives. What starts out as a simple situation gradually turns into a definite ideology, because the way of life in which man thinks he is so indisputably well off becomes a criterion of value for him. This does not mean that objectively he *is* well off, but that, regardless of the merits of his actual condition, he *thinks* he is. He is perfectly adapted to his environment, like "a fish in water." From that moment on, everything that expresses this particular way of life, that reinforces and improves it, is *good;* everything that tends to disturb, criticize, or destroy it is *bad.*

This leads people to believe that the civilization representing their way of life is best. This belief then commits the French to the same course as the Americans, who are by far the most advanced in this direction. Obviously, one tries to imitate and catch up to those who are furthest advanced; the first one becomes the model. And such imitation makes the French adopt the same criteria of judgment, the same sociological structures, the same spontaneous ideologies, and, in the end, the same type of man. Sociological propaganda is then a precise form of propaganda; it is comparatively simple because it uses all social currents, but is slower than other types of propaganda because it aims at long-term penetration and progressive adaptation.

But from the instant a man uses that way of life as his criterion of good and evil, he is led to make judgments: for example, anything un-American is evil. From then on, genuine propaganda limits itself to the use of this tendency and to leading man into actions of either compliance with or defense of the established order.

This sociological propaganda in the United States is a natural result of the fundamental elements of American life. In the beginning, the United States had to unify a disparate population that came from all the countries of Europe and had diverse traditions and tendencies. A way of rapid assimilation had to be found; that was the great political problem of the United States at the end of the nineteenth century. The solution was psychological standardization—that is, simply to use a way of life as the basis of unification and as an instrument of propaganda. In addition, this uniformity plays another decisive role—an economic role—in the life of the United States; it determines the extent of the American market. Mass production requires mass consumption, but there cannot be mass consumption without widespread identical views as to what the necessities of life are. One must be sure that the market will react rapidly and massively to a given proposal or suggestion. One therefore needs fundamental psychological unity on which advertising can play with certainty when manipulating public opinion. And in order for public opinion to respond, it must be convinced of the excellence of all that is "American." Thus conformity of life and conformity of thought are indissolubly linked.

But such conformity can lead to unexpected extremes. Given American liberalism and the confidence of Americans in their economic strength and their political system, it is difficult to understand the "wave of collective hysteria" which occurred after 1948 and culminated in McCarthyism. That hysteria probably sprang from a vague feeling of ideological weakness, a certain inability to define the foundations of American society. That is why Americans seek to define the American way of life, to make it conscious, explicit, theoretical, worthy. Therefore the soulsearching and inflexibility, with excessive affirmations designed to mask the weakness of the ideological position. All this obviously constitutes an ideal framework for organized propaganda.

We encounter such organized propaganda on many levels: on the government level, for one. Then there are the different pressure groups: the Political Action Committee, the American Medical Association, the American Bar Association, the National Small Business Men's Association—all have as their aim the defense of the private interests of the Big Three: Big Business, Big Labor, and Big Agriculture. Other groups aim at social and political reforms: the American Legion, the League of Women Voters, and the like. These groups employ lobbying to influence the government and the classic forms of propaganda to influence the public; through films, meetings, and radio, they try to make the public aware of their ideological aims.

Another very curious and recent phenomenon (confirmed by several American sociologists) is the appearance of "agitators" alongside politicians and political propagandists. The pure agitator, who stirs public opinion in a "disinterested" fashion, functions as a nationalist. He does not appeal to a doctrine or principle, nor does he propose specific reforms. He is the "true" prophet of the American Way of Life. Usually he is against the New Deal and for laissez-faire liberalism; against plutocrats, internationalists, and socialists—bankers and Communists alike are the "hateful other party in spite of which well-informed 'I' survives." The agitator is especially active in the most unorganized groups of the United States. He uses the anxiety psychoses of the lower middle class, the neo-proletarian, the immigrant, the demobilized soldier—people who are not yet integrated into American society or who have not yet adopted ready-made habits and ideas. The agitator uses the American Way of Life to provoke anti-Semitic, anti-Communist, anti-Negro, and xenophobic currents of opinion. He makes groups act in the illogical yet coherent, Manichaean universe of propaganda, of which we will have more to say. The most remarkable thing about this phenomenon is that these agitators do not work for a political party; it is not clear which interests they serve. They are neither Capitalists nor Communists, but they deeply influence American public opinion, and their influence may crystalize suddenly in unexpected forms.

The more conscious such sociological propaganda is, the more it tends to express itself externally, and hence to expand its influence abroad, as for example in Europe. It frequently retains its sociological character, and thus does not appear to be pure and simple propaganda. There is no doubt, for example, that the Marshall Plan—which was above all a real form of aid to underdeveloped countries—also had propaganda elements, such as the spreading of American products and films coupled with publicity about what the United States was doing to aid underprivileged nations. These two aspects of indirect propaganda are altogether sociological. But they may be accompanied by specific propaganda, as when, in 1948, subsidies of fifteen million dollars were poured into American publications appearing in Europe. The French edition of the New York *Herald Tribune* stated that it received important sums in Marshall credits for the purpose of making American propaganda. Along with reviews specializing in propaganda, such as *France-Amérique,* and with film centers and libraries sponsored by the Americans in Europe, we should include the *Reader's Digest,* whose circulation has reached millions of copies per issue in Europe and is so successful that it no longer needs a subsidy.

However, the success of such American propaganda is very uneven. Technical publications have an assured audience, but bulletins and brochures have little effect because the Americans have a "superiority complex," which expresses itself in such publications and displeases foreigners. The presentation of the American Way of Life as the only way to salvation exasperates French opinion and makes such propaganda largely ineffective in France. At the same time, French opinion has been won over by the obvious superiority of American technical methods.

All forms of sociological propaganda are obviously very diffuse, and aimed much more at the promulgation of ideas and prejudices, of a style of life, than of a doctrine, or at inciting action or calling for formal adherence. They represent a penetration in depth until a precise point is struck at which action will occur. It should be noted, for example, that in all the French *départements* in which there were Americans and propaganda bureaus, the number of Communist voters decreased between 1951 and 1953.

# NOTE

1. This notion is a little broader than that of Doob on unintentional propaganda. Doob includes in the term the involuntary effects obtained by the propagandist. He is the first to have stressed the possibility of this unintentional character of propaganda, contrary to all American thought on the subject, except for David Krech and Richard S. Crutchfield, who go even further in gauging the range of unintentional propaganda, which they even find in books on mathematics.

# Propaganda and Democracy

## JACQUES ELLUL

**J**ust as Galbraith argued that the technological-industrial system needs propaganda to plan the public response to the products of the system, so Ellul argues that democracy has need of propaganda if it is to work. If it is an evil, and that too is open to question, it is a necessary evil for a democracy. This is true, he believes, because the thoughts and responses of the masses must to some degree be organized toward a problem or patterned from the center if social order is to be maintained and the basic needs of society are to be met.

In this selection, Ellul also shows why modern democracies have become expressly committed to using propaganda as part of their international relations. The democratic faith that democracy is the truth and that any rational man, when exposed to it, will see it as the truth has been contradicted innumerable times. This seems incomprehensible in terms of the basic assumptions of the

*Reprinted from Jacques Ellul,* Propaganda, *by permission of Alfred A. Knopf, Inc. Copyright © 1965 by Alfred A. Knopf, Inc.*

democratic faith, so the believers in democratic ideas decide to use "information" to show others their mistaken ways. While democratic nations do not make use of the same degree of information control used by more totalitarian societies, they have become involved in the same kind of "rational control of information." As Ellul argues, democratic propaganda is truthful propaganda. It is factual propaganda which works and this is a basic reason for relying primarily on truthful propaganda. Ellul also shows other important differences between authoritarian propaganda and democratic propaganda. Yet, in spite of these important differences, propaganda is still an attempt to control men's thought and, as such, is destructive of other basic democratic beliefs.

Ellul ends this work on a somewhat more optimistic note than he did *The Technological Society.* He sees some chance that we can exercise free choice and, thereby, change this course of events. But how is not made clear.

## Democracy's Need of Propaganda

On one fact there can be no debate: the need of democracy, in its present situation, to "make propaganda." [1] We must understand, besides, that private propaganda, even more than governmental propaganda, is importantly linked to democracy. Historically, from the moment a democratic regime establishes itself, propaganda establishes itself alongside it under various forms. This is inevitable, as democracy depends on public opinion and competition between political parties. In order to come to power, parties make propaganda to gain voters.

Let us remember that the advent of the masses through the development of the democracies has provoked the use of propaganda, and that this is precisely one of the arguments of defense of the democratic State—that it appeals to the people, who are mobilized by propaganda; that it defends itself against private interests or anti-democratic parties. It is a remarkable fact worthy of attention that modern propaganda should have begun in the democratic States. During World War I we saw the combined use of the mass media for the first time; the application of publicity and advertising methods to political affairs, the search for the most effective psychological methods. But in those days German propaganda was mediocre: the French, English, and American democracies launched big propaganda. Similarly, the Leninist movement, undeniably democratic at the start, developed and perfected all propaganda methods. Contrary to some belief, the authoritarian regimes were not the first to resort to this type of action, though they eventually employed it beyond all limits. This statement should make us think about the relationship between democracy and propaganda.

For it is evident that a conflict exists between the principles of democracy—particularly its concept of the individual—and the processes of propaganda. The notion of rational man, capable of thinking and living according to reason, of controlling his passions and living according to scientific patterns, of choosing freely between good and evil—all this seems opposed to the secret influences, the mobilizations of myths, the swift appeals to the irrational, so characteristic of propaganda.

But this development within the democratic framework can be understood clearly if we look at it not from the level of principles but from that of actual situations. If, so far, we have concluded that inside a democracy propaganda is normal and indispensable, even intrinsic in the regime, that there are one or more propagandas at work, nothing seems to make propaganda obligatory in *external* relations. There the situation is entirely different. There the democratic State will want to present itself as the carrier of its entire public opinion, and the democratic nation will want to present itself as a coherent whole. But that creates some difficulty because such desire does not correspond to a true and exact picture of democracy. Moreover, this implies an endemic, permanent state of war. But, whereas it is easy to show that permanent wars established themselves at the same time as democratic regimes, it is even easier to demonstrate that these regimes express a strong desire for peace and do not systematically prepare for war. By this I mean that the economic and sociological conditions of the democracies possibly provoke general conflicts, but that the regime, such as it is, is not organically tied to war. It is led there, *volens nolens*. And it adjusts poorly to the situation of the Cold War, which is essentially psychological.

Another circumstance imprisons democracy in the ways of propaganda: the persistence of some traits of the democratic ideology. The conviction of the invincible force of truth is tied to the notion of progress and is a part of this ideology. Democracies have been fed on the notion that truth may be hidden for a while but will triumph in the end, that truth in itself carries an explosive force, a power of fermentation that will necessarily lead to the end of lies and the shining apparition of the true. This truth was the implicit core of the democratic doctrine.

One must stress, furthermore, that this was in itself a truth of an ideological kind that ended by making history because it imposed itself on history. This attitude contained the seeds of, but was at the same time (and still is) the exact opposite of, the current Marxist attitude that history is truth. Proof through history is nowadays regarded as *the* proof. He in whose favor history decides, was right. But what is "to be right" when one speaks of history? It is to win, to survive, *i.e.,* to be the strongest. This would mean that the strongest and most efficient, nowadays, is the possessor of the truth. Truth thus has no content of its own, but exists only as history produces it; truth receives reality through history.

One can easily see the relationship between the two attitudes and how one can pass easily from one to the other: for if truth possesses an invincible power that makes it triumph through itself alone, it becomes logical —by a simple but dangerous step—that triumph is truth. But—and this is frightening—the consequences of the two attitudes are radically different.

To think that democracy must triumph because it is the truth leads man to be democratic and to believe that when the democratic regime is opposed to regimes of oppression, its superiority will be clear at first sight to the infallible judgment of man and history. The choice is thus certain. What amazement is displayed again and again by democrats, particularly Anglo-Saxon democrats, when they see that a man selects something else, and that history is indecisive. In such cases they decide to use information. "Because democratic reality was not known, people have made a bad choice," they say, and even there we find the same conviction of the power of truth. But it is not borne out by facts. We will not establish a general law here, to be sure, but we will say that it is not a general law that truth triumphs automatically, though it may in certain periods of history or with respect to certain verities. We cannot generalize here at all. History shows that plain truth can be so thoroughly snuffed out that it disappears, and that in certain periods the lie is all-powerful.

Even when truth triumphs, does it triumph through itself (because it is truth)? After all, the eternal verities defended by Antigone would, in the eyes of history, have yielded to Creon even if Sophocles had not exited.

But in our time, the conviction of democracy and its claim to inform people collide with the fact that propaganda follows an entirely different mechanism, performs a function entirely different from that of information, and that nowadays facts do not assume reality in the people's eyes unless they are established by propaganda. Propaganda, in fact, creates truth in the sense that it creates in men subject to propaganda all the signs and indications of true believers.

For modern man, propaganda is really creating truth. This means that truth is powerless without propaganda. And in view of the challenge the democracies face, it is of supreme importance that they abandon their confidence in truth as such and assimilate themselves to the methods of propaganda. Unless they do so, considering the present tendencies of civilization, the democratic nations will lose the war conducted in this area.

## Democratic Propaganda

Convinced of the necessity for using the means of propaganda, students of that question have found themselves facing the following problem. Totalitarian States have used propaganda to the limit, domestically in order to create conformity, manipulate public opinion, and adjust it to the decisions of the government; externally to conduct the Cold War, undermine the public opinion of nations considered enemies, and turn them into willing victims. But if these instruments were used principally by authoritarian States, and if democracies, whose structure seemed made for their use, did not use them, can they now be used by democracies? By that I mean that the propaganda of the authoritarian State has certain special traits, which seem inseparable from that State. Must democratic propaganda have other traits? Is it possible to make democratic propaganda?

Let us quickly dismiss the idea that a simple difference of content would mean a difference in character. "From the moment that propaganda is used to promulgate democratic ideas, it is good; if it is bad it is only because of its authoritarian content." Such a position is terribly idealistic and neglects the principal condition of the modern world: the primacy of means over ends. But one may say—and this is a matter worthy of reflection—that democracy itself is not a good "propaganda object." Practically all propaganda efforts to promulgate democracy have failed. In fact, one would have to modify the entire concept of democracy considerably to make it a good propaganda object, which at present it is not.

Also, in passing, I will mention the following thought: "From the moment that democracy uses this instrument (propaganda), propaganda becomes democratic." This thought is not often expressed quite so simply and aggressively, but it is an implicit notion found in most American writers. Nothing can touch democracy: on the contrary, it impresses its character on everything it touches. This prejudice is important for understanding the American democratic mythology and the tentative adoption of this principle by other popular democracies.

Such positions are so superficial and so remote from the actual situation that they do not need to be discussed. Besides, they usually come from journalists or commentators, and not from men who have seriously studied the problem of propaganda and its effects. Even the majority of the latter, however, retain the conviction that one *can* set up a propaganda system that expresses the democratic character and does *not* alter the working of democracy. That is the double demand that one must make of propaganda in a democratic regime.

It is argued that the first condition would be met by the absence of a monopoly (in a democracy) of the means of propaganda, and by the free interplay of various propagandas. True, compared with the State monopoly and the unity of propaganda in totalitarian States, one finds a great diversity of press and radio in democratic countries. But this fact must not be stressed too much: although there is no State or legal monopoly, there is, nevertheless, indeed a private monopoly. Even where there are many newspaper publishers, concentration as a result of "newspaper chains" is well established, and the monopolization of news agencies, of distribution and so on, is well known. In the field of radio or of motion pictures the same situation prevails: obviously not everybody can own propaganda media. In the United States, most radio and motion picture corporations are very large. The others are secondary and unable to compete, and centralization still goes on. The trend everywhere is in the direction of a very few, very powerful companies controlling all the propaganda media. Are they still private? In any event, as we have already seen, the State must make *its* propaganda, if only under the aspect of disseminating news.

Assuming that information is an indispensable element of democracy, it is necessary that the information promulgated by the State be credible. Without credibility, it will fail. But what happens when a powerful private propaganda organization denies facts and falsifies information? Who can tell where truth lies? On whom can the citizen rely to judge the debate? It is on this level that the dialogue really takes place. The problem then is whether the State will support a private competitor who controls media equal or superior to its own but makes different propaganda. It may even be entirely legitimate for the State to suppress or annex such a competitor.

Some will say: "Freedom of expression is democracy; to prevent propaganda is to violate democracy." Certainly, but it must be remembered that the freedom of expression of one or two powerful companies that do not express the thoughts of the individual or small groups, but of capitalist interests or an entire public, does not exactly correspond to what was called freedom of expression a century ago. One must remember, further, that the freedom of expression of one who makes a speech to a limited audience is not the same as that of the speaker who has all the radio sets in the country at his disposal, all the more as the science of propaganda gives to these instruments a shock effect that the non-initiated cannot equal.

I refer in this connection to the excellent study by Rivero,[2] who demonstrates the immense difference between the nineteenth and twentieth centuries in this respect:

> In the nineteenth century, the problem of opinion formation through the expression of thought was essentially a problem of contacts between the State and the *individual,* and a problem of *acquisition of a freedom.* But today, thanks to the mass media, the individual finds himself outside the battle . . . the debate is between the State and powerful groups. . . . Freedom to express ideas is no longer at stake in this debate. . . . What we have is mastery and domination by the State or by some powerful groups over the whole of the technical media of opinion formation . . . the individual has no access to them . . . he is no longer a participant in this battle for the free expression of ideas: he is the stake. What matters for him is which voice he will be permitted to hear and which words will have the power to obsess him. . . .

It is in the light of this perfect analysis that one must ask oneself what freedom of expression still means in a democracy.

But even if the State held all the instruments of propaganda (and this becomes increasingly probable for political, economic, and financial reasons—particularly so far as TV [3] is concerned), what characterizes democracy is that it permits the expression of different propagandas. This is true. But it is impossible to permit the expression of all opinion. Immoral and aberrant opinions are justifiably subject to censorship. Purely personal opinions and, even more, certain political tendencies are necessarily excluded. "No freedom for the enemies of freedom" is the watchword then. Thus the democracies create for themselves a problem of limitation and degree. Who then will exclude certain propaganda instruments?

For the Fascist, the Communists are the enemies of truth. For the Communists, the enemies of freedom are the bourgeois, the Fascists, the cosmopolitans. And for the democracy? Obviously all enemies of democracy.

Matters are even more serious. In time of war, everybody agrees that news must be limited and controlled, and that all propaganda not in the national interest must be prohibited. From that fact grows a unified propaganda. The problem that now arises is this: We have talked of the Cold War. But it seems that the democracies have not yet learned that the Cold War is no longer an exceptional state, a state analogous to hot war (which is transitory), but is becoming a permanent and endemic state.

There are many reasons for that. I will name only one: propaganda itself.

Propaganda directed to territories outside one's borders is a weapon of war. This does not depend on the will of those who use it or on a doctrine, but is a result of the medium itself. Propaganda has such an ability to effect psychological transformations and such an impact on the very core of man that it inevitably has military force when used by a government and directed to the outside. There is no "simple" use of propaganda; a propaganda conflict is hardly less serious than an armed conflict. It is inevitable, therefore, that in cold war the same attitude exists as in the case of hot war: one feels the need to unify propaganda. Here democracies are caught in a vicious circle from which they seem unable to escape.

The other principal aspect of democratic propaganda is that it is subject to certain values. It is not unfettered but fettered,[4] it is an instrument not of passion but of reason.[5] Therefore, democratic propaganda must be essentially truthful. It must speak only the truth and base itself only on facts. This can be observed in American propaganda: it is undeniable that American information and propaganda are truthful. But that does not seem to me characteristic of democracy. The formula with which Americans explain their attitude is: "The truth pays." That is, propaganda based on truth is more effective than any other. Besides, Hitler's famous statement on the lie is not a typical trait of propaganda. There is an unmistakable evolution here: lies and falsifications are used less and less. We have already said that. The use of precise facts is becoming increasingly common.

Conversely, the use of nuances and a certain suppleness reveals an attitude peculiar to democracy. At bottom there is a certain respect for the human being, unconscious perhaps, and becoming steadily weaker, but nevertheless still there; even the most Machiavellian of democrats respects the conscience of his listener and does not treat him with haste or contempt. The tradition of respecting the individual has not yet been eliminated, and this leads to all sorts of consequences. First, it limits propaganda. The democratic State uses propaganda only if driven by circumstances—for example, traditionally, after wars. But whereas private and domestic propaganda is persistent in its effects, governmental and external propaganda evaporate easily. Besides, such propaganda is not total, does not seek to envelop all of human life, to control every form of behavior, to attach itself ultimately to one's person. A third trait of democratic propaganda is that it looks at both sides of the coin. The democratic attitude is frequently close to that of a university: there is no absolute truth, and it is acknowledged that the opponent has some good faith, some justice, some reason on his side. It is a question of nuances. There is no strict rule—except in time of war—about Good on one side and Bad on the other.

Finally, the democratic propagandist or democratic State will often have a bad conscience about using propaganda. The old democratic conscience still gets in the way and burdens him; he has the vague feeling that he is engaged in something illegitimate. Thus, for the propagandist in a democracy to throw himself fully into his task it is necessary that he believe— *i.e.,* that he formulate his own convictions when he makes propaganda.

Lasswell has named still another difference between democratic and totalitarian propaganda, pertaining to the technique of propaganda itself, and distinguishing between "contrasted incitement" and "positive incitement." The first consists of a stimulus unleashed by the experimenter or the authorities in order to produce in the masses an effect in which those in power do not participate. This, according to Lasswell, is the customary method of despotism. Conversely, the positive incitement, symbolizing the extended brotherly hand, is a stimulus that springs from what the powers that be really feel, in which they want to make the masses participate. It is a communal action. This analysis is roughly accurate.

All this represents the situation in which democracies find themselves in the face of propaganda, and indicates the differences between democratic and authoritarian propaganda methods. But I must now render a very serious judgment on such activity (democratic propaganda): all that I have described adds up to ineffectual propaganda. Precisely to the extent that the propagandist retains his respect for the individual, he denies himself the very penetration that is the ultimate aim of all propaganda: that of provoking action without prior thought. By respecting nuances, he neglects the major law of propaganda: every assertion must be trenchant and total. To the extent that he remains partial, he fails to use the mystique. But that mystique is indispensable for well-made propaganda. To the extent that a democratic propagandist has a bad conscience, he cannot do good work; nor can he when he believes in his own propaganda. As concerns Lasswell's distinction, the technique of propaganda demands one form or the other, depending on circumstances. In any event, propaganda always creates a schism between the government and the mass, that same schism I have described in the book *The Technological Society,* and that is provoked by all the techniques, whose practitioners constitute a sort of aristocracy of technicians and who modify the structures of the State.

According to Lasswell's analysis, propaganda based on contrasted incitation expresses a despotism. I would rather say that it expresses an aristocracy. But the famous "massive democracy" corresponds to that, *is* that. Ultimately, even if one tries to maintain confidence and communion between the government and the governed, all propaganda ends up as a means by which the prevailing powers manipulate the masses.

The true propagandist must be as cold, lucid, and rigorous as a surgeon. There are subjects and objects. A propagandist who believes in what he says and lets himself become a victim of his own game will have the same weakness as a surgeon who operates on a loved one or a judge who presides at a trial of a member of his own family. To use the instrument of propaganda nowadays, one must have a scientific approach—the lack of which was the weakness that became apparent in Nazi propaganda in its last few years: clearly, after 1943, one could see from its content that Goebbels had begun to believe it himself.

Thus, some of democracy's fundamental aspects paralyze the conduct of propaganda. There is, therefore, no "democratic" propaganda. Propaganda made by the democracies is ineffective, paralyzed, mediocre. We can say the same when there is a diversity of propagandas: when various propagandas are permitted to express themselves they become ineffective with respect to their immediate objective. This ineffectiveness with regard to the citizens of a democracy needs more analysis. Let us merely emphasize here that our propaganda is outclassed by that of totalitarian States. This means that ours does not do its job. But in view of the challenge we face, it is imperative that ours be effective. One must therefore abandon the traits that are characteristic of democracy but paralyzing for propaganda: the combination of effective propaganda and respect for the individual seems impossible.

There is a last element, which I shall mention briefly. Jacques Driencourt has demonstrated that propaganda is totalitarian in its essence, not because it is the handmaiden of the totalitarian State, but because it has a tendency to absorb everything. This finding is the best part of his work.[6] It means that when one takes that route, one cannot stop halfway: one must use all instruments and all methods that make propaganda effective. One must expect—and developments over the past dozen years show it— that the democracies will abandon their precautions and their nuances and throw themselves wholeheartedly into effective propaganda action. But such action will no longer have a special democratic character.

We must now examine the effects that the making of propaganda has on democracy. To measure that, we must distinguish between external and domestic propaganda. We must not retain the illusion that propaganda is merely a neutral instrument that one can use without being affected. It is comparable to radium, and what happens to the radiologists is well known.

## Effects of International Propaganda

In the domain of external politics and the propaganda that is directed toward the outside, there is practically no more private propaganda or any diversity of propagandas. Even parties indentured to a foreign government, and thus making propaganda different from that of their own national government, direct their propaganda to the interior. But what character does this unique form of propaganda (directed to the outside) take, and what repercussions has it on a democracy that conducts it? Can it be that it really exists in the domain of information?

We have abundant proof nowadays that straight information addressed to a foreign country is entirely useless.[7] Where the problem is to overcome national antipathies (which exist even between friendly nations), allegiance to a different government, to a different psychological and historical world, and finally to an opposite propaganda, it is fruitless to expect anything from straight information: the bare fact (the truth) can accomplish nothing against such barriers. Facts are not believed. Other than in exceptional cases (military occupation and so on), people believe their own government over a foreign government. The latter's facts are not believed. In fact, propaganda can penetrate the consciousness of the masses of a foreign country only through the myth. It cannot operate with simple arguments pro and con. It does not address itself to already existing feelings, but must create an image to act as a motive force. This image must have an emotional character that leads to the allegiance of the entire being, without thought. That is, it must be a myth.

But then democracy takes a path that needs watching. First of all, it begins to play a game that drives man from the conscious and rational into the arms of irrational and "obscure forces"; but we already know that in this game the believer is not the master, and that forces thus unleashed are rarely brought under control again. To put it differently: mythical democratic propaganda in no way prepares its listeners for democracy, but strengthens their totalitarian tendencies, providing at best a different direction for those tendencies. We will have to come back to this. But above all we must ask ourselves what myth the democracies should use. From experience we have seen that the democracies have used the myths of Peace, of Freedom, of Justice, and so on.

All that has now been used, and is all the more unacceptable because everybody uses these words. But the myth used by propaganda must be specific: the myth of Blood and Soil was remarkable. What specific myths are left for democracy? Either subjects that cannot possibly form the content of a myth, such as well-being or the right to vote, or democracy itself.

Contrary to what one may think, the myth of democracy is far from exhausted and can still furnish good propaganda material. The fact that Communist authoritarian regimes also have chosen democracy as the springboard of propaganda tends to prove its propagandistic value. And to the extent that democracy is presented, constructed, and organized as a myth, it can be a good subject of propaganda. Propaganda appeals to belief: it rebuilds the drive toward the lost paradise and uses man's fundamental fear. Only from this aspect does democratic propaganda have some chance of penetration into non-democratic foreign countries. But one must then consider the consequences.

The first consequence is that any operation that transforms democracy into a myth transforms the democratic ideal. Democracy was not meant to be a myth. The question arose early—in 1791 in France. And we know what, shortly after, Jacobinism made of French democracy. We must understand this: Jacobinism saved the country. It claimed to have saved the Republic, but it is clear that it only saved the Jacobin regime by destroying all that was democratic. We cannot analyze here at length the influence of the myth on the abolition of democracy during 1793–5. Let us merely say that democracy cannot be an object of faith, of belief: it is expression of opinions. There is a fundamental difference between regimes based on opinion and regimes based on belief.

To make a myth of democracy is to present the opposite of democracy. One must clearly realize that the use of ancient myths and the creation of new ones is a regression toward primitive mentality, regardless of material progress. The evocation of mystical feelings is a rejection of democratic feelings. Considerable problems arise in the United States because of such diverse myths as, for example, the Ku Klux Klan, the American Legion, or Father Divine. These are anti-democratic, but they are localized, only partial, and private. The matter becomes infinitely more serious when the myth becomes public, generalized, and official, when what is an anti-mystique becomes a mystique.

Of course, we have said that such democratic propaganda is created for external use. People already subjected to totalitarian propaganda can be reached only by the myth, and even that does not change their behavior or mentality; it simply enters into the existing mold and creates new beliefs there. But looking at things this way implies two consequences.

First, we accept the fact that such external democratic propaganda should be a *weapon,* that we are dealing here with psychological warfare, and that we adjust ourselves to the enemy's train of thought; and that, proceeding from there, the people that we subject to our propaganda are not those whom we want to see become democratic but whom we want to defeat. If we actually work on such a nation with the help of the myth, we confirm it in a state of mind, in a behavior, and in a concept of life that is anti-democratic: we do not prepare it to become a democratic nation, for on the one hand we reinforce or continue the methods of its own authoritarian government; and on the other, we cannot give the people, by such means, the desire to adhere to something else in another way. We are simply asking for the same *kind* of acceptance of something else, of another form of government. Is this sufficient to make people switch allegiance? That is the democratic propaganda problem in Germany and Japan.

In the second place, such methods imply that we consider democracy an abstraction; for if we think that to cast different ideas in the mold of propaganda is sufficient to change the nature of propaganda, we make a mere theory or idea of democracy. Propaganda, whatever its content, tends to create a particular psychology and a determined behavior. Superficially there can be differences, but they are illusory. To say, for example, that

Fascist propaganda, whose subject was the State, and Nazi propaganda, whose subject was the race, were different from each other because of their difference in content, is to become a victim of unreal and academic distinctions. But "the democratic idea" when promulgated by means that lead to non-democratic behavior only hardens the totalitarian man in his mold.

This does not take into account that this democratic veneer and the myth of democracy as a propaganda subject are very fragile. It is, in fact, one of propaganda's essential laws that its objects always adjust themselves to its forms. In this, as in so many other domains of the modern world, the means impose their own laws. To put it differently: the objects of propaganda tend to become totalitarian because propaganda itself is totalitarian. This is exactly what I said when I spoke of the necessity to turn democracy into a myth.

Thus, such propaganda can be effective as a weapon of war, but we must realize when using it that we simultaneously destroy the possibility of building true democracy.

I have said that such propaganda was for external use, that the myth was directed to the outside. But it is not certain that one can impose such a limitation. When a government builds up the democratic image in this fashion, it cannot isolate the external and internal domains from each other. Therefore the people of the country making such propaganda must also become convinced of the excellence of this image. They must not merely know it, but also follow it. This, incidentally, sets a limit to the degree to which propaganda can lie; a democratic government cannot present to the outside world a radically inexact and mendacious picture of its policies, as can a totalitarian government.

But one must qualify this thought in two ways: on the one hand a democratic nation is itself more or less in the grip of propaganda and goes along with the idealistic image of its government because of national pride; on the other, even authoritarian governments are aware that in propaganda the truth pays, as I have said: this explains the final form of propaganda adopted by Goebbels in 1944.

From there on, the myth created for external use becomes known at home and has repercussions there; even if one does not try to influence people by making propaganda abroad, they will react indirectly. Therefore, the repercussions on a democratic population of the myth developed by its government for external use must be analyzed; these repercussions will lead primarily to the establishment of unanimity.

This is a primary and very simple consequence. A myth (an image evoking belief) can stand no dilution, no half-measures, no contradictions. One believes it or does not. The democratic myth must display this same form, incisive and coherent; it is of the same nature as other myths. In order for the myth to be effective abroad, it must not be contradicted at home. No other voice must arise at home that would reach the foreign propaganda target and destroy the myth.

Can anyone believe that it was possible to make effective propaganda, for example, toward Algeria, when it was immediately contradicted at home? How could the Algerians—or any other foreigners—take seriously a promise made by General de Gaulle in the name of France when the press immediately declared that one part of France was in disagreement with it? [8]

This will lead to the elimination of any opposition that would show that the people are not unanimously behind the democracy embodied by the government. Such opposition can completely destroy all effectiveness of democratic propaganda. Besides, such propaganda is made by a government supported by a majority. The minority, though also democratic, will tend to be against such propaganda merely because it comes from the government (we saw this in France after 1945). From there on, though in accord with the idea of democracy, this minority will show itself hostile to the democratic myth. Then the government, if it wants its propaganda to be effective, will be forced to reduce the possibility of the minority's expressing itself—*i.e.,* to interfere with one of democracy's essential characteristics; we are already used to this from wartime, as with censorship. Here we are face to face with the fact discussed above: propaganda is by itself a state of war; it demands the exclusion of opposite trends and minorities—not total and official perhaps, but at least partial and indirect exclusion.

If we pursue this train of thought, another factor emerges: for the myth to have real weight, it must rest on popular belief. To put it differently: one cannot simply project a myth to the outside even by the powerful modern material means; such an image will have no force unless it is already believed. The myth is contagious because beliefs are contagious. It is indispensable, therefore, that democratic people also believe the democratic myth. Conversely, it is not useful that the government itself should follow suit; but the government must be sure that its propaganda abroad is identical with its propaganda at home, and understand that its foreign propaganda will be strong only if it is believed at home. (The United

States understood this perfectly between 1942 and 1945.) And the more the myth will appear to be the expression of belief of the entire nation, the more effective it will be. It thus presumes unanimity.

We have seen how all propaganda develops the cult of personality. This is particularly true in a democracy. There one exalts the individual, who refuses to be anonymous, rejects the "mass," and eschews mechanization. He wants a human regime where men are human beings. He needs a government whose leaders are human beings. And propaganda must show them to him as such. It must create these personalities. To be sure, the object at this level is not idolatry, but idolatry cannot fail to follow if the propaganda is done well. Whether such idolatry is given to a man in uniform bursting with decorations, or a man in work shirt and cap, or a man wearing a business suit and soft hat makes no difference; those are simple adaptations of propaganda to the feelings of the masses. The democratic masses will reject the uniform, but idolize the soft hat if it is well presented. There can be no propaganda without a personality, a political chief. Clemenceau, Daladier, De Gaulle, Churchill, Roosevelt, MacArthur are obvious examples. And even more, Khrushchev, who, after having denounced the cult of personality, slipped into the same role, differently, but with the same ease and obeying the same necessity. The nation's unanimity is necessary. This unanimity is embodied in one personality, in whom everyone finds himself, in whom everyone hopes and projects himself, and for whom everything is possible and permissible.

This need for unanimity is accepted by some of those who have studied the problem of propaganda in democracy. It has been claimed that this unanimity indicates the transition from an old form of democracy to a new one: "massive and progressive democracy." In other words, a democracy of allegiance; a system in which all will share the same conviction. This would not be a centrifugal conviction, *i.e.,* one expressing itself in diverse forms and admitting the possibility of extreme divergences. It would be a centripetal conviction with which everything would be measured by the same yardstick; democracy would express itself in a single voice, going further than just forms—all the way to rites and liturgies. It would, on the other hand, be a democracy of participation in which the citizen would be wholly engaged; his complete life, his movements would be integrated into a given social system. And one of the authors gives as an example the Nuremberg Party Congress! What a strange example of democracy.

It is true that only such a unanimous and unitary society can produce propaganda that can be effectively carried beyond the borders. But we must ask ourselves whether such a society is still democratic. What is this democracy that no longer includes minorities and opposition? As long as democracy is merely the interplay of parties, there can be opposition; but when we hear of a massive democracy, with grandiose ceremonies in which the people participate at the prompting of the State, that signifies, first of all, a confusion between the government and the State, and indicates further that anyone who does not participate is not merely in opposition, but excludes himself from the national community expressing itself in this participation. It is a truly extraordinary transformation of the democratic structure, because there can no longer be any respect for the minority opposition to the State—an opposition that, lacking the means of propaganda—or at least any means that can compete with those of the State—can no longer make its voice heard.

The minority is heard even less because the effects of the myth, inflated by propaganda, are always the same and always antidemocratic. Anyone who participates in such a socio-political body and is imbued with the truth of the myth, necessarily becomes sectarian. Repeated so many times, being driven in so many different forms into the propagandee's subconscious, this truth, transmitted by propaganda, becomes for every participant an absolute truth, which cannot be discussed without lies and distortion. Democratic peoples are not exempt from what is vaguely called "psychoses." But such propaganda, if it is effective, predisposes people to—or even causes—these psychoses.

If the people do not believe in the myth, it cannot serve to combat totalitarian propaganda; but if the people do believe in it, they are victims of these myths, which, though democratic on the surface, have all the traits of all other myths, particularly the impossibility, in the eyes of believers, of being questioned. But this tends to eliminate all opposing truth, which is immediately called "error." Once democracy becomes the object of propaganda, it also becomes as totalitarian, authoritarian, and exclusive as dictatorship.

The enthusiasm and exaltation of a people who cling to a myth necessarily lead to intransigeance and sectarianism. The myth of democracy arose, for example, during the period of the Convention; there we had forms of massive democracy, with great ceremonies and efforts at unanimity. But was that still democracy? Are there not also changes in the mores of the United States when everything is called un-American that is not strict conformism? This term, *un-American,* so imprecise for the

French, is in the United States precise to the extent that it is a result of the belief in the myth. To provoke such belief and launch a people on the road to such exaltation, without which propaganda cannot exist, really means to give a people feelings and reflexes incompatible with life in a democracy.

This is really the ultimate problem: democracy is not just a certain form of political organization or simply an ideology—it is, first of all, a certain view of life and a form of behavior. If democracy were only a form of political organization, there would be no problem; propaganda could adjust to it. This is the institutional argument: propaganda is democratic because there is no unitary State centralized by propaganda. If, then, we were merely in the presence of an ideology, there still would be no problem: propaganda can transmit any ideology (subject to the qualifications made above) and, therefore, also the democratic ideology, for example. But if democracy is a way of life, composed of tolerance, respect, degree, choice, diversity, and so on, all propaganda that acts on behavior and feelings and transforms them in depth turns man into someone who can no longer support democracy because he no longer follows democratic behavior.

Yet propaganda cannot "create" democratic behavior by the promulgation of a myth—which is the only way of making propaganda on the outside, but which modifies the behavior of the people at home. We shall find the same problem in examining certain effects of domestic propaganda.

## Effects of Internal Propaganda

I have tried to show elsewhere that propaganda has also become a necessity for the internal life of a democracy. Nowadays the State is forced to define an official truth. This is a change of extreme seriousness. Even when the State is not motivated to do this for reasons of action or prestige, it is led to it when fulfilling its function of disseminating information.

We have seen how the growth of information inevitably leads to the need for propaganda. This is truer in a democratic system than in any other.

The public will accept news if it is arranged in a comprehensible system, and if it does not speak only to the intelligence but to the "heart." This means, precisely, that the public wants propaganda, and if the State does not wish to leave it to a party, which will then provide explanations for everything (i.e., the truth), it must itself make propaganda. Thus, the democratic State, even if it does not want to, becomes a propagandist State because of the need to dispense information. This entails a profound constitutional and ideological transformation. It is, in effect, a State that must proclaim an official, general, and explicit truth. The State can then no longer be objective or liberal but is forced to bring to the overinformed people a *corpus intelligentiae.* It can no longer tolerate competition, because a State that assumes this function no longer has the right to err; if it did, it would become the laughing stock of the citizenry, and its information would lose its effect, together with its propaganda. For the information it dispenses is believed only to the extent that its propaganda is believed.

This State-proclaimed truth must be all-embracing: the facts, which are the subjects of information, are becoming more and more complex, are covering larger segments of life; thus the system into which they are arranged must cover all of life. This system must become a complete answer to all questions occurring in the citizens' conscience. It must, therefore, be general and all-valid: it cannot be a philosophy or a metaphysical system—for such systems appeal to the intelligence of a minority. To describe the system, we must go back to an ancient primitive notion: the etiological myth. In fact, a propaganda that corresponds to the body of information in a democratic State, and aims at alleviating the troubles of its citizens, must offer them an etiological myth.

This would not be necessary if the citizens were to work only three or four hours a day and devote four hours daily to personal reflection and cultural pursuits, if all citizens had a similar cultural level, if the society were in a state of equilibrium and not under the shadow of tomorrow's menace, and if the moral education of the citizens enabled them to master their passions and their egotism. But as these four conditions are not fulfilled, and as the volume of information grows very rapidly, we are forced to seek explanations *hic et nunc,* and publicly parade them in accordance with popular demand.

But the creation of the etiological myth leads to an obligation on the part of democracy to become religious. It can no longer be secular but must create its religion. Besides, the creation of a religion is one of the indispensable elements of effective propaganda. The content of this religion is of little importance; what matters is to satisfy the religious feelings of the masses; these feelings are used to integrate the masses into the national collective. We must not delude ourselves: when one speaks to us of "massive democracy" and "democratic participation," these are only veiled terms that mean "religion." Participation and unanimity have always been characteristics of religious societies, and only of religious societies. Thus we return by another route to the problem of intolerance and the suppression of minorities.[9]

On the other hand, democracy is more and more conceived as a simple external political structure, rather than as a complete concept of society, of behavior of man. This concept, this Way of Life, is tied to political democracy. Certain qualities on the part of the citizens are needed if democracy is to exist. It is easy to see that democracy wants to preserve this treasure that is its reason for, and its way of, existing. The government must maintain this Way of Life, without which democracy would no longer be possible. It thus becomes understandable and consistent that American prisoners, repatriated from Korea, were put in quarantine and subjected to mental and psychological treatment to detoxicate them of Communism. They had to be given an American brainwashing, corresponding to the Chinese brainwashing, to make them fit to live once again according to the American Way of Life.

But what is left of a man after that? We understand that democracy wants to control the mental and psychological state of the people who serve it, according to the notion of the Security Risk. Public servants cannot be permitted criminal or immoral conduct, alcoholism, dope-addiction, or the like; they would be so far removed from the virtues a democratic citizen must exhibit that this exercise of control and the massive education by propaganda for a life congruous with democracy are easy to understand. The civic virtues created by the mass media will guarantee the maintenance of democracy. But what remains of liberty?

I want to touch upon one other fact: I have tried to show, in my book *The Technological Society,* that modern technical instruments have their own weight and by themselves change political structures. Here I will ask only one question: What will be the effect on democracy of the use of TV for propaganda?

One can see the first effects: TV brings us close to direct democracy. Congressmen and cabinet members become known; their faces and utterances come to be recognized; they are brought closer to the voter. TV permits political contact to extend beyond election campaigns and informs the voters directly on a daily basis. More than that, TV could become a means of control over public servants: In his capacity as TV viewer, the voter could verify what use his representatives make of the mandate with which he has entrusted them. Certain experiments conducted in the United States showed that when sessions of Congress were televised, they were much more dignified, serious, and efficient; knowing that they were being observed, the congressmen took greater pains to fulfill their function. But one must not hope for too much in this respect:[10] there is little chance that governing bodies will accept this control. In reality, statesmen fully understand how to use it for *their* propaganda, and that is all. In fact, TV probably helped Eisenhower to win over Stevenson, the Conservatives to win over Labour.[11] The problem is first one of money, second of technical skill. But the use of TV as a democratic propaganda instrument entails the risk of a profound modification of democracy's "style."

What can democracy use for TV propaganda? Democracy is not well adapted to that. So far, the technical instruments are in accord with democratic activities: democracy speaks, and its entire being is expressed in words (this is not meant ironically; I believe that speech, in the most powerful and rhetorical sense, is one of the highest expressions of man). The instruments of propaganda, particularly press and radio, are made for words.

Conversely, democratic propaganda made by motion pictures is weak. Democracy is not a visual form of government. The ceremony of the Flame under the Arc de Triomphe—one of the most successful pictures—has little propaganda impact even though it is spectacular. Actually, when democracy wants to use the film for propaganda, it can think of nothing but military parades, which cannot be presented too often. Propaganda needs both repetition and diversity. So far, democracy's inability to use motion pictures for its propaganda has not seemed serious, the films being a secondary arm. But it seems that TV is destined to become a principal arm, for it can totally mobilize the individual without demanding the slightest effort from him. TV reaches him at home, like radio, in his own setting, his private life. It asks no decision, no a priori participation, no move from him (such as going to a meeting). But it holds him completely and leaves him no possibility of engaging in other activities (whereas radio leaves a good part of the individual unoccupied). Moreover, TV has the shock effect of the picture, which is much greater than that of sound.

But in order to use this remarkable arm, one must have something to show. A government official giving a speech is not a spectacle. Democracies have nothing to show that can compare with what is available to a dictatorship. If they do not want to be left behind in this domain, which would be extremely dangerous, they must find propaganda spectacles to televise. But nothing is better than massive ceremonies, popular marches —the Hitler youth and the Komsomols—or an entire population enthusiastically assembled to build new ships or a new university (as in Yugoslavia). The exigencies of TV will lead democracy to engage in such hardly democratic demonstrations.

We are now reaching the most important problem. Earlier, I examined the psychological transformations that the individual undergoes when subjected to an intense and continuous propaganda. We have also seen that the existence of two contradictory propagandas is no solution at all, as it in no way leads to a "democratic" situation: the individual is not independent in the presence of two combatants between whom he must choose. He is not a spectator comparing two posters, or a supreme arbiter when he decides in favor of the more honest and convincing one. To look at things this way is childish idealism. The individual is seized, manipulated, attacked from every side; the combatants of two propaganda systems do not fight each other, but try to capture *him*. As a result, the individual suffers the most profound psychological influences and distortions. Man modified in this fashion demands simple solutions, catchwords, certainties, continuity, commitment, a clear and simple division of the world into Good and Evil, efficiency, and unity of thought. He cannot bear ambiguity. He cannot bear that the opponent should in any way whatever represent what is right or good. An additional effect of contradictory propagandas is that the individual will escape either into passivity or into total and unthinking support of one of the two sides.

It is striking to see how this current, which is the point of departure of totalitarian parties, is beginning to take hold in the United States. These two different reactions—passivity or total commitment—are completely antidemocratic. But they are the consequence of some democratic types of propaganda. Here is the hub of the problem. Propaganda ruins not only democratic ideas but also democratic behavior—the foundation of democracy, the very quality without which it cannot exist.

The question is not to reject propaganda in the name of freedom of public opinion—which, as we well know, is never virginal—or in the name of freedom of individual opinion, which is formed of everything and nothing—but to reject it in the name of a very profound reality: the *possibility* of choice and differentiation, which is the fundamental characteristic of the individual in the democratic society.

Whatever the doctrine promulgated by propaganda, its psycho-sociological results are the same. To be sure, some doctrines are more coherent subject matter for propaganda than others, and lead to a more efficient and insistent propaganda; other doctrines—republican and democratic—are rather paralyzing and less suitable. But the only result is the progressive weakening of the doctrine by propaganda.

Conversely, what gives propaganda its destructive character is not the singleness of some propagated doctrine; it is the instrument of propaganda itself. Although it acts differently, according to whether it promulgates a closed system or a diversity of opinions, it has profound and destructive effects.

What am I saying then? That propaganda can promulgate a democratic doctrine? Absolutely. That it can be used by a government elected by majority vote? Absolutely. But this gives us no guarantee that we still are dealing with democracy. With the help of propaganda, one can disseminate democratic ideas as a *credo* and within the framework of a myth. With propaganda one can lead citizens to the voting booth, where they seemingly elect their representatives. But if democracy corresponds to a certain type of human being, to a certain individual behavior, then propaganda destroys the point of departure of the life of a democracy, destroys its very foundations. It creates a man who is suited to a totalitarian society, who is not at ease except when integrated in the mass, who rejects critical judgments, choices, and differentiations because he clings to clear certainties. He is a man assimilated into uniform groups and wants it that way.

With the help of propaganda one can do almost anything, but certainly not create the behavior of a free man or, to a lesser degree, a democratic man. A man who lives in a democratic society and who is subjected to propaganda is being drained of the democratic content itself—of the style of democratic life, understanding of others, respect for minorities, re-examination of his own opinions, absence of dogmatism. The means employed to spread democratic ideas make the citizen, psychologically, a totalitarian man. The only difference between him and a Nazi is that he is a "totalitarian man with democratic convictions," but those convictions do not change his behavior in the least. Such contradiction is in no way felt by the individual for whom democracy has become a myth and a set of democratic imperatives, merely stimuli that activate conditioned reflexes. The word *democracy,* having become a simple incitation, no longer has anything to do with democratic behavior. And the citizen can repeat indefinitely "the sacred formulas of democracy" while acting like a storm trooper.

All democracy that is maintained or propagated through propaganda eventually scores this success, which is its own negation with regard to the individual and the truth.

But can things really be that way?

I said above that, generally, those who tend to deny propaganda's efficacy unconsciously hold a concept of the inalienable value of the individual. Those who accept its efficacy hold a materialistic concept. So far as I am concerned, I would much prefer to be able to assert that man is invulnerable, that few dangers exist for him in present-day society, that propaganda can do nothing to him. Unfortunately, the experiences of the last half century are not encouraging in this respect. Moreover, it seems to me that the belief in propaganda's harmlessness and the spreading of this belief are ultimately detrimental to man. For man then is reassured in the face of attacks, he believes in his invulnerability and in the ineffectiveness of the attack, and his will to resist is greatly diminished. Why lose one's time and waste one's efforts defending oneself against propaganda if propaganda is merely child's play and empty talk by ridiculous tyrants? Why exert one's mind, one's personality, one's strength of character if the tigers are paper tigers, if the methods are so absurd and obvious that even the biggest fool can manage to escape them? Why make discerning choices if propaganda, using only what is already there and leading me along roads I would have traveled without it, can in no way modify my actions? If the propagandee takes that attitude, he is in the most favorable position to obey without knowing it, to drift into the routine of propaganda while claiming to be supremely superior.

The only truly serious attitude—serious because the danger of man's destruction by propaganda is serious, serious because no other attitude is truly responsible and serious—is to show people the extreme effectiveness of the weapon used against them, to rouse them to defend themselves by making them aware of their frailty and their vulnerability, instead of soothing them with the worst illusion, that of a security that neither man's nature nor the techniques of propaganda permit him to possess. It is merely convenient to realize that the side of freedom and truth for man has not yet lost, but that it may well lose—and that in this game, propaganda is undoubtedly the most formidable power, acting in only one direction (toward the destruction of truth and freedom), no matter what the good intentions or the good will may be of those who manipulate it.

# N O T E S

1. Perceptive authors agree that without propaganda a democratic State is disarmed at home (vis-à-vis the parties) and abroad, the latter as a result of the famous "challenge" that sets the democracies and the totalitarian States against each other. But one must not overlook the many setbacks that democracy has suffered for lack of propaganda. Maurice Mégret shows (in *L'Action psychologique* [Paris: A. Fayard; 1959]) that the crisis in which the French Army found itself from 1950 on was in large part caused by an absence of psychological action on the part of the government, and he demonstrates that the famous Plan was less than a great success for the same reasons. Finally, we must remember that if the democratic State is denied the right to make propaganda, such propaganda appears in the form of Public Relations at the expense of the State, and is all the more dangerous because camouflaged.

2. "Technique de formation de l'opinion publique," in *L'Opinion Publique* (1957).

3. In France. (Trans.)

4. Propaganda as such is limited in the democracies by law, by the separation of powers, and so on.

5. See, for example, "Trends in Twentieth-Century Propaganda," by Ernst Kris and Nathan Leites, who contrast the appeal to the super-ego and to the irrational by authoritarian propaganda with democratic propaganda, which is directed at the ego.

6. *La Propagande, nouvelle force politique* (Paris: A. Colin; 1950).

7. We are talking here primarily of propaganda directed at the Communist countries.

8. This non-coherence, leading to the ineffectuality of the myth, was the cause—among many others—of years of unsuccessful negotiations.

9. Let us recall another effect of such propaganda on democracy: an aristocratic category of men arises which has no common bond with democracy. The propagandist is a technician and a member of an aristocracy of technicians that establishes itself above the institutions of a democracy and acts outside its norms. Besides, the employment of propaganda leads the propagandist to cynicism, disbelief in values, non-submission to the law of numbers, doubts on the value of opinions, and contempt for the propagandee and the elected representatives: he knows how public opinion is fashioned. The propagandist cannot subject himself to popular judgment and democracy. Finally, the propagandist is privy to all State secrets and acts at the same time to shape opinions: he really has a position of fundamental direction. The combination of these three elements makes the propagandist an aristocrat. It cannot be other-

wise. Every democracy that launches propaganda creates in and by such propaganda its own enemy, an aristocracy that may destroy it.

10. John Albig states correctly that this "personification" by TV corrodes and inhibits personal, analytical reflection, standardizes personal images, and transmits a "false reality": a televised session of Congress or the Cabinet is not a *true* session, *cannot* be a true session. In such a televised session, "the public sees the responsible government in action, but only as a political show performed by humanized stars who play a role." This seems an excellent description.

11. This has been challenged by Angus Campbell (in "Television and the Election"). Campbell, on the other hand, gives important indications of TV's decisive influence on elections.

# PART IV

# The Control of Information and Power in the Technological Society

# Intelligence, Freedom, and Justice

## HAROLD L. WILENSKY

In this selection Wilensky examines the basic relations
that exist among the control of information, social values,
and the control of human beings. He believes that certain
patterns of practical action which we have created to
solve problems have inadvertent, or unintended, effects,
on our basic values and our general way of life, especially
our individual freedoms. He is especially concerned with
what he sees as the basic dilemma existing between the
demands for organizational secrecy and the need for
disclosure of information for help in making rational
decisions to maintain our freedoms.

All organizations seek to control information about
their activities, just as individuals seek to control
information about themselves. Over the last hundred
years in the United States we have created numerous
official organizations of control to maintain some kind of
central control over the activities of members of our society.

*Reprinted from Harold L. Wilensky,* Organizational Intelligence, *by
permission of Basic Books, Inc.* © *1967 by Harold L. Wilensky.*

These organizations are bureaucracies, and like all bureaucracies they seek to extend their own power and to increase their own wealth. One of the primary strategies used has been to control the information which the public receives. They have become deeply involved in public relations and, therefore, in manipulating information. To some degree they have all become secret societies. The police are an excellent example of this kind of organization.

Wilensky argues that at the same time we have presented police organizations and other control organizations with impossible demands. We insist that they enforce various laws against such activities of questionable morality as gambling and prostitution, engaged in by many people in our society, perhaps a majority. This brings the police into conflict with public morality and forces them to compromise. Yet they have to hide these compromises, to pretend they don't exist. By requiring the police to enforce various laws, and at the same time restricting their powers to do so, we have often put them in a situation of having to commit illegal actions. They have in fact carried out these illegal activities and have then maintained secrecy to prevent our learning about it.

There are many other practical constraints on organizations that lead to such secret curtailments of individual freedom. All organizations have limited resources and time to carry out extensive demands. Because of this, they compromise by making use of experts who perform quasi-judicial functions. That is, these experts decide on the fates of individuals by making use of their own commonsense understandings and their own morality. They do so in a way that is most conducive to their own best interests and to those of their organizations. They need not be very concerned with the relatively powerless clientele whose interests they are administering. They carry out these quasi-judicial functions in almost total secrecy from the general public and then present us with their decisions as if they were subject to expert knowledge, when, in fact, they are only commonsense decisions.

One of the most important examples of this is the gigantic system of bargain justice that has grown up in the courts. The vast majority of individuals accused, convicted, and sentenced for crimes in our society plead guilty to lesser charges than might otherwise be brought against them by prosecuting attorneys. From the standpoint of the prosecuting attorneys, this is seen as a necessary compromise with the demands of justice because any other method would lead to a collapse of the courts. It would indeed be impossible to have jury trials, or even lengthy administrative trials of the many criminal charges in our society. They, therefore, bring extensive charges against any individual so that he must fear being sentenced for long periods of time if he does not plead guilty. Eighty percent act rationally and plead guilty for consideration, that is, for lower sentences. In this way, ''justice'' is carried out. And yet the public is unaware that this happens. Bargain justice goes on unobstructed by public opinion, or by a possible public demand for justice. Similar situations can be found in the methods of legal commitment for insanity, in juvenile courts, family courts, and other judicial procedures.

Wilensky argues that only governmental investigations involving full disclosure of the conflicts between the various experts can help assure us of free and rational decision making on such public issues. But this is expensive. Meanwhile, the public seems intent on putting less money into serious government and at the same time demanding more enforcement, more control, more services. If unchecked the inevitable consequences will be further compromises with our ideas of justice and further curtailments of individual freedoms. The most serious consequence of all could be a tyranny of experts—technological experts, of course.

What we think and do in the quest for useful knowledge affects the fate of such values as individual freedom, justice, and privacy. For instance, the intelligence doctrine of "all the facts" lends itself to the demand for publicity; the belief in "short-run estimates" and "inside dope" lends itself to the demand for secrecy. The tension between publicity and secrecy permeates administration, where the executive must deliberate in private at the same time that he keeps his employees informed, and politics, where the policy-maker must tap expert knowledge and protect secret sources at the same time that he briefs reporters and honors the public's "right to know."

The dilemmas of intelligence in a democratic society are most evident in three areas: the maintenance of democratic control of secret intelligence agencies and secret police; the effects of patterns of secrecy and publicity on the development of an enlightened public opinion; and the efficacy of alternative means for discovering truth in the administration of justice— adversary and inquisitorial procedures, the testimony of unchecked experts, and scientific methods. The ideal is to strike a balance in which constraints on the proliferation of secret police, secret agents, and secret files are matched by constraints on the spread of punishing publicity and, further, to devise procedural safeguards that insure the privacy and liberty of the individual confronting a bureaucratic world.

## Police Secrecy

That the police—private or public, secret or open—are a potential threat to constitutional liberties and to the rule of law has been a strong feeling in the Anglo-American world, especially in early-nineteenth-century England and in twentieth-century America. Nevertheless, there has been in both countries a rise in the power and prestige of the police.[1]

London remained without a police force of any kind until 1829; the individual citizen was to maintain civic order and guard property. If carried out at all, police functions were performed by citizens acting as sheriffs, constables, or magistrates, or as members of militia, posses, watch-and-ward committees, or the Yeomanry (a cavalry force composed largely of small landowners). From the perspective of urban workers these citizen volunteers were particularly vicious in suppressing mobs, riots, and the "dangerous classes" (the poor) by means of volley-firing and saber-charging. Forming a common front with the leaders of the masses, London merchants, too, proclaimed that a police force would mean tyranny, espionage, destruction of individual liberty. In fact, they concerned themselves less about civil liberties than about protecting the mobs that they manipulated and incited to riot in order to embarrass the government when legislation inimical to commercial interests was proposed. Finally, the burgeoning urban industrialists, frightened by the rapid spread of crime, violence, and class conflict, nevertheless perceived that the Yeomanry and similar citizen police were exacerbating all three. (Parish constables were paying deputies to serve for them and the latter soon formed a confederacy in league with professional criminals.) However diverse the sources of hostility to the police, the appearance of the New Police in London in 1829 united all classes in near-universal demand that the Force be immediately disbanded. It is thus remarkable that the British eventually established a centralized efficient, metropolitan police, centered in New Scotland Yard. From a storm of criticism and hatred emerged the most respected police force in the world. Today—although some close observers note a slight deterioration in the relationship between police and public—it is still safe to say that the relatively benign, unarmed "bobby" is held in almost affectionate esteem.

The parish-constable police system was transferred to the American colonies. Although it failed in the mother country, it survived in the United States and can be seen today in the form of no less than 40,000 separate independent police forces. There is little evidence of public abhorrence of the police in nineteenth-century America to match that in Britain. Except for bursts of indignation at the use of private police, state police, and federal troops in strikes and riots, law enforcement officials were not generally objects of hatred. To respectable citizens in rural areas, the sheriff and his deputies—though lacking the omniscience bestowed by their television images—were often heroes. In cities where police were controlled by corrupt political machines, they were nevertheless often responsive to the needs of the immigrant masses—even providing prized careers for them. Hostility comparable to the early British response was delayed until racial minorities migrated to the big cities and, more recently, until the civil rights movement took hold. On the one hand, the police have become the symbol of white oppression of Negroes. On the other hand, the nineteenth-century British image of the "dangerous classes" is now being revived in the United States: anxiety about "crime in the streets" and the corresponding demand for public order and safety have risen, thereby strengthening the position of the police. This is evident in the successful

1966 campaign of white policemen in New York City against Mayor John Lindsay's civilian-dominated police review board. In general, professional police have become a larger fraction of the labor force, more trained in technique and demeanor, more skilled in accommodating themselves to legal constraints. The dramatic rise in their prestige and authority in Britain, the more modest rise in the United States, has paralled the swift expansion in their command of modern technology. Systematic, scientific investigating machinery—from fingerprinting and ballistics to forensic medicine and toxicology—has proliferated in every society, whether free or not, and everywhere it has increased police capacity for surveillance and control.

In democratic societies, the growth of secret police and secret intelligence agencies has until very recently met with greater resistance or at least with greater dismay. Power, if invisible and therefore not effectively accountable, is generally considered subversive in a duly constituted government. From his experience with the German underground in World War II, Allen W. Dulles observed that "an intelligence service is the ideal vehicle for a conspiracy" [2]—a theme repeated in many attacks on the Central Intelligence Agency.[3] All students of totalitarian societies note that the secret police, drawing on secret dossiers on rulers and ruled alike, is a prime means of social control, at once a way of intimidating the underlying population and ferreting out dissenters within the ruling regime.

We have seen that the technology and manpower for developing a police state are widely available not only to external intelligence agencies such as the CIA and various military intelligence branches but to agencies mainly devoted to domestic intelligence or policing or both, and in government and industry—the Federal Bureau of Investigation (FBI), the Federal Narcotics Bureau, the Secret Service, the up-to-date metropolitan police department or industrial security consultant. Such organizations are becoming self-consciously "professionalized." Insofar as they find their definition of professionalism in efficient crime control, unmodified by a strong commitment to due process of law, they will subvert freedom and justice, or, at best, be indifferent to democratic values.

In the United States, the overcriminalization of the substantive law encourages abuses in the detection of crime. If we declare as crimes numerous acts that many or most citizens do not feel are morally wrong; if these acts do not harm others; and if few know about them or complain about them, we pose an intelligence problem for the police. In a case of murder or car theft the police have initial evidence that the act occurred; in a case of a Saturday-night poker game, they usually have no complaint to lead the way. Without a complainant the police are under pressure to seek out, if not provoke, the crime. Thus, the most frequent and spectacular instances of unconstitutional search and seizure, assembly-line arrest and screening, and advanced electronic eavesdropping occur in the pursuit of prostitutes, numbers runners, drug users, medical abortionists, homosexuals, chronic alcoholics, "vagrants and loiterers"—persons whose conduct, while offensive to the community-at-large, seldom evokes complaints from their purported victims.[4]

Illegal techniques of investigation are also prominent in the search for "subversives." Most important in the present context, the elaborate and typically covert intelligence machinery mobilized by federal detectives and metropolitan police, whatever it accomplishes in the control of professional criminals, is weak for discovering the truth about political crimes or vaguely defined misconduct. The FBI, in its celebrated pursuit of alleged spies and subversives, has stolen letters, tapped the phones of suspects and defense attorneys, protected perjurers, and relied heavily on the evidence of anonymous informers.[5] So faulty is the information it thus obtains that at the height of the McCarthy era in 1954—after years of FBI screening of hundreds of thousands of government workers and after sensational congressional exposés—only three of the "at least 75" federal employees formally accused of Communist activities from 1948 through 1953 by the House Un-American Activities Committee and the Senate Internal Security Committee had been brought to trial for any crime. Of the scores accused and subjected to trial by publicity, Alger Hiss, William Remington, and Judith Coplon were the only three who could be brought into court. Two others had died. Hiss and Remington were convicted of perjury. Miss Coplon's conviction on two counts of espionage was set aside because the FBI, at first vigorously denying wiretapping, was later forced to admit that some thirty agents had participated in a vast operation of electronic eavesdropping.[6] Even if we accept the argument that illegal means were justified for reasons of national security, the box score for those five years of hysteria does not inspire confidence in the truth of confidential dossiers on political beliefs and activities.

Belief in the informer's evidence, faith in the efficacy of undercover operations, and the weakness of outside criticism and control can sometimes produce absurd results. By the 1960's FBI undercover agents were so numerous in the Communist Party U.S.A. (one source claims that they were approaching a dominant position in the membership[7]) that they unwittingly began to inform on one another.

The FBI is more than a repository of unevaluated "facts" on the political opinions and affiliations of ordinary citizens. As an operating agency it apprehends violators of federal laws within its jurisdiction (kidnappers, bank robbers) and cooperates with local, county, and state law enforcement agencies in crime control. As an intelligence agency it reports information on sabotage, subversion, and miscellaneous matters to other agencies of government. Not enough is known about the work of the FBI in record keeping, operations, or intelligence to judge its conformity to due process in any of these missions. It is likely that as an operating agency its interrogation procedures are at least as lawful, if not more so, than those of municipal police. The FBI's collection and use of unevaluated information is the mission that presents the greatest danger to the rule of law. The temptation to feed the files selectively to political friends in the executive and legislative branches must be very strong and, as we shall see, the use of these files is not always relevant to law enforcement.

In free societies and totalitarian societies alike, there is a general tendency for agencies charged with gathering intelligence on internal security to magnify the internal threat and for agencies responsible for external security to magnify the power of the outside enemy. Thus, the FBI has vigorously publicized a succession of menaces: white slavery beginning in 1910, spies in World War I, the Red Menace of the Palmer era, kidnapping and bank robbery during the 1930's, followed by the most glamorous menaces of all, sabotage and espionage in World War II and internal subversion in the Cold War. While these menaces were of course not fictional, the publicity given them was not closely related to their magnitude. In its sensational exaggerations, the FBI is like its counterparts elsewhere— intelligence agencies that try to persuade administrative leaders that they are imminently threatened by one conspiracy or another, one crime wave or another. What is perhaps unique is the FBI's success in publicizing its secret activities as a national cause beyond criticism and its chief as "Public Hero Number One." [8] In 1940, in the days when U.S. senators felt that it was politically safe to complain publicly of FBI activities, Senator Norris castigated J. Edgar Hoover as "the greatest hound for publicity on the American continent today." Extralegal extensions of FBI power have plainly been enhanced by skillful press agents. And there is no question that this agency, spurred on by its fans on Capitol Hill, has intruded the police power into the realm of ideas.

.  .  .

## Administrative Devices for Truth-Finding

That the excesses of unwarranted secrecy and punishing publicity at once obstruct justice for individuals and stifle the criticism necessary for enlightened public opinion; that government officials, however limited in their promotion of domestic civilian programs, can dominate debate on national security; that the media vacillate between silence in honor of security and competitive screaming about undifferentiated crises and pseudo-events—these developments unmistakably affect the quality of intelligence. Less dramatic is the erosion of devices for truth-finding in everyday administrative life. The adversary principle, in courts and administrative agencies alike, for instance, is slowly losing its pre-eminent place—a tendency related to the elaboration of the intelligence function.

Informal adjudication and fact-finding are becoming more prominent in all modern societies. Overloaded with work and information, modern governments are moved to settle things expertly and informally; the regulated parties, in turn, want to avoid the expense, uncertainty, and publicity of formal litigation and to cultivate the good will of regulatory officials. To the extent that quasi-judicial procedures are pivotal to administration, it is vital to learn more about them. The relative merits of various devices for symbolizing justice and fairness (the consumer counsel, the Ombudsman) and for discovering "facts" (reliance on technical experts, legislative investigations, public commissions, and courts) are little understood.

Because legal contexts illuminate more general problems in truthfinding, consider first the adversary process typified by a jury trial. Through partisan contest conducted according to rules each counsel makes the strongest case he can before an impartial judge and jury. The deficiencies of adversary procedure are obvious. A circus atmosphere may develop as attorneys become preoccupied with press releases rather than legal briefs, with courtroom histrionics rather than reasoned argument ("When you can't win a case, jaw it"). Further, adversary procedure, because it rests on partisan initiative, limits the kind of evidence presented; the contending parties define the issue and say what is relevant. Finally, the procedure is limited for resolving technical issues; a trial ". . . is not well adapted to the intelligible sequential ordering of complex factual data. . . . Either it leaves out too much to be informative or it includes too much to be orderly." [9] It may bog down in well-established, trivial detail. But these limitations, not inevitable, are offset by the overriding advantages of partisan advocacy, including the opportunity to test the credibility of witnesses through cross-examination. In or out of court, the adversary process is the best way to assure that assertions are exposed to systematic scrutiny by men with countervailing interests who are motivated to press hard.

In the popular view, science is a more disinterested and, therefore, better institution for uncovering truth. But major advances in scientific theory often come from men insisting on opposing models of physical or social nature. They are often polemical; their debate is sometimes carried on in the spirit of armies at war, as Priestley's holding action against Lavoisier's theory of chemical elements, Marx's invective about German idealism, and Weber's insistence on the role of religious ethics in economic life all illustrate.[10] Three characteristics of science, however, mark it as different from adversary procedure and limit its use in everyday administrative life as well as in the court. First, although individual scientists may be contentious, they are oriented more toward truth than power. The judge or the official must give some weight to political consequences of decisions; the scientist is ideally oblivious of such considerations. Second, differences in science are settled by colleagues; scientific truths rest ultimately on the consensus of the competent. It is thus too technical for many administrative purposes; the capacity to assess scientific truth is well developed only among those immersed in its traditions and techniques. Finally, because scientific propositions take a long time to establish, science is not an ideal procedure for urgent organizational and judicial decisions. In short, although adversary proceedings do not involve critical experimental tests, they resemble science in their systematic regulation of the clash of views, and they have the additional advantage of sensitivity to political interests, greater availability to non-expert officials and judges, and speed.

Despite their considerable merit for truth-finding, and even greater merit for justice, adversary systems are being weakened or eliminated in several areas of modern life. This is evident in four developments: the bypassing of courts; the movement to incorporate vague social and moral purposes in specialized courts; the use of nonlegal knowledge and processes; and the substitution of inquisitorial for adversary methods in many contexts.

The first problem is rooted in shortages of judicial manpower and budget. Sheer crowding of the court calendar has forced litigants with urgent problems to turn to other tribunals. Commercial arbitration is neither as fair nor as accurate as court procedure, but it is quicker and cheaper; business finds it expedient for settling a huge volume of controversy. Similarly, legislators unhappy about slow-moving justice have set up scores of quasi-judicial agencies.[11] Some of these arrangements reduce adversariness; others, like arbitration, retain it.

Remaining controversies still overload the courts, evoking pressures to find substitutes for adversariness. The case for substitutes is strong—for example, in personal injury and accident cases, which constitute the core of the court calendar. In a perceptive examination of the traffic safety problem, Moynihan[12] argues that it is not merely that the auto industry's venality has assured that an estimated one out of every three automobiles manufactured in Detroit ends up with blood on it; not merely that the public is ambivalent about the dangers of driving and the question of safety; nor even that until 1966 the government evaded the problem by substituting exhortation for the collection of data on accidents and safety design and for money and experts to devise serious programs. The root of the difficulty is that we have never applied the necessary standards of evidence and self-criticism; we have instead treated the automobile as a source of taxes and, with the rise of the State Police and the spread of insurance company doctrines of individual liability, as an issue of criminal law enforcement. The result is an intense concentration on the guilt of individual drivers, a futile effort to punish the violator, and a paralyzing overcrowding of court calendars. Great gains are possible if we ". . . put to an end the present idiocies of armed police arresting and often imprisoning hordes of citizens who are then hauled before courts incompetent to judge a problem that is in any event impossible to define in legal terms." [13] In many, perhaps in most cases we simply cannot ascertain just how an accident occurs, much less apportion the blame among the manufacturer, the victim, the accused, and a host of poorly understood and sometimes unavoidable mechanical, chemical, thermal, and electrical causes. The best principle is to seek the truth only where there is a reasonable chance of finding it. It might be desirable to set up a compensation system for victims of accidents which does not depend on determination of fault—a system already in effect in the province of Saskatchewan.

Excluding traffic safety, an increasing part of the criminal law system is being removed from the safeguards of adversary procedures—notably the time after arrest and before trial when the police and the district attorney decide whether the suspect will go to court or not. That more than 80 per cent of suspects plead guilty suggests considerable pressure to "cop a plea"—that is, accept informal promises of lesser charges and lighter penalties in exchange for reducing the workload of the DA and the courts.[14]

To explain his heavier sentence on the one of five defendants who refused to plead guilty, a federal judge remarked: ". . . if in one year, 248 judges are to deal with 35,517 defendants, the district courts must encourage pleas of guilty. One way to encourage pleas of guilty is to establish or announce a policy that, in the ordinary case, leniency will not be granted to a defendant who stands trial." [15] That some innocent men are thus persuaded to plead guilty is plain.[16]

Another threat to adversariness is the need of the courts to incorporate nonlegal knowledge into the process of decision. Part of the humanitarian trend of the twentieth century has been the infusion of social and moral purposes, particularly the rehabilitative ideal, into judicial and police procedures. This is evident in juvenile courts, in family courts, and in the occasional use of psychiatric-clinical knowledge and social science in all courts. The danger lies in an increasing reliance on unchecked experts.

Now that we have set up children's courts with the ideology of treatment and rehabilitation rather than punishment and revenge, we face a new dilemma. Even in the well-run, well-staffed court for children, there is a conflict of values between paternalism and justice, linked to a conflict between two approaches to the truth—the clinical therapeutic truth of the psychological sciences and the adversary truth of the lawyer. An enlightened juvenile court judge in Pittsburgh sums up the distinctive philosophy of the juvenile court in a way that highlights the problem. He points to the difference between the question, " 'Did you or did you not?' " and the quite different question of the juvenile court, " 'Why, under what circumstances, and what can be done to help?' " [17] The conflict in functions is not hard to see, though it is extremely difficult to resolve. Should the court assume that the delinquent act is a symptom of underlying psychological or family maladjustment, take jurisdiction over an increasing variety of cases, and seek to operate as a sympathetic substitute parent, with adjustment of any youngster who comes before it as the aim? Should it, in short, be a generalized social agency? Or should it instead be primarily a dispenser of justice, giving careful attention to whether it has a right to intervene in the first place and, if so, respecting the rules of evidence. Are not the facts of delinquent behavior often in dispute? By virtue of its authority and the training of its functionaries, is not the court on firmer ground when it sticks to the legal questions (what is the legal status of the child, who shall have custody, does the community have the right to intervene in his life, and so on), leaving social services to agencies specially equipped to diagnose and plan treatment? [18]

Most critics of the children's court feel that some balance between the conflicting goals of due process and rehabilitation of the young is possible and desirable. They suggest the following procedural reforms: "regulate detention practices, advise parents and children of the right to counsel, circumscribe the use of questionable evidence, separate out determination of jurisdiction from treatment, protect the confidentiality of records, and at the same time maintain an informal and private atmosphere consistent with the best protection of children." [19]

Family courts present similar problems. Under restrictive divorce laws, the application of the adversary principle in a search for the guilty party is misplaced. More liberal divorce laws recognize the large number of non-contending parties for whom separation or divorce is desirable for everyone involved, for parents and for children for whom the continued marriage is also a punishment. Even under the most liberal divorce laws, however, there are numerous cases in which conflicts between husbands and wives over the desirability of divorce, over custody of children, or over alimony are severe and where the best interests of the spouses and children are difficult to determine. If these cases are not to be dealt with as just another form of litigation but as social-clinical problems, whose values shall prevail, what knowledge is relevant, and what safeguards for justice shall be used? The marriage counseling and reconciliation procedures now gaining ground—on the surface a civilized approach to family breakup—depend entirely on the availability of well-trained personnel, which does not now exist and which legislators would be reluctant to pay for if it did exist.[20]

The need to avoid premature confidence in "scientific" testimony is even more apparent in the use of psychiatrists in commitment proceedings or in the determination of criminal insanity, and in the use of social workers and criminologists in the administration of probation and parole. At the heart of the controversy regarding psychiatric testimony is the fact that the psychiatrist is attempting to get the community to accept a highly tentative theory of behavior and behavior change. Like the advocates of children's courts, psychiatrists focus attention on the criminal not the crime, seek to rehabilitate rather than punish, and want to replace prisons with hospitals. They despair of the legal definitions of insanity because they are obsolete, because legal rules are posited on the theory of free will and responsibility rather than on a theory of psychological determinism, and because they are forced to testify in legal rather than psychiatric terms.[21]

At the other extreme, critics like Dr. Thomas S. Szasz discount psychiatric claims. They argue that there is no evidence that mental disease causes criminal behavior; that there is no evidence that traditional psychiatry can reform criminals *or* noncriminals.[22] Further, they think that the law should not attempt to abrogate its own responsibility by shifting the burden of proof onto the expert.

Courts maintain a position short of full acceptance of psychiatric testimony.[23] And it is likely that jurors who hear insanity cases, while they pay careful attention to psychiatric testimony, decide whether or not the person is sane primarily on their own assessment of whether the defendant was able to act rationally in the commission of legally proscribed acts. Jurors tend to think that the psychiatrist has an investment in finding something wrong with everybody.[24] Where the judge acts without a jury, as in commitment hearings, there may be greater willingness to accept the psychiatrist or other physician's opinion as conclusive. In 1965 over 13,000 Californians were committed to mental hospitals. Commitment generally progresses through four stages. First, the person is brought to a hospital observation ward for seventy-two hours. Next, two medical examiners diagnose and make recommendations to the court. They need not be psychiatrists, but "may be drawn from a panel of local physicians, staff doctors from a mental hospital, private psychiatrists, or any combination of these and others, including retired general practitioners." [25] It is necessary only that they be medical doctors. These examinations frequently take place on an assembly-line basis, and in general they average less than ten minutes.[26]

Third, the examiner makes a recommendation to the court. The California Assembly Subcommmittee on Mental Health Services noted that the criteria for commitment are vague and that there is a presumption of mental illness and a tendency to recommend commitment. "In the Subcommittee's Survey of Commitment Courts, observers reported that in 78 per cent of the cases the examining physicians recommended commitment. In only 11 per cent of the hearings were alternatives even discussed by the examining physicians. In contrast, the observers administering the Subcommittee's questionnaire stated a belief that alternatives to commitment would have been desirable in 47 per cent of the cases." [27]

The final step is the court hearing. The survey found that the average length of commitment hearings in California was 4.7 minutes; one-third took less than two minutes each.[28] Judges are inclined to accept the examiners' recommendation, because, among other things, those committed are generally too poor to hire contending lawyers, and the public defender is overworked.[29] Thus an average professional assessment of less than fifteen minutes may result in a lifetime incarceration in a mental institution.

Similarly, in post-conviction dispositional proceedings—when probation as an alternative to imprisonment is granted or revoked or when a prisoner is released on parole—the administrative agencies often use no adversary procedure. They rely on probation officers with varying degrees of training whose reports are largely beyond the challenge of the defendant.[30]

A final kind of expert knowledge that would diminish the adversary quality of the trial is that provided by social science. The Supreme Court's attention to the "Brandeis Brief" set the precedent that judges may take notice of nonauthoritative, extra-legal sources of social information—"all matters of general knowledge." [31] The Brandeis Brief was designed to establish that a legislative act was reasonable, as shown by the fact that responsible persons held opinions and made assertions which supported its judgments. In principle, however, social-science evidence could go as well to the truth of the facts asserted, and increasingly is admitted for that purpose. Nevertheless the influence of social science on legal decision-making is still limited. Lawyers generally object to the use of social-science data in court on the grounds that the judge has neither the time nor the skill to make an independent investigation of the data he notes and, more important, when data are submitted in a brief and not as evidence presented for the record, they cannot be impeached nor can countervailing data be offered.[32] Social scientists who have written on this issue tend to feel that the courts should take more cognizance of social-science expertise than they do. They argue that the rules of evidence lag far behind scientific standards of evidence and that adversary procedure is better for discovering values than for discovering matters of fact.[33]

The issues in the use of data from psychiatry and social science are not fundamentally different from issues in the use of any expert testimony; they are difficult questions of the state of knowledge in the relevant discipline and the degree of consensus among the competent. Toxicologists can disagree about the effects of a poison as much as sociologists might disagree about the meaning of a survey of prejudice. Indeed, the court might on some issues place more confidence in expert social-science data that it now excludes and reject some of the opinions of leading citizens that it now admits. For instance, in 1952 the NAACP asked the Elmo Roper organization to undertake an objective survey of public sentiment in Marion County, Florida, the scene of a pending retrial of Walter Irvin, a Negro accused of raping a white woman.[34] The survey aimed to provide a basis for concluding either that Irvin could obtain a fair trial in Marion County or that the community had so prejudged guilt or innocence that a fair trial would be impossible. The survey also included adjoining Lake County (the scene both of the alleged crime and of the first trial) and two counties in northern Florida (Gadsden and Jackson) far from the action. In the context of an interview on national and state issues, a cross-section of whites in each county was asked questions about the rape case and about the contrast case of Sheriff Sullivan, a white man accused of taking bribes in Dade County. A small cross-section of Negro adults (N = 151) was interviewed in Marion County only. Selected results revealed that prejudgment among whites in the Irvin case was significantly higher in Lake and Marion counties (43 and 63 per cent said, " 'I feel sure he is guilty' ") than in Jackson County (17 per cent) and Gadsden County (25 per cent). Prejudgment in the Sullivan case did not exceed 18 per cent in any county and within each county was lower than prejudgment in the rape case. Negroes were more worried about what might happen to a juror in both cases than were whites, but Negro fears were very much higher in the Irvin case than in the Sheriff Sullivan case (e.g., in answer to the question " 'Do you think anybody on the jury in the Irvin case would get away with it if they voted "not guilty" or do you think something might happen to them if they did?' " 84 per cent of the Negroes vs. 16 per cent of the whites expressed fear that something might happen). In general, the pattern of response for a variety of questions was consistent with the argument of the defense for a change in venue. The judge allowed the survey director and field supervisor to describe their methods in court, but when the findings were to be introduced, he sustained the district attorney's objection: since the interviews were anonymous, no respondent could be connected with opinions recorded on the questionnaire, and therefore no cross-examination was possible. The survey results were ruled out as hearsay evidence. Later a parade of leading citizens testified that the state of opinion in the county was such that a fair trial could definitely be had. Change of venue was denied; Irvin received his "fair trial" and was convicted.

My argument, then, is not that social science provides weaker evidence than that commonly admitted into court. Nor is it that social research is necessarily "softer" than physical science, sample surveys always less rigorous than forensic ballistics, the clinical insight of a psychiatrist less valuable than the practiced eye of a handwriting expert. It is instead that in all the examples discussed above—in juvenile court and in family court, in psychiatry, social work, and social science alike—there is danger that the claims of experts will be accepted uncritically. Where inquisitorial procedures replace adversary procedures—that is, where the judge himself takes responsibility for eliciting truth—it is important that the inquisitor be expert enough to evaluate the uses and limits of the knowledge he extracts. There is the further need to find equivalents to adversary procedures so that experts do not remain unchallenged.

The question of court use of nonlegal knowledge in nonadversary proceedings is part of a broader problem in public administration: what institutional arrangements will improve the quasi-judicial and fact-finding operations of all branches of government?

The ultimate assurance that experts will be questioned fruitfully lies in a pattern of political pluralism: a diversity of strong, independent interest groups representing a significant division of values and engaged in open conflict and competition. Perhaps the epitome is labor-management relations. A great many officials, flanked by their experts, undertake visible confrontations, using techniques of private negotiation, conciliation, and arbitration, as well as public propaganda and persuasion. Clashing goals are rather well defined; adversary methods of truth-finding are dominant.

Two radical contrasts to this pluralist pattern are most dangerous for the purposes of intelligence and justice. In the first case an organization has or seems to have a monopoly of information and relies on its own unchecked expertise. We see this in the making of foreign policy and in such agencies as the CIA and the FBI; the pathologies of secrecy combine with excessive reliance on specialized house intelligence to maximize the power of preconceptions. In the second case, the public interest is diffuse, and a purported expertise is given heavy weight, not because there is a monopoly of information—real or fancied—but because no contending groups provide diverse versions of the truth. Into the void pour the most parochial pressures. For instance, the public interest in highways is mixed and vaguely defined. Everyone wants them but not if they sweep through one's backyard. The downtown businessman is pleased that automobiles have access to his business, but suspicious that they might have better access to some suburban shopping center; in any case, he is unhappy about the rush-hour crush and the parking scramble. The average American is delighted by the $47 billion plan to build nonstop, limited-access, high-speed freeways. But his dream of going anywhere quickly and conveniently at the touch of an accelerator is shattered when too many others have the same idea at the same time; the psychological wear and tear of the journey to work is oppressive. City officials and urban planners favor roads, too, but they are concerned when highway programs eat up valuable land and displace people without providing new sources of city tax revenues. They are also vaguely uneasy about air pollution. In such situations, it is imperative to devise administrative structures that invite the clash of expert opinion and include an adversary system to dramatize issues and define the public interest. In the absence of such safeguards, a potent nationwide lobby in 1956 was able to mobilize public sentiment for the Interstate Highway System embracing both urban and rural areas. The lobby included auto manufacturers and their 64,000 local car dealers, gasoline companies, tire producers, the state motor clubs, highway contractors and highway department officials in city halls and state capitols, the trucking industry, the cement and asphalt companies, and the many businesses and industries that profit from cars and roads. Described as "old-fashioned" were plans to rebuild rapid transit facilities; ignored was the unwritten law that added roads demand added parking space and the two together merely invite a new overflow of automobiles.

That highway engineers became so powerful during the subsequent decade can be attributed in part to the vacuum of intelligence and power created by the typical state highway commission as well as by the continued failure to formulate broad national and state transportation policies. In California, the Highway Commission, a group of laymen appointed by the governor, has final responsibility for route locations. Although in the mid-sixties this Commission was one of the more independent-minded in the nation and although the San Francisco Bay Area was the scene of a lively highway revolt, the technical people of the Division of Highways continued to dominate the decisions. As in many other states, the Commissioners have no staff of their own to develop critical evaluations of proposals from the highway engineers who, left to their own devices, would put a highway through the Washington Monument.[35]

In official fact-finding for public enlightenment the problem is not merely to open up a wide range of policy alternatives but to create incentives for persistent criticism of evidentiary value. None of the major administrative alternatives is perfect; each has some advantages.

A legislative investigation has two advantages over a court: first, because it is nonadversary, it is broader in scope; second, it more effectively engages public attention. Theoretically, winning or losing is not the immediate problem. So witnesses speak more freely; what appears to be a coherent narrative is recorded. But politics and publicity and the occasional temptation to use unverifiable information from unidentified witnesses are crippling disadvantages.[36] Preparation by legislators and their staff is typically casual and unsystematic. The proceedings are too often free-ranging but fuzzy, free-wheeling but incompetent, public but unfair, effective but irresponsible.

The advantage of an agency hearing over a jury trial is its expertise. Instead of a group of twelve people assembled for one case, it is a continuing body whose cumulative experience presumably gives it competence. If the issue is complex and technical, as in rate and route proceedings in regulated industries—indeed, as in all government decisions regarding the allocation of economic resources—and the aim is to arrive at guidelines for future behavior rather than to judge past behavior in the individual case, administrative hearings are a good compromise between the trial and the legislative investigation. Even here, however, if the administrative agency is removed from the general constraints of political pluralism (the CIA, the FBI) or lacks enough independence to render a critical judgment (the ICC, the FCC and other government commissions staffed by the industries they regulate), it is a weak source of justice in individual cases and only moderately useful for public enlightenment.

For official fact-finding and public education, a more meaningful compromise is to move out of conventional channels of investigation and communication toward men of independent mind and stature—a strategy commonly used to overcome the pathologies of hierarchy and specialization. The British provide two models: the Tribunal of Inquiry and the Royal Commission of Inquiry. The United States has used a variety of government commissions, with varying composition, function, and result. And, although its scope is narrow, the review boards set up by a few American labor unions deserve attention as sources of organizational intelligence and justice.

The British use commissions to find facts rather than to apply sanctions; they keep such bodies more or less free of political pressures. A Tribunal of Inquiry is the device for investigating serious government scandals. It is typically chaired by a Justice of the High Court; its members are in effect appointed by the Cabinet. Its fact-finding, mainly adjudicative, aims to provide an orderly account of what happened. Facing quasi-political issues, these Tribunals adopt methods of procedure somewhat more flexible than those of the courts. But they almost always observe such normal safeguards for witnesses as the right of cross-examination by counsel. At the end, they issue public reports of their findings. Their record of thoroughness, objectivity, and respect for the rights of the accused has excited

the admiration of a number of students of government.[37] The British seldom resort to the device of the Tribunal; in recent years one investigated
an allegation that public officials had accepted gifts in return for favorable
official action, another investigated the improper disclosure of financial information.

An older and more common investigatory instrument is the Royal Commission of Inquiry, used chiefly to investigate social problems or new problems of policy and to prepare the way for major legislative innovations.[38]
It may exist for a few months or several years. Its members are drawn from
all segments of the British elite outside Parliament; they are sophisticated
experts or persons of eminence in the judiciary, universities, government,
labor unions, business, the professions, and welfare.[39] Where there are
strong conflicts of interest on the issue, the members are likely to be representative—the Commission on Liquor Licensing included representatives
of unions, temperance societies, the liquor industry, and social workers, as
well as government experts—but even in such cases they see service more
as a civic duty than as a means to fight traditional battles. The Royal Commission is designed to bring disinterested common sense, data, and good
judgment to bear on major social issues. Its fact-finding, mainly educative
and legislative, aims to provide a basis for public policy. Reinforcing its
independence, it usually employs its own staff and counsel.

The typical Royal Commission transcends current "political realities";
it is years ahead of what is currently acceptable. Although a few Commissions may have been diversionary—using studies as a way to avoid action
—many have stimulated major social reforms. Two impressive recent examples are the Wolfenden Report on sexual deviance, whose recommendations touched off eight years of public debate culminating in legislation
that abolished all penalties for homosexual behavior between consenting
adults, and the report of Lord Robbins in British universities, which questioned traditional elitist assumptions and became the basis for a marked
expansion of British higher education.[40]

A combination of expertise, independence, and access to the highest
councils of state makes the Royal Commission an indispensable source of
intelligence for both the public and the government. Several observers note,
however, that the adaptation of British experience to American needs
would be difficult.[41] Rivalry between the White House and Congress means
that an investigation set up by one is viewed as a threat to the other. And
Congress zealously guards its traditional investigatory powers. In the absence of a parliamentary form of government to mitigate conflict between

legislative and executive branches, dispassionate fact-finding is politically dangerous.[42] Yet many American government commissions have been able to perform impressive services. In the early decades of this century, the findings of numerous Industrial Commissions studying labor conditions led to significant reforms. In recent years, such commissions have provided continuous expert advice (the President's Science Advisory Committee, a statutory body with fixed-term memberships), evaluation of government operations (the committee headed by Emanuel Piore of IBM to assess the work of government science laboratories), and fact-finding (presidential boards established to deal with emergency strikes).[43] Perhaps the closest approximation to the British Royal Commission is the "blue-ribbon" study commission that confronts a big social problem and makes policy recommendations. One of the best of these in recent years was the national Commission on Technology, Automation, and Economic Progress. Despite its mixed labor-management-public composition (members included Walter P. Reuther of the United Autoworkers, Thomas J. Watson, Jr., of the IBM Corporation, and Whitney M. Young, Jr., of the National Urban League), it issued a trenchant statement of domestic economic problems.[44] Sociology Professor Daniel Bell, a member of this commission, describes its operations and lists some general functions of all such study groups, which cannot be adequately performed by other government agencies or by Congress. First, the study commission provides a means for direct representation of "functional constituencies," increasingly important in the power structure of modern society. Second, it permits the government to explore the limits and possibilities of action with groups that can prevent or facilitate change. Third, it focuses public attention on certain issues and mobilizes support for particular policies without closing off discussion and hardening positions. Finally, it involves nongovernmental elites in the formulation of public policy.[45]

These functions are more difficult to execute but also more essential in a decentralized political system characterized by a strong division of powers and by erratic swings between excessive secrecy and excessive publicity. Illustrating the difficulties is the controversial Gaither Committee, a group of distinguished citizens who in 1957 presented to the President and the National Security Council a classified report on American defense requirements.[46] The report differed sharply from government policy in its estimate of the Soviet threat and the appropriate size of the defense budget. Drawing upon RAND's research on the effectiveness and vulnerability of air bases and upon other data, the Gaither Report forcefully urged that American missile sites be hardened and dispersed and that our limited-war capacity be increased, thereby indirectly challenging Secretary Dulles's policy of massive retaliation. The Eisenhower administration tried to keep the report secret. Operating agencies saw the civilian outsiders as too far out of touch with their problems and resented their interference. Although the Gaither Report significantly influenced the analysis of strategy by defense intellectuals, although its new interpretation of the facts may have encouraged the administration to take a fresh look at our defense posture, it naturally did not have an instantaneous impact on administration policy. Instead, the Report was used by the pro-spending groups within the administration against the more powerful anti-spending groups and by the opposition Democrats in Congress against the executive. Adopting the typical American counterbalance to secrecy, the losing faction leaked the Report to the newspapers and to critics of administration policy. In a system characterized by the ambivalent love-and-fear of secrecy and the ready resort to publicity, in circumstances where top leadership is weak and consequently unwilling to use the results of independent thought to overcome internal bureaucratic opposition by means of appeals to the public—in such a situation the effectiveness of blue-ribbon study commissions is reduced and the response to their findings is unpredictable.

It is a plausible hypothesis that administrative leaders with the best experts on the payroll make the best use of external sources of intelligence —partly because such leaders are already exposed to professionally independent staff and partly because that staff is a recruitment link to sophisticated outsiders. The point is evident in the strong academic ties of the U.S. government's Council of Economic Advisers—analyzed at length above. And it can be seen indirectly in a new development in the American labor movement. One of America's best-staffed unions, the UAW-AFL-CIO, has exposed itself systematically to outside criticism of its internal operations by a public review board.[47] Established by labor leaders unusually anxious to protect the rights of union members, this board of independent labor relations experts provides a final "court of appeals" in rights cases. Through its decisions, annual reports, and contacts with the union's own staff, the Board has made officials at every level aware of constitutional provisions, of decisions of the international executive board, and of procedural lapses within the union hierarchy. By acting to remove threats to members' rights, top UAW leaders not only promote internal democracy and their own reputation among members and the public; they learn more of what goes on inside their union. At least two other unions—the Upholsterers' International Union and the United Packinghouse Workers' Union—have established review boards.

The principle underlying the government commission and the review board—to go outside the established bureaucracy for truth on a social issue or for justice in an individual case—is the basis for an institution now spreading throughout the Western world, the Ombudsman.[48] In Scandinavia, the Ombudsman is an officer of Parliament who investigates citizens' complaints about unfair treatment by government departments or officials and who seeks a remedy, if he finds a complaint justified. His powers are confined to investigation and recommendation. Hearings are private; decisions, public. Although the Ombudsman can bring cases of administrative abuse to public attention and although questions of the confidentiality of files are variously resolved, the use of publicity as punishment is minimal.[49] In Scandinavia the Ombudsman is exclusively an agent of the legislature, but this is not an essential feature of the system. What counts in its success is a unique blend of expertise, political independence, the power to investigate, easy access for citizens, and speedy disposition of cases. In general, as a close observer of the impact of government on the individual, the Ombudsman is both an outside check on administrative negligence or abuse and an invaluable source of intelligence for executive agencies and the legislature. In the United States somewhat similar functions are served by the Inspector General of the Army. Even grievancemen or shop stewards in labor unions, despite their partisan roles, often serve as a channel of upward communication ("information feedback") for management as well as processors of complaints. But they lack the independence of an Ombudsman. Non-judicial civilian review boards for citizens' grievances against the police also perform similar functions. But they single out a polarized conflict between one occupational group and one minority; they lack the generality of a municipal grievance commissioner with authority to examine any complaint by any citizen against any agency, the police along with everyone else.

In sum, the possible administrative devices for approaching the truth are as diverse as they are important. Whatever its political risks, as a means to counter the expanding influence of unchecked experts, to preserve open discussion of complex issues, and to mobilize elite support for innovations, the independent government commission has no peer. We need to institutionalize the use of such commissions. At the same time we must make a greater attempt to preserve adversary safeguards in quasi-judicial decision-making as well as in courts—or to find approximations that assure intelligent inquiry. Commissions, *ad hoc* tribunals, administrative courts, Ombudsmen—none of these are panaceas for any problem in public administration, but all can help make the values of truth, freedom, and justice less precarious.

# NOTES

1. On British police see Charles Reith, *A Short History of the British Police* (London: Oxford University Press, 1948); Frederick C. Mather, *Public Order in the Age of the Chartists* (Manchester: University of Manchester Press, 1959), pp. 75–140, 182–225; and Jürgen Thorwald, *The Century of the Detective*, trans. by Richard and Clara Winston (New York: Harcourt, Brace and World, 1965), pp. 35–43. On the police in the United States, see Michael Banton, *The Policeman in the Community* (New York: Basic Books, 1964) and Charles Reith, *The Blind Eye of History: A Study of the Origins of the Present Era* (London: Faber and Faber, n.d. [1952]), pp. 54–129—two British students of law enforcement. Reith is plainly shocked by the American scene; his incredulous tone as he reports police practices underscores the differences between our armed, decentralized constabulary and the unarmed, centralized British police—differences more objectively analyzed by Banton. American police cope with a more heterogeneous, mobile population, operate in a context of weaker consensus regarding morals and laws, and have been more subject to outside political influence.
2. Allen W. Dulles, *Germany's Underground* (New York: The Macmillan Company, 1947), p. 70.
3. David Wise and Thomas B. Ross, *The Invisible Government* (New York: Random House, 1964).
4. Cf. Schur.
5. Rourke, pp. 92 ff.; and Cook, pp. 239 ff., 248, 362, 366–381. Cook shows an insufficient appreciation of the character of the Communist Party when it functioned as an important force in American life; his account is burdened with liberal clichés (e.g., dark hints that Alger Hiss was framed are not persuasive in light of an earlier study—Herbert L. Packer, *Ex-Communist Witnesses: Four Studies in Fact Finding* [Stanford: Stanford University Press, 1962]). *The FBI Nobody Knows* is, nevertheless, a serious indictment of the FBI as a subverter of the law. A similar attack comes to the same conclusions for an earlier period: Max Lowenthal, *The Federal Bureau of Investigation* (New York: William Sloane Associates, 1950). For a more scholarly treatment, unfortunately more restricted in scope, see Bontecou. Other sources provide little more than semi-official celebration of the FBI and its director since 1924, J. Edgar Hoover—e.g., Don Whitehead, *The FBI Story: A Report to the People* (New York: Random House, 1956). Besides using

the investigative techniques described above, the FBI has apparently engaged in a good deal of informal intimidation of its critics in Congress and the press—which may account for the paucity of published analyses of its activities, in proportion to the record of responsible criticism of other government agencies, including the CIA. A prime reason that the FBI is so free to intimidate men of power is that it has no strong institutionalized competition. The CIA faces a sometimes resentful State Department and an equally resentful Defense Department. The FBI faces only local police who are unlikely sources of public criticism; the police depend on the FBI for its fingerprint collection, its laboratories for analyzing physical clues, and its training opportunities at the National Police Academy.

6. Packer, *Ex-Communist Witness;* Cook, pp. 288, 358–362; and Lowenthal, pp. 434 ff.
7. Cook, pp. 38–45.
8. *Ibid.,* pp. 34–35, 163 ff.; Lowenthal, pp. 388–400.
9. Packer, *Ex-Communist Witnesses,* p. 230.
10. Cf. Kuhn, pp. 150, 158, 165–171, *passim.*
11. E. Eugene Davis, "Legal Structures in a Changing Society," in *Society and the Law,* ed. by F. James Davis *et al.* (New York: The Free Press, 1962), p. 220. Occasionally legislators create new tribunals that bypass the court because they hope to produce more favorable decisions. The impetus behind workmen's compensation boards and commissions, for instance, was the hope of progressive law-makers and their constituents that such agencies would take the worker's side. See the unpubl. diss. (University of California, Berkeley, 1966) by Philippe Nonet, "Administrative Justice: A Sociological Study of the California Industrial Accidents Commission."
12. Daniel P. Moynihan, "The War Against the Automobile," *The Public Interest,* No. 3 (Spring, 1966), pp. 10–26.
13. *Ibid.,* p. 26.
14. Donald J. Newman, "Pleading Guilty for Considerations: A Study of Bargain Justice," in *The Sociology of Punishment and Correction,* ed. by Norman Johnson, *et al.* (New York: John Wiley & Sons, 1962), pp. 24–32; Skolnick, pp. 13–14.
15. *United States v. Wiley,* 184 F. Supp. 679 (N. D. Ill., 1960). This decision was reversed on appeal.
16. In 1959, again in response to overcrowding of the court calendar, a special committee of the American Bar Association suggested ten remedies, three of which would reduce adversariness: (1) encouragement of jury waivers; (2) use of pretrial conferences; and (3) disposition of some cases by lawyers acting as referees, commissioners, auditors, or arbitrators. E. Eugene Davis, p. 221. For the case against such measures see the data and arguments in Hans Zeisel, Harry Kalven, Jr., and Bernard Buchholz, *Delay in the Courts* (Boston: Little, Brown, and Company, 1959). They claim that the time that would be saved is grossly exag-

gerated and, in any case, the gain would not offset the erosion of the ideal that litigants should have free access to courts and qualified judges.

17. Gustav L. Schramm, "Philosophy of the Juvenile Court," *Annals of the American Academy of Political and Social Science,* CCLVI (January, 1949), 107.

18. H. L. Wilensky and C. N. Lebeaux, *Industrial Society and Social Welfare* (New York: Russell Sage Foundation, 1958), pp. 220–222. For an extended, recent statement of the conflict between due process of law and individualized treatment, see David Matza, *Delinquency and Drift* (New York: John Wiley & Sons, 1964), ch. 4. Cf. Alfred J. Kahn, *A Court for Children: A Study of the New York City Children's Court* (New York: Columbia University Press, 1953), especially chs. 10 and 11; and Paul W. Tappan, *Juvenile Delinquency.* (New York: McGraw-Hill Book Co., 1949).

19. Alex Elson, "Juvenile Courts and Due Process," in *Justice for the Child: The Juvenile Court in Transition,* ed. by Margaret K. Rosenheim (New York: The Free Press, 1962), p. 99.

20. W. Friedmann, *Law in a Changing Society* (Berkeley and Los Angeles: University of California Press, 1959), p. 228.

21. C. Ray Jeffrey, "Criminal Justice and Social Change," in Davis *et al., Society and the Law,* pp. 290–298. See cases and comments in Monrad G. Paulsen and Sanford H. Kadish, *Criminal Law and Its Processes* (Boston: Little, Brown, and Company, 1962), pp. 312–353.

22. Thomas S. Szasz, *Law, Liberty, and Psychiatry* (New York: The Macmillan Company, 1963), especially pp. 91–190. See also George Dession, "Psychiatry and the Conditioning of Criminal Justice," *Yale Law Review,* XLVII (January, 1938), 319–340.

23. Friedmann, pp. 166–177.

24. Rita M. James, "Jurors' Assessment of Criminal Responsibility," *Social Problems,* VII (Summer, 1959), 58–69.

25. *The Dilemma of Mental Commitments in California: A Background Document.* Subcommittee on Mental Health Services, California Assembly (Sacramento: Department of General Services, Documents Section, 1966), p. 27.

26. *Ibid.,* pp. 29–31. See also Thomas J. Scheff, "The Societal Reaction to Deviance: Ascriptive Elements in the Psychiatric Screening of Mental Patients in a Midwestern State," *Social Problems,* XI (Spring, 1964), 401–413.

27. California Assembly, *The Dilemma,* pp. 42–43.

28. *Ibid.,* p. 43.

29. *Ibid.,* pp. 43–50.

30. For an excellent analysis of the tension between a system of individualized disposition and a fair hearing in an adversary proceeding, see Sanford H. Kadish, "The Advocate and the Expert: Counsel in the Peno-Correctional Process," *Minnesota Law Review,* XLVII (January, 1961), 803–841. For discussion of the legal problems, see Ernst W.

Puttkammer, *Administration of Criminal Law* (Chicago: University of Chicago Press, 1953), pp. 220–230; and Paulsen and Kadish, pp. 168–181, 198–209.

31. *Muller v. Oregon,* 208 U.S. 412 (1908). The case involved a law on hours of work for women. Brandeis, as a consulting attorney to the state of Oregon, cited reports of public investigating committees, books and articles by medical authorities and social workers.

32. Paul Freund, "The Brandeis Brief," *On Understanding the Supreme Court* (Boston: Little, Brown, and Company, 1951), pp. 86–92. Anon. note, "Social and Economic Facts—Appraisal of Suggested Techniques for Presenting Them to the Courts," *Harvard Law Review,* LXI (February, 1948), 692–702.

33. Edward W. Cleary, "Evidence as a Problem in Communicating," *Vanderbilt Law Review,* V (April, 1952), 277–281. Cf. Arnold M. Rose, "The Social Scientist as an Expert Witness," *Minnesota Law Review,* XL (February, 1956), 205–218.

34. Julian L. Woodward, "A Scientific Attempt to Provide Evidence for a Decision on Change of Venue," *American Sociological Review,* XVII (August, 1952), 447–452.

35. For discussion of the effects of the technical nature of decisions on the quality of intelligence, see above, pp. 79–81. For an excellent case study of the role of engineers, planners, and private interests in the location and design of an intercity freeway in and around St. Paul, see Alan A. Altshuler, *The City Planning Process: A Political Analysis* (Ithaca: Cornell University Press, 1965), pp. 17–83. The apparent clarity of technical standards of the engineers (traffic service and cost) and their sense of rectitude overwhelmed less-focused and less-coordinated interests and beliefs.

36. Cf. Packer, *Ex-Communist Witnesses,* pp. 221–231.

37. Lindsay Rogers, "Congressional Investigations: The Problem and Its Solution." *University of Chicago Law Review,* XVIII (Spring, 1951), 464–477; Herman Finer, "Congressional Investigations: The British System." *University of Chicago Law Review,* XVIII (Spring, 1951), 564, 568–570; Telford Taylor, *Grand Inquest: The Story of Congressional Investigations* (New York: Simon and Schuster, 1955), pp. 292–294; and Packer, *Ex-Communist Witnesses,* pp. 236–237.

38. Charles J. Hanser, *Guide to Decision: The Royal Commission* (Totowa, New Jersey: The Bedminster Press, 1965); and Hugh M. Clokie and J. W. Robinson, *Royal Commissions of Inquiry: The Significance of Investigations in British Politics* (Stanford: Stanford University Press, 1937). Cf. Finer, p. 554; Taylor, pp. 290–291. Among other issues, Commissions have dealt with national health insurance (1924), awards to inventors (1946), control and ownership of the press (1947), capital punishment (1949), taxation (1951), marriage and divorce (1951), the law relating to mental illness and mental deficiency (1954), and doctors' and dentists' remuneration (1957).

39. Hanser, pp. 182, 258–259.
40. Martin Trow, "Second Thoughts on Robbins: A Question of Size and Shape," *Universities Quarterly,* XVIII (March, 1964), 136–152. The Robbins Committee was not technically a "Royal Commission" officially appointed by the Crown, which cannot be discharged by a succeeding Government. It was the second level in the ranking of advisory bodies; in this instance, the government felt no need for the prestige of "Royal" origin. But such special committees have the same high-caliber, unpaid membership, independence, and standards as the Royal Commission. The several kinds of British commissions are alike in their broad functions. Cf. Hanser, pp. 35 ff., 51–53, 86.
41. Telford Taylor, pp. 285–287; Packer, *Ex-Communist Witnesses,* pp. 241–246.
42. Packer suggests a system of *ad hoc* tribunals that permits initiation by either branch subject to a speedy check by the other (e.g., a veto within a fixed time). To reduce conflict and increase independence, members would be drawn from a standing panel of one or two hundred persons from private life, designated in equal numbers by the President, a Senate leader, and the Speaker of the House; each tribunal would have its own staff and counsel and "the power to subpoena witnesses and documents, to take testimony under oath, to compel testimony as to which the privilege against self-incrimination is invoked by granting immunity from criminal prosecution, and to obtain such material from the files of the FBI and other Government agencies as it may deem pertinent to the subject of inquiry and to the testimony of witnesses called before the tribunal" (p. 245). Procedures would depend on whether the purpose is to investigate alleged misdeeds of individuals or to analyze a social issue. Presumably each purpose would require a different approach to the facts. Where damage may be inflicted on the individual, he must be accorded the opportunity to participate in the process meaningfully and effectively by presenting evidence concerning his particular case; where legislative rules are to be formulated, it is appropriate to rely on more general knowledge, statements of probability, and representative cases. Cf. Kenneth Culp Davis, *Administrative Law Treatise,* Vol. II (St. Paul: West Publishing Company, 1958), pp. 353–363.
43. Daniel Bell, "Government by Commission," *The Public Interest,* No. 3 (Spring, 1966), p. 6.
44. *Technology and the American Economy,* I, February, 1966 (Washington: Government Printing Office, 1966).
45. Bell, p. 7. Cf. Hanser, p. 144.
46. For a shrewd account of the Gaither episode see Morton H. Halperin, "The Gaither Committee and the Policy Process," *World Politics,* XIII (April, 1961), 360–384.
47. Jack Stieber, Walter E. Oberer, and Michael Harrington, *Democracy and Public Review: An Analysis of the UAW Public Review Board* (Santa Barbara: Center for the Study of Democratic Institutions, 1960).

48. A long-needed survey of experience with various versions of this idea has recently been published. *The Ombudsman: Citizen's Defender,* ed. by Donald C. Rowat (London: George Allen & Unwin, 1965). The institution originated in Sweden in 1809; it later developed in Finland, was adopted by Denmark in 1955, and spread to Norway and New Zealand in 1962. By 1966, proposals to establish the Ombudsman system were being discussed in Canada, Britain, the Netherlands, India, Ireland, and the United States.

49. Even in Sweden and Finland, where there is free access to most official documents, information on security matters, trade secrets, and the treatment of alcoholics or the mentally ill is kept secret. *Ibid.,* pp. 7, 49–50, 84, 103–105.

# Value Dilemmas and Computerized Systems

## ROBERT BOGUSLAW

**M**ost experts make use of some form of scientific
rhetoric to give them greater control over the public. The
public trust in the methods and the conclusions of science
make them willing to accept almost any idea that is
presented under the aegis of science. Science is God, and
the word of God is not questioned by mortals. There is no
question because mortals cannot understand God.

Today one of the most powerful rhetorics of science is
that of systems theory and computers. The computer is
taken today as one of God's prime symbols. The computer
is the power of science made manifest to mortals. Anything
presented in terms of computers and systems theory is apt
to be generally believed by the public. Computers and
systems analyses, therefore, are extremely useful to
officials or anyone else who wishes to control the public.

A few members of the public understand the language

*Reprinted from Robert Boguslaw,* The New Utopians: A Study of
System Design and Social Change, *by permission of Prentice-Hall,
Inc.* © *1965.*

of computers and the nature of systems analysis. The public cannot see
that most systems analyses involve secret or taken-for-granted value
assumptions which become primary determinants of the outcome of
the analysis. As Boguslaw argues in this selection, systems analyses can
have great power in determining the future of our society, in part
precisely because the directions of the analyses are left almost completely
out of question. The ideas of justice and morality, the feelings of
individuals, the happiness of individuals—all can be overlooked by a
general ''scientific'' systems analysis. The dangers are especially great
in the area of urban social planning because more and more systems
analyses are being used by urban planners to decide how we should go
about solving our urban social problems.

Only by becoming more aware of the dangers implicit in the use of
systems analyses and by gaining greater knowledge of systems analyses
can the public protect itself against these dangers. If such protections
can be guaranteed, and if systems analyses are done in such a way as to
take into consideration our basic values and needs, then certainly few
would reject the use of this method of analyzing our complexly
interrelated problems.

Replying to arguments about the possible superiority of computers over
human beings can be an upsetting experience—if one happens to identify
with the perspective of people. Sociologists, anthropologists, and other
students of human behavior are familiar with this experience. In countless
other contexts they have seen it as an indication of ethnocentrism—the
view that one's own life or tribe or customs are to be preferred over all
others. Anthropologists have long been familiar with the curious phenomenon that in the language of many nonliterate people the name of the tribe
frequently means "human beings." Implicitly, everyone to whom the tribal
name does not apply is outside the pale of humanity. And, for example,
"When the Suriname Bush-Negro is shown a flashlight, admires it, and
then quotes the proverb, 'White man's magic isn't black man's magic,' he

is merely reaffirming his faith in his own culture. He is pointing out that the stranger, for all his mechanical devices, would be lost in the Guiana Jungle without the aid of his Bush-Negro friends, at ease among its dangers." [1]

So, it comes as a very small surprise indeed to those who believe that the crucial ingredient of the human condition is high-order intelligence that an argument such as Paul Armer's (purporting to demonstrate that computers are potentially just as smart as the rest of us) must be rejected out of hand. We all tend to be somewhat ethnocentric about the tribe of humanity. We *know* we have magic that Armer's cottonpickin' machine couldn't possibly have.

What precisely is it that we have in addition to that mechanistic kind of IQ which Armer implies is our last remaining talent?

As a minimum, we have a sense of values. Some things are important to us. Other things are not so important. As sophisticates of twentieth-century civilization rather than members of a nonliterate tribe, we can accept the possibility that Paul Armer's computer might not only be able to replicate our values, but might even dream up a set demonstrably better for us than our own. But they wouldn't be ours. And they wouldn't be the machine's. They would be Paul's. And that's the rub.

On the face of it this seems almost insulting to Paul Armer and his colleagues in the information-processing profession. These men do not have any readily discernible political axes to grind. They are neither politicians, labor leaders, nor representatives of big business. They are scientists and engineers—objective experts whose only concern is technical efficiency and scientific detachment. It seems grossly unfair to imply that they act with devious motivations and for the promotion of hidden causes.

The point, of course, is simply that values are not derived either scientifically, logically, or intellectually. They are simply prime factors. And even if Armer's values were those of a saint, we might well wish to promote our own saint with a somewhat different set of values to be implemented. But, says the information processor, "I do only what the customer tells me to do. I implement the values of someone else, rather than my own. And in the absence of specific instructions, I use as a guide line the criterion of technical efficiency or cost, or speed or something similar."

All this is true, and it brings us once again to the inescapable fact that power in the design of large-scale computer-based systems resides to an increasing degree with 1) the customer—to the extent that he can specify in complete and rigorous detail exactly what decisions he wishes to see implemented by his bureaucracy under every conceivable set of conditions, or, 2) the system designer and computer programmer, who insure that *some* decision is made in every case whether that case has been clearly anticipated or not, and 3) the hardware manufacturer, whose technology and components determine what kind of data can be sensed and processed by computers, display equipment, and other system equipment.

To the extent that customers (and these may include government agencies or private industry) abdicate their power prerogatives because of ignorance of the details of system operation, de facto system decisions are made by equipment manufacturers or information-processing specialists. The customers may find it impossible to specify all future situations; they may be unable to devise foolproof heuristics; they may fail to specify detailed operating unit characteristics; they may be unable to devise appropriate ad hoc plans. Under each of these conditions, de facto decisions are again made for them by system designers or other technical specialists.

As computer-based systems become increasingly more significant in shaping the realistic terms of existence in contemporary society, it becomes increasingly more relevant to inquire about the implications contained for expression of individual values. The process of obtaining representation for individual values is one of the specific notions contained in popular conceptions of democracy. However, the central idea of democracy has been penetratingly described as "one particular way in which the authority to govern is acquired and held." [2] Thus, "A man may be said to hold authority democratically when he has been freely chosen to hold such authority by those who must live under it, when they have had, and will have, the alternative of choosing somebody else, and when he is accountable to them for the way in which he exercises this authority." [3]

It is, of course, clear that there are limits on the democratic principle and that legal and institutional safeguards must exist to protect values other than those of democracy itself. It is equally clear that at best the democratic principle can be only approximated. No one in our society seriously suggests that every person must be absolutely equal to every other person in power and influence. [4] But, "the working touchstone of a 'democratic' system of authority is simply the degree to which it gives individuals legitimate instruments for reaching those who make the decisions that affect them, and for bringing influence to bear upon them. A system is more or less 'democratic' depending on the number, availability, and effectiveness of these instruments, and on the proportion of the population entitled and able to use them." [5]

Now, whether the "masses" are denied legitimate access to decision makers by reason of despotism, bureaucratic deviousness, or simple technical obfuscation, the resultant erosion of democratic process can be much the same. To the extent that decisions made by equipment manufacturers, computer programmers, or system designers are enshrouded in the mystery of "technical" detail, the persons most affected by these decisions (including customers, publics, and employees) will be denied the opportunity to participate or react to the decision made. The spectrum of values represented in the new decision-making order can and is being increasingly more circumscribed by fiat disguised as technological necessity. The paramount issues to be raised in connection with the design of our new computerized utopias are not technological—they are issues of values and the power through which these values become translated into action.

A major difficulty is the lack of clarity involved in efforts to specify values in exact terms. Frequently, values are expressed in terms of principles or heuristics. Thus, some of us value property rights, others value political, social, or more generally, "human" rights. Partisans of the extreme political right as well as those of the left and many in between insist upon their espousal of values which, when stated as heuristics, all sound the same. Yet it is clear that the value orientations of "conservative" political groups are fundamentally different from the value orientations of "liberal" political groups. It is clear that such differences include at least the following:

1. Differences in the implicit priorities each group would assign to a set of specifically stated heuristics. Indeed, it has been pointed out that a stranger in a new society may become progressively more confused about the operating values of a society as he learns more about the formal statements the inhabitants make about their values. "The explicit formulations are effective guides only to those who have already so fully internalized the multitude of situational directives that they have become dulled to the . . . logical implications of the explicit value statements of the society." [6]

2. Differences in the elements of society to which they would each award power prerogatives. The historic guffaw that accompanied the assertion that, "What's good for General Motors is good for America," is perhaps primarily attributable to the fact that it is not considered in good taste to place on public display one's own private power aspirations. The fact that the statement might or might not be true in some global societal sense was beside the point. The sight of a corporation executive betraying a possible slip of his power tongue

was inevitably perceived as a possible violation of the unwritten canons of good taste.

3. Differences in the specific scenarios of situations that the two groups have in mind as they espouse their individual causes. To the stereotype of an economic "conservative" in American society, the economic situations to be dealt with are seen as consisting of firms and individuals willing and able to engage in free competition for markets, resources, and profits. Under these conditions, "government interference" is seen as a barrier to "freedom." To the stereotype of an economic "liberal," on the other hand, the situations are characterized by monopolistic control of the economic process by mammoth corporations, under conditions in which freedom of competition is impossible. To such a liberal, "government interference" can be seen as a method for insuring that freedom of competition will be permitted. People with identical value orientations can be found classified as either conservative or liberal depending upon their perception of empirical reality.

4. Differences in notions about the structure of operating units within this society. Are the human operating units motivated primarily by wishes to maximize their individual fortunes, at the expense of their neighbors if necessary? Or are they motivated primarily by codes of religion and morality to maximize the search for a more common welfare? In a specific situation, would these operating units prefer to surrender some national prerogatives rather than to insure total devastation of their own and other nations? Under what specific circumstances would they choose to press the nuclear war button or refrain from doing so?

5. Differences in perceptions of the environments within which the respective causes attempt to provide design solutions. Is the outer world essentially hostile? Or is it peopled by persons approximately as sincere in their search for solutions as our own? Are we trying to solve only our own problems? Or are we trying to help solve problems for persons living in other countries of this world? Who is the customer?

In short, value differences are sometimes nothing more than differences in ways of looking at reality. Sometimes they consist of honest differences in opinion about the most effective way to achieve mutually agreed-upon goals. Sometimes they reflect fundamental differences in primary orientation to the world we live in. These differences may be as simple as a preference for the Martins over the Coys; they can be as complex as the choice between egoism and humanitarianism.

Probably the most distinctive characteristic of classical utopian designs is the basic "humanitarian" bent of their value structures. In Sir Thomas More's *Utopia,* the inhabitants are more concerned with the welfare of their fellow men than with furthering their individual fortunes. The phalanstery designed by Charles Fourier provides environments and procedures calculated to undo the more undesirable human consequences of unbridled individualism. And even in Francis Bacon's *New Atlantis,* where the major emphasis is presumably placed upon scientific programs, the fundamental goal of scientific activity is seen as the solution of social problems and the welfare of human beings—rather than the advancement of science for its own sake.

And perhaps the most notable difference to be found between the classical system designers and their contemporary counterparts (system engineers, data processing specialists, computer manufacturers, and system designers) consists precisely in the fact that the humanitarian bent has disappeared. The dominant value orientation of the utopian renaissance can best be described as "efficiency" rather than "humanitarianism."

The powerful appeal of the efficiency concept is a well-known and well-documented feature of contemporary Western civilization. It is more efficient to ride in an automobile than it is to walk. It is more efficient to fly in an airplane than it is to ride in an automobile. It is more efficient to use a guided missile than it is to use a manned bomber, and so on. The fundamental challenge of efficiency arises in connection with the struggle for ascendancy over man's physical environment. This struggle may be rationalized as a necessity for the survival of man. More frequently these days it is simply attributed to the sport of satisfying man's insatiable curiosity about the universe in which he finds himself. For the American schoolboy, learning to exert mastery over the mysterious forces of nature has become every bit as much a challenge as the problem of overcoming rival princes ever was for Machiavelli's Lorenzo de Medici. But just as no de Medici could seriously be expected to learn his politics from pre-Machiavellian books, it is not reasonable to expect American schoolboys to learn the facts of the utopian renaissance exclusively from contemporary computer journals and works on system engineering. The strength of Machiavelli, as the first of the modern analysts of power, consisted of the fact that, "Where others looked at the figureheads, he kept his eyes glued behind the scenes. He wanted to know what made things tick; he wanted to take the clock of the world to pieces to find out how it worked." [7]

Information necessary to take apart the clock of the contemporary world is simply not underscored in contemporary computer journals and works on system engineering, which remain devoted to the idols of physical efficiency. The central consequences of the utopian renaissance involve fundamental changes not only in the value structure of Western people, but redistributions of power concentrations made possible through the use of system control mechanisms. The resurgence of intellectual and political orientations such as "conservative" and "liberal" must be re-examined in the light of these newly emerging, altered power relationships.

Classical utopias received their impetus from a dissatisfaction with existing reality. They represented attempts to design systems more consistent with notions about what was really "good" for the mankinds they knew or dreamed about. They were unsuccessful largely because their designers, in attempting to transcend the limits of their own environmental realities, severed the threads between their brave new systems and the system control or power mechanisms of their times.

Our own utopian renaissance receives its impetus from a desire to extend the mastery of man over nature. Its greatest vigor stems from a dissatisfaction with the limitations of man's existing control over his physical environment. Its greatest threat consists precisely in its potential as a means for extending the control of man over man.

# NOTES

1. Cf. Melville J. Herskovits, *Man and His Works* (New York: Alfred A. Knopf, Inc., 1948), p. 68.
2. Charles Frankel, "Bureaucracy & Democracy in the New Europe," *Daedalus* (Proceedings of the American Academy of Arts and Sciences), XCIII, No. 1 (Winter 1964), 476.
3. *Ibid.*
4. Cf. *ibid.*, 476–477.
5. *Ibid.*, 477.
6. Ralph H. Turner, "Social Disorganization, Deviance, and Social Problems," *Sociology: The Progress of a Decade,* ed. Seymour Martin Lipset and Neil J. Smelser (Englewood Cliffs, N.J.: Prentice-Hall, Inc., 1961), p. 526.
7. Max Lerner, "Introduction to Niccolò Machiavelli," *The Prince and the Discourses* (New York: Random House, 1950), p. xxvi.

PART V

# The Tyranny of
# Experts in the
# Technological Society

# The Servants of Power

## LOREN BARITZ

One of the greatest dangers of "expert" control in our society today is that of expert social science control. Lacking the precision and the formal validity of the natural sciences, the social sciences are far more adaptable to the individual desires and values of officials and of social scientists themselves. The social sciences can more easily be manipulated by such individuals in order to control the public. This danger has grown as the social scientists have achieved greater respectability among the public, especially as the social scientists have made increasing use of the symbols of science, that is, quantitative measures and systems analyses.

In this selection, Baritz shows how the social scientists over many years have used their methods and the rhetoric of science to support the power of administrators. His argument shows that private organizations of individuals can use such means of expert control as well as government officials can. In fact, we might argue, in line with some of Wilensky's earlier suggestions, that one of the greatest sources of protection against such expert control would be the use of private organizations dedicated to providing such protection by expert knowledge to counteract the expert knowledge of government officials and of other private organizations.

Henry Ford, II, 1946: "If we can solve the problem of human relations in industrial production, we can make as much progress toward lower costs in the next 10 years as we made during the past quarter century through the development of the machinery of mass production." [1] By the middle of the twentieth century, industrial social science had become one of the most pregnant of the many devices available to America's managers in their struggle with costs and labor, government and the consuming public. But, even then, industrial social science remained richer in its promise than in its accomplishments, impressive as these had been. It was often what social science *could* do in the next five, ten, or twenty years that justified to managers their current support of its practitioners. Thus far, social scientists had contributed to management a useful array of techniques, including testing, counseling, attitude research, and sociometry. All to the good, certainly; but much was left to do. And most of what was left, as Henry Ford correctly pointed out, was centered in the area of human relations. The reason that an understanding of human relations assumed such monumental proportions was that, in an age of governmental regulations and more powerful unions, costs continued to rise. American management came to believe in the importance of understanding human behavior because it became convinced that this was one sure way of improving its main weapon in the struggle for power, the profit margin.

The promise of industrial social science has not been a subject about which America's managers have had to guess. The industrial social scientists themselves have, throughout their professional history, made explicit their aspirations, their hopes for the future, and their unbounded faith in the centrality of their discipline to the problems of modern life. The history of this explication of faith began, appropriately enough, with Walter Dill Scott, who argued in 1911 that a knowledge of the laws of psychology would make it possible for the businessman to control and therefore raise the efficiency of every man in his employ, including his own. At about the same time, a lecturer at the University of Wisconsin's School of Commerce assured his students that a knowledge of psychology would increase their "commercial proficiency by fifty per cent." Workers, according to Hugo Münsterberg's 1913 statement, would have their wages raised, their working hours reduced, mental depression and dissatisfaction with work eliminated, all through the application of psychology to industry. He assured Americans that a "cultural gain . . . will come to the total economic life of the nation." A knowledge of psychology, reported another psychologist, would provide the business executive with the skills needed to influence the behavior of his workers. Psychologist G. Stanley Hall went all out: "Our task," he said, "is nothing less than to rehumanize industry." [2]

During the 1920's and 1930's psychologists reported that "the fate . . . of mankind" depended on the help they could give to managers. Indeed, according to James McKeen Cattell, the founder of the Psychological Corporation, "The development of psychology as a science and its application to the control of human conduct . . . may in the course of the coming century be as significant for civilization as has been the industrial revolution." Specific tasks were also outlined for the psychology of the future. For example, General Motors' sit-down strikes of 1937 could have been avoided through the use of psychology, said a psychologist. If psychologists were as effective in industry as they had been in education, said another, "something akin to an industrial Utopia would arise." Over and over again these men assured anyone who cared to listen that many of the world's problems would disappear if only executives would be more receptive to the advances of psychology.[3]

Even problems of general moment were thought to be solvable through the work of industrial psychologists; the factory, said M.I.T. psychologist Douglas McGregor, "is a microcosm in which we may well be able to find answers to some of the fundamental problems of modern society." Industrial conflict would disappear, reported other psychologists, if their conclusions were implemented in industry. In fact, said still another, if psychology were more widely accepted by management, "the advancement of our emotional, social, and economic life" would be more certain. *"Potentially the most important of sciences for the improvement of man and of his world-order"* is the way Robert M. Yerkes, a psychologist at Yale, described his discipline in 1946.[4]

Sociologists, too, tried to make clear what they could do if they were given the chance, though they were usually more restrained than the psychologists. They recognized that managers determined the kinds of opportunities the sociologists had, and hence, if the claims of sociology were frustrated, the managers themselves would be at fault. If all was in order, however, if managers cooperated, sociologists could "provide useful analytical tools and profitable guides for activity." Other sociologists believed that they could help managers "think more effectively about their human problems." Perhaps this was why one sociologist accepted employment with a petroleum company in 1943 to explain why the CIO was able to organize its men. Margaret Mead thought her colleagues could help make the anonymous industrial worker feel important. Focusing on the top echelon of the business hierarchy, some sociologists were dissatisfied with what they saw. A different type of social control was needed, and they believed that they were the men to point the way to the future. The powers of the sociological elite would be concentrated on the subelite of managers who needed to be led and "clarified." All that was needed was some cooperation from those who wielded managerial power.[5]

It was precisely this need for managerial cooperation that made the social scientists' conception of what they could do in the future seem at best a trifle grandiose and at worst silly. As part of the bureaucratization of virtually every aspect of American life, most industrial social scientists labored in industry as technicians, not as scientists. Not professionally concerned with problems outside the delimited sphere which management had assigned to them, not daring to cross channels of communication and authority, they were hemmed in by the very organization charts which they had helped to contrive. And the usual industrial social scientist, because he accepted the norms of the elite dominant in his society, was prevented from functioning critically, was compelled by his own ideology and the power of America's managers to supply the techniques helpful to managerial goals. In what should have been a healthful tension between mind and society, the industrial social scientist in serving the industrial elite had to abandon the wider obligations of the intellectual who is a servant of his own mind.

Casting his characteristically wide net, sociologist C. Wright Mills pointed out that "the intellectual is becoming a technician, an idea-man, rather than one who resists the environment, preserves the individual type, and defends himself from death-by-adaption." Unless psychologists raised their sights and became concerned with broader social problems, said another observer, they would not "rise to the level of professional persons but will degenerate into mere technicians." [6]

The technician's role was literally forced upon industrial social scientists by the nature of their industrial positions. Hired by management to solve specific problems, they had to produce. The problem was best stated by two of the most astute psychologists of the 1920's: "Research, to be successful, has to be carried out under the most favorable conditions, and only the business man himself can say whether these conditions shall be provided." [7]

A few industrial social scientists learned that they could not even rely on the much touted practicality of business executives. One psychologist employed by an advertising agency said in 1955 that he "had expected that the businessman would be hard headed and practical. . . . To my surprise and frustration," he went on, "they have accepted an awful lot of research mish mush. . . . Hard headed businessmen hell!" [8] Managers, however, have usually been sufficiently practical, from their own point of view, to realize that controls over research programs were necessary. Demanding that the social scientists in their employ concentrate exclusively on the narrow problems of productivity and industrial loyalty, managers made of industrial social science a tool of industrial domination. Some social scientists warned that this procedure would result in a "distorted view of industry," but failed to see that this was precisely what sophisticated managers wanted.[9]

Even Elton Mayo, of Hawthorne fame, feared that the forced status of technician would seriously limit the effectiveness of industrial social scientists, whose science would thereby be strangled. Because of the control of management over the nature and scope of their work, Mayo said, "the interesting *aperçu,* the long chance, may not be followed: both alike must be denied in order that the [research] group may 'land another job.' " The long-range effects would be even worse, because the "confusion of research with commercial huckstering can never prosper: the only effect is to disgust the intelligent youngster who is thus forced to abandon his quest for human enlightenment." [10]

Management, in short, controlled the industrial social scientists in its employ. Managers did not make use of social science out of a sense of social responsibility, but out of a recognized need to attack age-old problems of costs and worker loyalty with new weapons designed to fit the needs and problems of the twentieth century. Thus the recent arguments that American industry has entered a new era of social obligations and responsibilities[11] have missed the main point in the motivation of managers. When fulfilling putative social obligations became smart business, smart managers became socially conscious. Walter Reuther is characteristic of the small group that has refused to be seduced by the sophisticated rhetoric of managers, their spokesmen, and the articulate academicians who insist that the American business civilization is the best of all possible worlds. Trying to educate a congressional committee, Reuther said that his extensive experience with employers had taught him that "the one sure way of making them [employers] socially responsible is to make them financially responsible for the social results of what they do or fail to do." [12] Because of the general climate of opinion today, it is perhaps necessary to repeat what in previous years would have been a cliché unworthy of serious argument: managers, as managers, are in business to make money. Only to the extent that industrial social scientists can help in the realization of this goal will management make use of them.

Managers are forced by the necessities of the business world to measure their personal success or failure by the yardstick of the balance sheet; they have occasionally made considerable effort to clarify the thinking of industrial social scientists who just might be of help in improving the financial condition of the firm and therefore improving the position of the manager. It will be recalled that one of the main obstacles to easy interchange between managers and social scientists had long been the managers' conviction that social scientists were ignorant about the nature and purposes of industry. To employ an expert who did not recognize either the values or necessities of business might prove dangerous. Articulating what many managers felt, an executive of a large utility company, for example, in 1951 laid down the law to social scientists specifying the attitudes business expected of them:

> First—a willingness to accept the notion that businessmen perform a useful function in society, and that their methods may be necessary to accomplish this function. . . .
> Second—a willingness to accept the culture and conventions of business as necessary and desirable. . . .
> Third—a willingness to obtain personal satisfaction from being a member of a winning team, perhaps an anonymous member.
> Fourth—a willingness and ability to practice the good human relations principles that he knows.[13]

How unnecessary was this managerial fear of the industrial social scientist. The popular image of the impractical and absent-minded professor who was either a political liberal or perhaps even worse blurred the perception of the hard-headed managers of the business life of the nation. For, throughout their professional history, industrial social scientists, without prodding from anyone, have accepted the norms of America's managers. If this attitude had not tended to influence their work, it would deserve merely passing mention. But this commitment to management's goals, as opposed to the goals of other groups and classes in American society, did color their research and recommendations. These men have been committed to aims other than those of their professional but nonindustrial colleagues. Though the generalization has weaknesses, it seems that making a contribution to knowledge has been the essential purpose of only a few industrial social scientists. Reducing the pressures of unionism while increasing the productivity of the labor force and thereby lowering costs have been among their most cherished goals, because these have been the goals which management has set for them.

Managers, of course, had the power to hire and fire social scientists. If a social scientist was to be kept on the payroll, he had to produce. The judge of whether he was producing was his boss. His boss was interested in the specific problems of the business including those that threatened managerial control. Thus industrial social scientists have usually been salaried men, doing what they were told to do and doing it well—and therefore endangering those other personal, group, class, and institutional interests which were opposed to the further domination by the modern corporation of the mood and direction of American life. Endangered most have been the millions of workers who have been forced or seduced into submission to the ministrations of industrial social scientists. For these men and women there has been little defense, because organized labor generally has been apathetic to the movement, and because, even had labor been more active, management has played the game from a dominant position. Recently, however, there have been a few hints indicating that organized labor is beginning to make use of social-science techniques itself.[14] In any case, to date nothing seems to stand in the way of increased industrial exploitation of social science, and the industrial social scientists themselves have been especially willing.

The position these social scientists have taken regarding the ethics and politics of power obtrudes as a red thread in the otherwise pallid canvas on which they have labored. From the pioneers in industrial psychology to the sophisticated human-relations experts of the 1950's, almost all industrial social scientists have either backed away from the political and ethical implications of their work or have faced these considerations from the point of view of management. Aptly, it was Hugo Münsterberg who first formulated the comfortable and self-castrating position that industrial psychologists should concern themselves with means only, not with goals, aims, or ends, which could and should be determined only by the industrial managers themselves. Scientific method was clearly on Münsterberg's side, for science cannot solve political problems, and psychology, he argued, was a science which must be impartial. Thus he insisted that his colleagues should not pander "to selfish fancies of either side"—that is, capital or labor—but should remain detached and scientific observers of the industrial situation. Other early leaders in the development of industrial psychology quickly picked up Münsterberg's cue and explicated his position: "Psychology will always be limited by the fact that while it can determine the means to the end, it can have nothing to do with the determination of the end itself." [15]

During the 1920's the political stance desirable for social scientists was made even more clear. Moving from the justification by objectivity to a recognition of the industrial facts of life, psychologists were told that "business results are the main object." Objectivity was lifeblood to a true science, but the industrial manager would instruct his hired specialists about those problems or subjects that required analysis. "The pursuit and enlargement of psychological knowledge is merely a by-product of business efforts," psychologists were further cautioned. Confusion was compounded when, late in the decade, another industrial psychologist explained his position: workers who were justifiably dissatisfied were not fit subjects for psychological analysis because such a situation was an "economic or ethical problem." The obverse held: where workers were treated fairly and still were dissatisfied, there was the spot for psychological inquiry.[16] The controlling question of who determined the justification of employee dissatisfaction was unanswered, as of course it had to be. Moving from the academic to the industrial world, it seemed relatively clear that managers would at least suggest where psychological analysis should occur, which is to say that the decision about the justification of employee satisfaction or dissatisfaction was one that management made. The social scientist applied his tools where he was told to apply them.

Of major importance in this subordination of industrial social science to the pleasure of management were the assumptions made by the Hawthorne researchers. Perhaps this was the area in which the work of Elton Mayo was the most significant. For Mayo, more than any other single individual, directed the course of industrial research—obliquely, to be sure, through the statement of his attitudes and assumptions, which proved so comfortable that many disciples made them their own.

Mayo's unshakable conviction was that the managers of the United States comprised an elite which had the ability and therefore the right to rule the rest of the nation. He pointed out, for instance, that many of America's managers were remarkable men without prejudice.[17] According to one of his critics, Mayo believed that "management is capable, trained, and objective. Management uses scientific knowledge, particularly engineering knowledge, for making decisions. Political issues are illusions created by evil men. Society's true problems are engineering problems." [18] With this frame of reference, Mayo throughout his inquiring and productive life ignored labor, power, and politics. Indeed, he ignored the dignity that is possible in the age of the machine, despite his contrary arguments idealizing what for him was the soothing past, the preindustrial America. And in his myopia his colleagues and the larger movement of industrial human relations shared.[19]

But the commitment of social science to management derived not alone from Mayo's assumptions about the nature of the industrial world and of American civilization. Quite as important were the implications of the substantive research done at the Hawthorne Works of the Western Electric Company. The counseling program developed there, for example, led most industrial social scientists to conclude that, because workers felt better after talking to a counselor, even to the point of commenting about improved pay rates which the company had not changed, most workers did not have compelling obective problems. Much of industrial unrest was simply a function of faulty perception and conceptualization on the part of labor. One counselor, also an industrial consultant, put it this way:

> At least half of the grievances of the average employee can be relieved merely by giving him an opportunity to 'talk them out.' It may not even be necessary to take any action on them. All that they require is a patient and courteous hearing, supplemented, when necessary, by an explanation of *why* nothing can be done. . . . It is not always necessary to yield to the worker's requests in order to satisfy them.[20]

More and more industrial psychologists heeded the injunction of one of their colleagues who, in 1952, said that "the psychologist must reorient his thinking from what is good management of the individual to what is good personnel management and, ultimately, good business." [21]

The industrial social scientists' view of labor and unionism adds further depth to our understanding of their sweeping commitment to management. What kind of man is he who labors and why does he join a union? He is the kind of man, the early industrial psychologists agreed, who is stupid, overly emotional, class conscious, without recreational or aesthetic interests, insecure, and afraid of responsibility. He is a man who, when banded together in a union with others of like sort, is to be distrusted and feared. This blue-collar man joins a union, psychologists and sociologists eventually postulated, because of a personality maladjustment, one that probably occurred early in life.[22] The need for an equalization of power between labor and management, the need for economic sanctions, were not seen as the real reasons why men join unions. Rather, said psychologist Robert N. McMurry:

> The union also serves the worker in another way. Being somewhat authoritarian, *it may tell him what to do. He no longer has to think for himself.* . . . Once he has been relieved of personal responsibility for his actions, *he is free to commit aggressions which his conscience would ordinarily hold in check.* When this is the case, his conscience will trouble him little, no matter how brutal and anti-social his behavior may be.

Granting such premises, solely for the sake of discussion, one is forced to conclude with McMurry, whose position was rather typical, that "where management is fair and is alert to discover and remove sources of employee dissatisfaction, a union is not necessary." [23]

The social scientists' view of industrial conflict further illuminates their commitment to management. Throughout their professional history, the majority of industrial social scientists insisted that as soon as management took the trouble to study or to authorize studies of its workers, to learn their wants, instincts, desires, aspirations, and motivations, management would be able to do something about the demands of labor before such demands tied up the lifeline of industry and resulted in a strike. Understanding human relations, in short, was the only certain way to avoid conflict. Thus the demand of labor for wages was merely camouflage, argued the social scientists, masking more real and human needs of appreciation, understanding, and friendliness.[24]

Because of his impact, Elton Mayo's formulations have always been important, and his statement of the problem of conflict was no exception.

His early approach to conflict, and one that was to become rather representative of a large segment of industrial social science, was based on the postulate of the primacy of the individual in all social processes, including labor-management conflict. Before the Hawthorne researches broadened his vision, Mayo believed that " 'industrial unrest' has its source in obsessive preoccupation." And again: "There is a real identity between labor unrest and nervous breakdown." [25] Conflict to Mayo was neither inevitable nor economic. It was a result of the maladjustment of a few men on the labor side of the picture. Even after Hawthorne forced Mayo to grow, he remained firm in his conviction that conflict was an evil, a symptom of the lack of social skills. Cooperation, for him, was symptomatic of health; and, since there was no alternative in the modern world, cooperation must mean obedience to managerial authority. Thus collective bargaining was not really cooperation, but merely a flimsy substitute for the real thing.[26]

The nature of the social sciences in the twentieth century was, and is, such as to encourage the type of thinking of which Mayo is a good representative. His illusions of objectivity, lack of integrative theory, concern with what many have called the "wrong problems," and, at least by implication, authoritarianism, virtually determined the types of errors he committed. Such errors are built into modern social science.

The problem of objectivity has proved to be especially troublesome to modern social scientists. During the depression of the 1930's, for instance, some social scientists warned that a rigid insistence on objectivity would place power in the hands of partisans who would not trouble themselves with such matters. In other words, social scientists, by providing, without interpretation or advocacy, techniques and concepts useful to men engaged in struggles for power, became by default accessories to the power politics of American government and industry, while insisting that they were innocent of anything of the sort. The insistence on objectivity made an impartial *use* of their research findings virtually impossible.[27]

Only after World War II did many social scientists, including Mayo, blame their difficulties on a lack of theory.[28] But the more general belief that "the chief impetus to the field of industrial sociology has come from observational studies in industry rather than inference from theoretical principles" [29] discouraged a concentrated effort to tie together the many dissociated studies with some kind of underlying theory. Data were piled on data; statistical analyses were pursued with increasing vigor.

Only rarely was any attempt made to explain, in a broader framework, the significance and relationships of psychological and sociological research.

"Lacking an objective scale of values," said one industrial psychologist, "we have accumulated a vast body of data on what some of us suspect are either the wrong problems, or false or misstated questions, or altogether minor ones." [30] In 1947 the criticism was fully developed:

> The human problems of industry and economic relationships lie at the very heart of the revolutionary upheavals of our century. One might expect industrial psychologists to be fired by the challenge of these issues. But most of us go on constructing aptitude tests instead—and determining which of two advertising slogans "will sell more of our company's beauty cream." [31]

This concentration on wrong or trivial problems was a result of the fact that social scientists, especially those who applied their science to the desires or needs of power groups, were not in command of their activities. They have not been, and are not, free agents. Clearly, however, industrial social scientists have not been forced to accept the assumptions, biases, and frames of reference of America's industrial elite. These specialists, like virtually every other group in American society, freely shared the assumptions of this elite. Most managers have had no trouble in getting social scientists to grant managerial premises because such premises have also been assumed by the social scientists. According to some analysts, this acceptance and sanction of America's power status by social scientists can most easily be explained by reference to the social scientists themselves. Said a sociologist, "American social scientists have seldom, if ever, been politically engaged; the trend towards the technician's role has, by strengthening their a-political professional ideology, reduced, if that is possible, their political involvement, and often, by atrophy, their ability even to grasp political problems." Hence industrial social scientists have had no qualms about serving "the needs of the business side of the corporation as judged by the business manager." This, another sociologist believed, made "something less than a scientist" of any social scientist directly involved in the power relationships of the modern bureaucracies.[32]

The classic statement of the position of the industrial psychologist in relation to the powers for which he worked was made, in 1951, by the eminent industrial psychologist W. V. Bingham, who said that industrial psychology "might be defined as psychology directed toward aims other than its own." [33] Who, then, should set the aims for industrial psychologists? Obviously, managers would have no scruples against telling the social-science specialists on their payrolls how they should earn their money.

With Bingham's definition in mind, most industrial social scientists did not hesitate to do what they were told. "The result," reported one of *Fortune's* editors, "is not a science at all; it is a machine for the engineering of mediocrity. . . . Furthermore," he continued, "it is profoundly authoritarian in its implications, for it subordinates the individual to the group. And the philosophy," he concluded, "unfortunately, is contagious." [34]

A handful of industrial social scientists bitterly complained of this willing acceptance by almost all of their colleagues of the control of their science and their research by the managers and spokesmen of that ubiquitous concentration of power: the modern corporation. The psychologist Arthur Kornhauser was one of the first, when in 1947 he called industrial psychology a management technique rather than a social science, and complained that "psychological activities for industry . . . are characterized by the fact that business management constitutes a special interest group which manifests its special viewpoint in respect to research as in other matters. . . . Certain areas of research are tabu," he went on. "Certain crucial variables must not be dealt with. We must avoid," he concluded, "explicit analysis of the broad and basic problems of *power and authority* in economic life." On rare occasions an industrial sociologist expressed similar attitudes. In the same year, for instance, Wilbert E. Moore, then of Princeton, warned his audience of sociologists that the persistent managerial assumptions underlying so much of their work would reduce their profession to a refined type of scientific management dedicated to the exploitation of labor.[35] But such expressions were unusual and not representative of the opinions of most industrial social scientists. Most of these specialists remained content to develop and refine further the techniques in which management expressed an interest, and either did not bother about or approved of the implications of their research.

Despite the avowed or implicit hostility of virtually all industrial social scientists to organized labor, union leaders traditionally have been either unaware of or indifferent to the work of these specialists. With time, however, at least since the Second World War, a few labor leaders have spoken against the entire social-science movement as it was then implemented in industry. No major union has, however, taken action on the national level to counteract this movement.[36]

One labor leader has been especially troubled about the industrial use of social science; his formulation of the problem serves to highlight the basic difficulties of labor in a social-science world that is built on the assumptions of management. First of all, he wrote, social scientists so complicate the bargaining relationship that control is taken out of the hands of the inadequately informed workers and their representatives; experts are required to get through the maze of confusion, and democracy becomes impossible. "The essence of unionism," he continued, "is not higher wages, shorter hours or strikes—but self-government. If, as some unions apparently believe, higher benefits are the essential objective, then unionism becomes another, and more subtle, form of paternalism. . . . As for me," he concluded, "I would prefer to receive lower benefits than to lose control of my bargaining relationship. Unfortunately, and this is the nub of the problem, many workers prefer higher benefits to democracy." [37] The issues at stake in this man's dilemma are profound, and the impotence of all unions, including his own, to resist, as well as the general apathy of other labor leaders, causes rot at the heart of American unionism. But the industrialist's keen awareness of the problems pushes him forward in his use of social scientists to complicate and confuse bargaining, to reduce grievances, and to squelch militant unionism.

A final question remains. What difference does it make if social scientists have found a place in industry and generally have shared the points of view of management? Are not social scientists an esoteric group of academicians with little or no contact with reality? What if they have been hostile to interests other than those that pay them?

The difference is great. Many managers have not hesitated to make explicit the point that their use of social scientists and their skills is for the purpose of human control. Through group conferences, management hopes to pressure the recalcitrant individual into conforming with his more right-thinking colleagues. Cessna Aircraft and Atlantic Refining have furnished good examples of this approach. American Telephone & Telegraph has been convinced that it is possible through an understanding of motivation to "influence" a given employee. The Life Insurance Sales Research Bureau said that "in learning to shape people's feelings and control their morale, we shall be doing nothing more difficult than we have already done in learning how to fly. . . . We need not 'change human nature,' we need only to learn to control and to use it." General Foods took the position that "leadership" and persuasion would prove most effective in directing the thinking and conduct of its workers. Other businessmen and social scientists have agreed that the main business of business is the control of human conduct.[38]

A few social scientists were concerned, however, about the implications of their growing effectiveness with a science of behavior. Would this not lead to the most insidious and relentless form of exploitation ever dreamed of? One industrial social scientist argued that control in a complex and interdependent society is inevitable:

> Society has always outlawed certain techniques for getting people to do what one wants them to do. As our understanding of behavior becomes more and more refined, we will have to refine equally the moral judgment on the kinds of coercion—however subtle—that are approved and disapproved.[39]

Control, in other and more simple words, is a given; what needs to be changed is the system of morals that disapproves of control. Slim hope for the future, this. But *Business Week* has assured us that there is nothing to worry about. "There's no sign," reported this organ of business interests, "that the science of behavior is getting ready to spawn some monster of human engineering, manipulating a population of puppets from behind the scenes." [40]

*Business Week* is wrong. Social scientists by now have evolved a series of specific techniques whose results have delighted management. Especially through the use of group pressures has management shoved its people into line. Majority opinions, even when directly contrary to visual fact, sway the attitudes of others who would rather not trust their own eyes than suffer the stigma of being unusual. This social scientists have proved.[41] "If a manager's superior," said the personnel director of Continental Oil, "has had difficulty in developing a cooperative attitude within that manager, the group technique can frequently help in developing the appropriate attitude." Even *Business Week* was forced to admit that the pressures of the group on the individual members were so relentless that this was "one good way to change what they [managers] want." The Harwood Manufacturing Company and American Cyanamid both learned to lean heavily on group techniques to assure the continuation of management control.[42]

Through motivation studies, through counseling, through selection devices calculated to hire only certain types of people, through attitude surveys, communication, role-playing, and all the rest in their bag of schemes, social scientists slowly moved toward a science of behavior. Thus management was given a slick new approach to its problems of control. Authority gave way to manipulation, and workers could no longer be sure they were being exploited. Said C. Wright Mills:

> Many whips are inside men, who do not know how they got there, or indeed that they are there. In the movement from authority to manipu-

lation, power shifts from the visible to the invisible, from the known to the anonymous. And with rising material standards, exploitation becomes less material and more psychological.[43]

Many industrial social scientists have put themselves on auction. The power elites of America, especially the industrial elite, have bought their services—which, when applied to areas of relative power, have restricted the freedom of millions of workers. Time was when a man knew that his freedoms were being curtailed. Social scientists, however, are too sophisticated for that. The fires of pressure and control on a man are now kindled in his own thinking. Control need no longer be imposed. It can be encouraged to come from within. Thus the faith that if "people develop propaganditis" the effectiveness of control would be weakened [44] seems to miss the point. A major characteristic of twentieth-century manipulation has been that it blinds the victim to the fact of manipulation. Because so many industrial social scientists have been willing to serve power instead of mind, they have been themselves a case study in manipulation by consent.

Over the years, through hundreds and hundreds of experiments, social scientists have come close to a true science of behavior. They are now beginning to learn how to control conduct. Put this power—genuine, stark, irrevocable power—into the hands of America's managers, and the work that social scientists have done, and will do, assumes implications vaster and more fearful than anything previously hinted.

# N O T E S

1. Henry Ford, II, "Human Engineering Necessary for Further Mass Production Progress," *Automotive and Aviation Industries*, XCIV, 2 (Jan. 15, 1946), 39.
2. George R. Eastman, *Psychology for Business Efficiency* (Dayton, 1916), 9, 12; G. Stanley Hall, address to Vocational Educational Association of the Middle West, Jan. 17, 1919, in Lionel D. Edie (ed.), *Practical Psychology for Business Executives* (New York, 1922), 36; T. Sharper Knowlson, *Business Psychology* (Libertyville, Ill., 1912), 11, 12; Hugo Münsterberg, *Psychology and Industrial Efficiency* (New York, 1913), 244, 306–309; W. D. Scott, *Increasing Human Efficiency in Business* (New York, 1911), 6–7.
3. Floyd H. Allport *et al.*, "Psychology in Relation to Social and Political Problems," in Paul S. Achilles (ed.), *Psychology at Work* (New York, 1932), 252; Walter V. Bingham, "The Future of Industrial Psychology," *JCP*, I, *1* (Jan.-Feb., 1937), 9–11; George C. Brandenburg, "Personality

and Vocational Achievement," *JAP*, IX, *3* (1925), 282; Harold E. Burtt, *Principles of Employment Psychology* (Boston, 1926), 508; J. McKeen Cattell, "Retrospect: Psychology as a Profession," *JCP*, I, *1* (Jan.-Feb., 1937), 1; Edgar A. Doll, "Preparation for Clinical Psychology," *ibid.*, III, 5 (Sept.-Oct., 1939), 139–140; Eliott Frost, "What Industry Wants and Does Not Want from the Psychologist," *JAP*, IV, *1* (March, 1920), 23–24; George W. Hartmann, "Summary for Psychologists," in Hartmann and Theodore Newcomb (eds.), *Industrial Conflict* (New York, 1939), 544; Edward N. Hay, "Sizing Up Job Applicants," *Personnel Journal*, XVIII, 7 (Jan., 1940), 261; Harry W. Hepner, *Psychology in Modern Business* (New York, 1931), 436; Forrest A. Kingsbury, "Applying Psychology to Business," *Annals*, CX (Nov., 1923), 11; Morris Viteles, "The Clinical Viewpoint in Vocational Selection," *JAP*, IX, 2 (1925), 135; Viteles, *Industrial Psychology* (New York, 1932), 4; Robert M. Yerkes, "What is Personnel Research?" *Monthly Labor Review*, XIV, *1* (Jan., 1922), 11.

4. W. V. Bingham, "Industrial Psychology and Government," *JAP*, XXIV, *1* (Feb., 1940), 3; Milton L. Blum, *Industrial Psychology and its Social Foundations* (New York, 1949), 1; Orlo L. Crissey, "Personnel Selection," in *Current Trends in Industrial Psychology* (Pittsburgh, 1949), 81; George Katona, *Psychological Analysis of Economic Behavior* (New York, 1951), 282–283; C. H. Lawshe *et al.*, *Psychology of Industrial Relations* (New York, 1953), v; Douglas McGregor, "Foreword," *Journal of Social Issues*, IV, *3* (Summer, 1948), 4; Willard E. Parker and Robert W. Kleemeier, *Human Relations in Supervision* (New York, 1951), v, 11–12; May Smith, *An Introduction to Industrial Psychology* (London, 1943), 5–6; Harold C. Taylor, "Industrial Psychology and the Community," in *Current Trends*, 197; Robert M. Yerkes, "Psychology in World Reconstruction," *JCP*, X, *1* (Jan.-Feb., 1946), 2.

5. William F. Whyte to Elton Mayo, April 27, 1943, Mayo MSS; John S. Ellsworth, Jr., *Factory Folkways* (New Haven, 1952), 1; Delbert C. Miller and William H. Form, *Industrial Sociology* (New York, 1951), 100; Eugene Staley *et al.* (eds.), *Creating an Industrial Civilization* (New York, 1952), 180; W. F. Whyte, "Social Science and Industrial Relations,". *Personnel*, XXVII, *4* (Jan., 1951), 266; William H. Whyte, Jr., *Is Anybody Listening?* (New York, 1952), 219–220.

6. Warren W. Coxe, "Professional Problems of Applied Psychology," *JCP*, IV, *3* (May-June, 1940), 103; V. E. Fisher and Joseph V. Hanna, *The Dissatisfied Worker* (New York, 1931), 246; C. Wright Mills, *White Collar* (New York, 1953), 157.

7. Arthur W. Kornhauser and Forrest A. Kingsbury, *Psychological Tests in Business* (Chicago, 1924), 174–175.

8. Quoted from a personal letter whose author prefers to remain unidentified.

9. Frank W. Braden to L. Baritz, Sept. 13, 1955; John G. Darley, "An Overview of the Conference and its Controversies," in Harold Guetzkow

(ed.), *Groups, Leadership and Men* (Pittsburgh, 1951), 263–264; Arthur Kornhauser, "The Contribution of Psychology to Industrial Relations Research," *Proceedings of the First Annual Meeting, Industrial Relations Research Association, Cleveland, Dec. 29–30, 1948* (N.P., 1949), 174; Fred Massarik and Paula Brown, "Social Research Faces Industry," *Personnel*, XXX, 6 (May, 1954), 455; C. Wright Mills, "The Contribution of Sociology to Studies of Industrial Relations," *Proceedings of IRRA*, 204.

10. Elton Mayo in F. J. Roethlisberger and William J. Dickson, *Management and the Worker* (Cambridge, 1939), xiii–xiv.

11. See, e.g., Howard Bowen, *Social Responsibilities of the Businessman* (New York, 1953), *passim.*

12. Quoted in U.S. Congress, *Automation and Technological Change*, Hearings before Subcommittee on Economic Stabilization of the Joint Committee on the Economic Report, 84th Cong., 1st Sess., Oct. 14–28, 1955 (Washington, 1955), 105.

13. "Industry Appraises the Psychologist," *Personnel Psychology*, IV, 1 (Spring, 1951), 63–92.

14. See, e.g., Murray Kempton, "Pre-Tested Miracles," *New York Post*, Jan. 3, 1957, 26.

15. H. L. Hollingworth and A. T. Poffenberger, *Applied Psychology* (New York, 1917), 20; Hugo Münsterberg, *Business Psychology* (Chicago, 1915), 181–182.

16. Harold E. Burtt, *Psychology and Industrial Efficiency* (New York, 1929), 273; C. F. Hansen, "Psychology in the Service of the Life Insurance Business," *Annals*, CX (Nov., 1923), 190.

17. Elton Mayo, "The Fifth Columnists of Business," *Harvard Business School Alumni Bulletin*, XVIII, 1 (*Autumn*, 1941), 33.

18. William H. Knowles, *Personnel Management* (New York, 1955), 156.

19. See, e.g., Lewis Corey, "Human Relations Minus Unionism," *Labor and Nation*, VI, 2 (Spring, 1950), 48; W. A. Koivisto, "Value, Theory, and Fact in Industrial Sociology," *AJS*, LVIII, 6 (May, 1953), 564–567; Mills, "Contribution of Sociology," *Proceedings of IRRA*, 209n.

20. Robert N. McMurry, *Handling Personality Adjustment in Industry* (New York, 1944), 13–14.

21. John H. Gorsuch, "Industrial Psychology's Growing Pains," *Personnel*, XXIX, 2 (Sept., 1952), 154.

22. See, e.g., Hepner, *Psychology in Modern Business*, 578–583; Morris S. Viteles, "The Role of Industrial Psychology in Defending the Future of America," *Annals*, CCXVI (July, 1941), 157; C. R. Walker and R. H. Guest, *The Man on the Assembly Line* (Cambridge, 1952), 134; William F. Whyte, "Who Goes Union and Why," *Personnel Journal*, XXIII, 6 (Dec., 1944), 216–217.

23. McMurry, *Handling Personality Adjustment*, 15, 17.

24. E.g., Arthur W. Ayers, "Personality Considerations in Collective Bargaining," *JCP*, VIII, 3 (May-June, 1944), 144; George C. Homans,

"Industrial Harmony as a Goal," in Arthur Kornhauser *et al.* (eds.), *Industrial Conflict* (New York, 1954), 49; Elton Mayo, "The Great Stupidity," *Harper's,* CLI (July, 1925), 231; Ross Stagner, "Psychological Aspects of Industrial Conflict: II—Motivation," *Personnel Psychology,* III, *1* (Spring, 1950), 1; U.S. Bureau of Labor Statistics, *Strikes in 1941 and Strikes Affecting Defense Production* (B.L.S. Bull. No. 711; Washington, 1942), 17; B.L.S., *Strikes in 1942* (B.L.S. Bull. No. 741; Washington, 1943), 14; B.L.S., *Strikes in 1943* (B.L.S. Bull. No. 782; Washington, 1944), 18; B.L.S., *Strikes and Lockouts in 1944* (B.L.S. Bull. No. 833; Washington, 1945), 1; T. N. Whitehead, "Human Relations within Industrial Groups," *HBR,* XIV, *1* (Autumn, 1935), 2.

25. Elton Mayo, "The Irrational Factor in Human Behavior," *Annals,* CX (Nov., 1923), 122; Mayo, "Mental Hygiene in Industry," in Henry C. Metcalf (ed.), *The Psychological Foundations of Management* (New York, 1927), 276; Mayo, "Orientation and Attention," *ibid.,* 270–271.

26. Reinhard Bendix, "Bureaucracy," *ASR,* XII, *5* (Oct., 1947), 502; Bendix and Lloyd H. Fisher, "The Perspectives of Elton Mayo," *Review of Economics and Statistics,* XXXI, *4* (Nov., 1949), 314; Elton Mayo, "Research in Human Relations," *Personnel,* XVII, *4* (May, 1941), 265; Miller and Form, *Industrial Sociology,* 79.

27. Hadley Cantril and Daniel Katz, "Objectivity in the Social Sciences," in Hartmann and Newcomb, *Industrial Conflict,* 12; Robert S. Lynd, *Knowledge for What?* (Princeton, 1939), 116, 119–120, 128, 185–186.

28. E.g., Herbert Blumer, "Sociological Theory in Industrial Relations," *ASR,* XII, *3* (June, 1947), 272; Douglas McGregor, "Industrial Relations," *Advanced Management,* XIV, *4* (Dec., 1949), 2–6.

29. Wilbert E. Moore, "Current Issues in Industrial Sociology," *ASR,* XII, *6* (Dec., 1947), 651.

30. George W. Hartmann, "Summary for Psychologists," in Hartmann and Newcomb, *Industrial Conflict,* 541–542.

31. Arthur Kornhauser, "Industrial Psychology as Management Technique and as Social Science," *American Psychologist,* II, *7* (July, 1947), 224.

32. Mills, "Contribution of Sociology," *Proceedings of IRRA,* 206; Mills, *White Collar,* 82; Lynd, *Knowledge for What?* 178.

33. Walter V. Bingham, "Psychology as a Science, as a Technology, and as a Profession," in John Elmgren and Sigvard Rubenowitz (eds.), *Applied Psychology in Industrial and Social Life* (Göteborg, 1952), 24.

34. Whyte, *Is Anybody Listening?* 209.

35. Kornhauser, "Industrial Psychology," *American Psychologist* (1947), 225; Moore, "Current Issues," *ASR* (1947), 654.

36. Solomon Barkin to L. Baritz, Dec. 6, 1955; Otis Brubacker to L. B., Dec. 15, 1955; Sylvia B. Gottlieb to L. B., Dec. 2, 1955; Carl Huhndorff to L. B., Nov. 29, 1955; Solomon Barkin, "A Pattern for the Study of Human Relations in Industry," *Industrial and Labor Relations Review,* IX, *1* (Oct., 1955), 95–99; Barkin, "Technology and Labor," *Personnel Journal,* XVIII, *7* (Jan., 1940), 239.

37. Quoted from a personal letter whose author prefers to remain unidentified.

38. F. H. Allport, *Social Psychology* (Boston, 1924), 408; American Telephone & Telegraph Co., Personnel Relations Dept., "Motivation and the Job," *Human Relations in Management* (New York, 1949), 2; Atlantic Refining Co., *A Manual on Conference Leadership* (N.P., N.D.), 3–4, 6; Willard Beecher, "Industrial Relations in the Light of Individual Psychology," *American Journal of Individual Psychology,* XI, 2 (1955), 124; Cessna Aircraft Co., Personnel Dept., *How to Win Workers (Or— Hosswhippin' Won't Work)* (Wichita, [1942 (?)]), 4; General Foods Corp., Dept. for Personnel Administration, *Solving Problems by Practicing Consultative Supervision* (N.P. [1949]), 4; Knowles, *Personnel Management,* 59; Life Insurance Sales Research Bureau, *Morale and Agency Management,* Vol. I: *Morale: The Mainspring of Management* (Hartford, 1940), 22; U.S. Congress, Senate, *Violations of Free Speech and Rights of Labor,* Hearings before a Subcommittee of the Committee on Education and Labor, U.S. Senate, 75 Cong., 1st Sess., on S. Res. 266, Part 6, "Labor Espionage, General Motors Corp.," Feb. 15–19, 1937 (Washington, 1937), 2037.

39. Mason Haire, "Group Dynamics," in Kornhauser, *Industrial Conflict,* 384–385.

40. "People: "What's Behind Their Choices—in Buying, in Working," *Business Week,* Aug. 14, 1954, 50–60.

41. S. E. Asch, "Effects of Group Pressure upon the Modification and Distortion of Judgments," in Guetzkow, *Groups, Leadership and Men,* 189–190.

42. Richard Crow, "Group Training in Higher Management Development," *Personnel,* XXIX, 6 (May, 1953), 458; "Group Meetings Pay Off," *Business Week,* May 20, 1950, 82, 84; Alfred Marrow, "Group Dynamics in Industry," *Occupations,* XXVI, 8 (May, 1948), 476; "People," *Business Week,* Aug. 14, 1954, 50–60; "Psychologists at Work," *ibid.,* Sept. 19, 1953, 52–53.

43. Mills, *White Collar,* 110.

44. Harold L. Wilensky, "Human Relations in the Workplace," Industrial Relations Research Association, *Research in Industrial Human Relations* (New York, 1957), 40–41.

# Health Factories,
# the New Industrial Sociology

## ELIOT FREIDSON

**I**n this selection Freidson argues that in the modern world medicine, especially psychiatry, is operated in such a way as to depersonalize individuals. Individuals are controlled by administrators making use of expertise.

Freidson says that sociologists and other social scientists can make one of their greatest contributions to society by serving as experts to counteract the expertise of other such groups. Sociologists can and should become social ombudsmen.

*Reprinted from Eliot Freidson, ''Health Factories, the New Industrial Sociology,'' Social Problems, 14 (1967), 493–500, by permission of the author and The Society for the Study of Social Problems.*

"Do not clip, mark, fold, tear or staple this card." The IBM card, a polemical symbol of our time, represents the transforming of human beings the better to administer them. They are being administered services that are sometimes supposed to be of benefit to them. But in the course of being benefited they are transformed to ciphers which, it is felt, is no benefit. Nonetheless, rationalization proceeds in all service industries. Such rationalization requires breaking services up into standardized units, which in turn requires managing individuals as packages of standardized needs answerable by standardized units of service. Traditional industrial sociology has concerned itself with what the rationalization of manufacturing has done to the worker (and vice versa). The new industrial sociology concerns itself with what the rationalization of services has done to the people getting services and why.

But may we speak of service industries generically, or must we distinguish them into significant types of service industries? Is the hospital fully comparable to a hotel, or the college campus to an amusement park? I think there are critical differences. First, services competing with others in a relatively free consumer market must be distinguished from a monopoly of service. Second, frankly profit-making services may be distinguished from a nonprofit, ostensibly altruistic service. Taken together, the two distinctions may be used to discriminate between commercial and professionalized services. The distinctions are important for the customer because they point to different degrees of control over the selection of services that can be exercised by the recipient: whether he can choose *not* to use a service, and whether he can freely choose among alternatives of service.

The hospital belongs to that growing segment of organized service industries in which a number of systematic barriers to free choice exist, and in which, instead of being a customer, the consumer becomes a pupil, a client, a patient, or otherwise a member of a flock. Here, the responsibility for awareness of need for a service sometimes may be left to the customer, as well as some choice to use what is available, but the market is not left free to provide all that he may personally want. In health above all, but also in law, education, welfare and to a degree religion, the market is restricted to that which is licensed, certified, accredited or otherwise officially approved, and control over the definition of services is held by those who control the production of services rather than those who consume them.

Clearly, it is in this type of service industry that the fate of the consumer is most problematic. And it is this type of service industry that has stimulated the most dismay and rebellion on the part of the consumer, the most concern with reform on the part of society. Studies of hospitals reported by social scientists over the past thirteen years have faithfully reflected the problems of rationalizing non-commercial services. Let us look at some of them.

## The Prevalence of Depersonalization

One theme of some importance in many studies is the depersonalization of the patient. In the residential establishments called total institutions, Goffman asserts that the individual's self is stripped, trimmed, mortified, defaced and otherwise disfigured in the course of obtaining service.[1] And surely there is evidence of this in reports from mental hospitals in the United States,[2] homes for the aged in Great Britain[3] and general hospitals.[4] But the problem is not of the same magnitude in all kinds of establishments. For example, tax-supported hospitals seem to regiment and depersonalize the patient more than do private hospitals. And mental hospitals seem to strip and mortify patients considerably more than do general hospitals.

The analytical factor common to both of these contrasts is the status of the client. *Depersonalization is most marked when the client is most helpless, when the choice and arrangement of services is an exclusive prerogative of management.* In present day tax-supported service institutions, the client has a right as a citizen to obtain available services, but only if he is eligible. His "right" is only to services approved and financed by the state, and his eligibility is determined by the management's interpretation of the rules. The services themselves are underfinanced and frequently bare of what might be considered ordinary, everyday "necessities." The client can exercise choice most easily when he has the financial or socio-political resources that allow him to obtain special privileges in the system.[5] The point is not that tax-supported institutions are inevitably or generically depersonalizing, but that as they are *presently* constituted and financed they are likely to be. The generic variable underlying depersonalization is the status of the client: he is unable to choose and manage significant elements of his destiny.

Here is where the mental hospital, even when private, is relevant, for while there are differences in amenities, and while relatives who are paying the bills exercise more leverage in private than public hospitals, depersonalization nonetheless occurs. The client may be made helpless in many ways, one of the most important of which in our day is being defined as socially and intellectually incompetent by virtue of mental illness, or senility.[6] When his fundamental capacity to reason about reality is impugned, the patient becomes a ward of the service organization, public or private, and so becomes dependent upon the institution's choices made on his behalf.

## Utopian Tendencies in the Hospital

But the main thrust of most analyses is not to deplore the patient's helplessness so much as to deplore the unprofessional character of the decisions that are being made on the patient's behalf. The idea is that even if patients

are stripped of their ordinary freedom of choice, when managerial prerogatives of choice for the patient are exercised on a professional rather than lay
basis, the patient will be considerably better off. From Belknap, through
Dunham and Weinberg to Strauss and his associates[7] (not to speak of a
whole tradition of studies of "custodialism" in mental hospitals), attention
is paid primarily to the fact that non-professional or unprofessionalized
workers are largely responsible for the care of state mental hospital patients.
As Strauss and his associates have demonstrated, the issue is not really the
lack of a therapeutic orientation among those non-professional workers so
much as the lack of a professionally-approved orientation. If only there
would be more genuine psychiatrists dealing with patients, the argument
runs, things would be so much better for them.

This rather simple argument has been extended much farther. Great
impetus to the idea that there can be an organization which is wholly therapeutic in character, without significant "pathologies" in the form of depersonalizing bureaucracy, was given by Stanton and Schwartz' study, reported
in 1954.[8] The study's most celebrated findings (not fully borne out by later
investigators) were that psychiatric symptomatology and at least the short-
term progress of the patient in the small private hospital were related to the
disagreements and tensions among staff members—related, in fact, to the
total complex of relationships that makes up an organization as a whole.
The idea was that individual psychotherapy carried out with the patient
each day for an hour in the privacy of the consulting-room, insulated from
life on the ward, was no more and perhaps even less "therapeutic" than the
other hours of the day spent in interaction with semi-professional and non-
professional personnel during the round of life on the ward. The rather
more pallid and scattered study by Caudill,[9] and a succession of minor reports, have reinforced the general, even if not detailed, validity of the
observation.

The outcome of the observation was the notion that the whole organization must be administered as a therapeutic activity, and that everyone, professional and non-professional, must work together in order to be able to
provide the proper milieu.[10] The whole complement of institutional personnel must become a team, undivided by status distinctions and "blocked
communication" so as to create a therapeutic milieu. The patients themselves must be drawn into creating such a milieu, also serving as members
of the team. This ideology, closely akin to some in industrial sociology and
in liberal circles of penology, is essentially utopian, oriented toward blurring
and even dissolving such elementary axes of rational organization as hier-

archical and functional or task differentiation. Indeed, it is closely connected with utopian thought of the past, and with latter-day, non-medical utopians.

Rubenstein and Lasswell's book offers us an interesting commentary on the plight of the utopian therapeutic community.[11] In 1951–1952, Caudill studied a mental hospital in which he noted a "caste" system among the staff in which physicians were authoritarian, and the barriers between physician, nurse, and aide high and impermeable. In staff conferences participation was hierarchical. Without free and open communication among all staff members, much of what the patient did or said was misunderstood and mismanaged. Rubenstein and Lasswell describe how that same hospital began to move toward becoming a more "democratic" institution in subsequent years. In 1956 patients began attending staff meetings, and by 1960 patient-staff meetings were being held three times a week. As Rubenstein and Lasswell described it, nurses and residents were encouraged to take more active roles in therapy, and patients themselves were encouraged to assume responsibility for managing the hospital as well as their own wards.

There were definite moves toward wider participation in administration and therapy but, as the authors noted with some sadness, the basic structure remained authoritarian. Residents and nurses were uncomfortable in their new roles and the senior medical staff would not allow the patients to assume very much responsibility for their own affairs. A totally equalitarian community of patients and staff seemed not to be viable. Indeed, it may be argued that by its nature a hospital cannot be a community in which each person exercises to the full his individual qualities, for it is neither self-sufficient enough to be able to violate the expectations of the society surrounding it, nor able to overcome the constraints implicit in having a special mission or goal with special assumptions about the means of attaining it.

## The Hospital as Non-Community

Unlike historical utopias, the hospital lacks some of the essential conditions of community, and so can only be very loosely called a small society or a community. For one thing, even though power is exercised in the hospital just as it is exercised in the political community, the hospital is neither self-sufficient nor sovereign, and so cannot make its own rules for the exercise of power by "citizens," including patients. Hospitals depend on the community outside for financial support quite apart from patient fees.

Belknap and Steinle have shown that the relation of general hospitals to community leadership and financing is critical to the kind of hospital that can exist.[12] And in their narrative, Stotland and Kobler demonstrate graphically how the arrogance, jealousy and stupidity of a group of physicians and lay community leaders can destroy a hospital.[13]

Hospitals, then, are not true, self-sufficient communities. They are "communities" only in the special fashion defined by Goffman, composed of those who live in and try to make a life out of it, and those who live outside and carry on a job within. But there is an additional incompleteness in the American hospital that marks it off from virtually all other ordinary organizations. This is that excepting many publically supported hospitals, the prime members of the hospital staff are not employees, yet nonetheless exercise extensive influence in the organization. The physicians responsible for the care given to the patients by other members of the staff are not themselves members of the staff in the usual sense of the term. This is a very unusual structural arrangement that has not been examined as closely as it deserves. It is as if all professors were self-employed tutors, sending individual pupils to universities where they can themselves administer some special training briefly, but most particularly where they can count on having their pupils trained specially by lesser personnel employed by the university. The day-to-day service of the organization is supplied by people employed by the organization, but supervised by self-employed entrepreneurs committed to their own personal practice and to the individual clients of that practice. The commitment of physicians, therefore, is qualitatively and quantitatively different from that of other workers in the American hospital.

In being dependent on the professional community outside it for the voluntary supply of the basic services its activities need, then, the American hospital is considerably less self-sufficient than the usual industrial or service organization, which hires its experts. The physician constitutes a continuous breech in the walls of the organization. As Stotland and Kobler's case study showed so graphically, the organization cannot even survive without the cooperative approval of those who are necessary but uncommitted by employment.[14]

## Expertise and Authority

The hospital "community," then, cannot do its work without the company of those who are not members and who, in Georgopoulos and Mann's summary of findings on 10 hospitals, are "not too well integrated with the rest of the organization." [15] But why cannot doctors be dispensed with entirely, if they will not commit themselves wholly to the hospital? Obviously, quite apart from the fact that physicians often provide the customers needed by the hospital, they are needed because they are believed to have virtually exclusive possession of skill without which the essential tasks of the hospital cannot be performed adequately, without which the essential goals of the organization cannot be reached. And it is this that points to what is perhaps the most profound problem of utopian equalitarianism—how individuality and equal participation in communal decisions can be maintained in the face of special competencies.

Differences in *power* can be levelled by agreement or force. Differences in bureaucratic *authority* can be dissolved by the abolition of office. But in the face of a given goal, and belief that some special technique can gain the goal, *expertise* must be deferred to. The "authority" of expertise cannot go unheeded except at the expense of the goal. In this sense, I would argue that even if the hospital employed all its physicians (as is frequently the case in other nations) and had a most liberal endowment making it independent of the lay community, it could be either equalitarian or therapeutic but not both. So long as the goal of therapy is maintained, and physicians are held to know how to achieve it, physicians will maintain a place of privilege and "authority" by virtue of their expertise quite independently of bureaucratic office, and patients will hold a place of subordination by virtue of their helplessness and ignorance. Similarly, when occupations are imputed skills of varying degrees of complexity and responsibility, differentiation will not only be horizontal, by task, but also hierarchical, by "responsibility," even if not by bureaucratic office.

In this sense, even if bureaucratic administration were to dissolve itself by some acid equalitarian zeal, its structure would be recreated anew by the hierarchical and functional needs of the application and coordination of special skills in a division of labor. The essentially unilateral, therefore hierarchical, character of that division of labor was suggested by Georgopoulos and Mann's findings that "the extent to which the nursing staff understands the problems and needs of the medical staff, as seen by the latter, produces appreciably stronger relationships with each measure of patient care than the extent to which the medical staff understands the problems and needs of the nursing staff, as seen by the latter." [16]

## Technology and Organization

What seems to be implied by this clutch of hospital studies, then, is that the essential attributes of formal organization (hierarchy and task differentiation) are no less requisite for the production of health services by "professionals" than for the production of material goods by "workers." In this sense, the interaction among the workers and between workers and clients must take on some of the impersonality and social distance characteristic of any rationalized organization of work. This is not to say that only formal relations are the rule. As decades of industrial studies have shown since the Western Electric study, there is no doubt at all that formal organization— "official" positions and rules—is only part of reality, and sometimes only an ideological or "mock" part at that. However, neither is there any doubt that in all the hospitals studied, stable limits to what can be negotiated are posed by position in both administrative and task structure. Insofar as that structure varies, so will vary the content and amount of negotiation.

One element of structure limiting interaction has already been alluded to in the distinctions between state and private, mental and general hospitals. Those distinctions bear on the position of the patient as a ward of the system versus the patient as a well-paying customer in a buyer's market, and his position as a generally incompetent person versus that as a specifically incompetent or merely sick person. In the former, most extreme structural case, the patient is so little able to enter into negotiation as to be wholly depersonalized. At the other extreme—as in a luxurious rest home—the "patient" may dominate negotiations, being more a person than perhaps he deserves.

In addition to the status of the patient, there is another factor that has very important influence on the content and amount of free interaction among patients and staff—the character of the task, and the knowledge and technique actually available to accomplish it. It seems no accident that the most marked variations in organization and in staff-patient and staff relations are to be found in mental rather than general hospitals. It is not in general hospitals that conditions can so easily vary from those of a concentration camp to those of a partially self-governing community. The organization of mental hospitals can vary so markedly because there is no clearly efficacious method of "curing" the mentally ill.[17] It seems precisely the varied ideologies and technologies of psychiatry, and its extraordinary therapeutic uncertainty that permitted the existence of the unstructured situations studied by Strauss and his associates. In the public mental hospital they studied, different wards were managed by physicians with different philosophies of treatment, and in the private institution, psychiatrists hospitalizing patients were of varied therapeutic persuasions and needs.

In contrast, a surgical ward such as was studied by Coser is likely to vary considerably less in its organization, for its stable and frequently standardized therapeutic technology sets distinct limits on the degree of negotiation that can take place among the staff without interfering with the functional goals of the organization. Much the same regular and stable organization of authority and specialized task is likely to exist from one ward or hospital to another in such a case. The best of such organizations, in which one finds a smoothly operating team sustained by high morale, are nonetheless formal: good human relations must not mislead one into believing that members of the team are negotiating without limits. The task, the prerogatives of its practitioners, the equipment available to accomplish it, and administrative precedents all limit and constrain the behavior of the workers.

## The Prices of Depersonalization

Contrast between psychiatric and surgical tasks leads us to the final point suggested by this review of hospital studies—that depersonalization even of an extreme sort occurs in instances that are not protested or deplored. The deprivation of consciousness, the complete immobilization and the literal objectification of the surgical patient is a case in point. This depersonalization is even more extreme than occurs in total institutions, but it is acceptable nonetheless because it is seen to be a price worth paying for the benefits yielded. The depersonalization of the state mental hospital patient is an opposite case in point: while it may benefit the staff as an administrative convenience, and the community outside by its contribution to the inexpensive custody of unwanted people, it is a price many believe is not worth paying for the benefits accruing to the patient. Similar evaluations of whether depersonalization is worth the benefit to the customer no doubt underlie some of the contemporary protests surrounding educational and welfare service institutions, both of which have "soft" technologies similar to those of mental hospitals.

In this context one may note that the most important task of the sociologist is not to continuously and drearily document the mere fact of depersonalization as a consequence of the rationalization of services. Rather more valuable is it to evaluate the extent to which depersonalization is a necessary (or at worst on balance a mildly negative) consequence of the rationalization of a service sufficiently effective to make the price worth paying. For example, it is rather difficult to make much of an issue of Cartwright's findings that those who were patients in teaching hospitals reported more impersonality than patients in non-teaching hospitals, when she also cited findings that for selected diseases the mortality rates in teaching hospitals were lower than in non-teaching hospitals.[18]

Such crude calculations of cost are the least that may be done. The more subtle and complicated task lies in the analysis of the degree to which depersonalization is not related to the performance of an effective service at all, so much as related to the worker's attempt to perform the service in ways that are in accord with his unscrutinized commonsense notions of what is theoretically or technically sound, and compatible with his vested interests. The question is what elements in the organization and performance of work cannot be justified by the technical outcome of the work. Simple staff convenience that is of no benefit to the client is fairly easy to pick out if only because the worker himself is likely to label it such and defend it on non-technical grounds. Much more complicated is the task of assessing the justification of the mass of practices comprising the worker's activity, most of which he justifies on technical grounds even though such grounds are not always demonstrable.

In the special type of service industry of which the hospital is one instance, the prime workers claim to be professionals and therefore claim immunity from evaluation by others. Furthermore, if their claim to professional status is honored by others, along with it comes general belief in their expertise and concession of the authority of expertise. As noted earlier, it is the social establishment of expertise that then permits the organization of services around its authority independently of purely administrative organization. However, it must be noted that expertise is merely imputed, and may not in fact have a sound technical foundation. Even in the corpus of such a scientifically based profession as medicine one finds a heart of solid skill surrounded by a large fatty mass of unexamined practices uncritically honored because of their association with the core skills. Some of that mass is composed of the social prerogatives claimed by the expert because of his professional status, though on occasion they may be justified technologically. Another portion of that mass is composed of the expert's commonsense world.

The most important task of the sociologist in his studies of education and welfare no less than health factories is to dissect the fat from the muscle in the imputed skill of the professional service worker, and to determine the consequence of each for what is done to the client, with what price. This task is so important because it is a moot question whether or not the rigidification of services is due to purely administrative bureaucratization. As I have tried to show, some aspects of organization stem specifically from the institutionalization of expertise. And since what is special about the health, education and welfare factories is the great degree to which the prime worker is insulated both from outside influence and from inside, lay administrative influence by virtue of his professional status, the influence of expertise on depersonalization of services is particularly well worth evaluating. The first step to evaluation, of course, is finding out more about the expert himself.

Unfortunately, in the studies reviewed here there has been no trend at all toward undertaking detached examination of the expert's approach to his work. The earliest book reviewed—that of Stanton and Schwartz—presented a trenchant analysis of the individualistic ideology of psychotherapists and its bearing on staff policy decisions. Some time later came Roth's baleful look at the commonsense world of treatment in tuberculosis hospitals, and its bearing on the fate of the patient.[19] Finally, most recently came the analysis of the various ideologies of psychiatric workers by Strauss and his colleagues. But these are three of more than a dozen. Virtually all those remaining took as real and true most of the essential premises of the professionals whose domains they studied, at best differing with minor particulars. There is thus hardly yet a trend toward attacking the major task of the new industrial sociology, in which the problem lies not only in management but also in the worker.

# NOTES

1. Erving Goffman, *Asylums, Essays on the Social Situation of Mental Patients and Other Inmates,* Garden City, New York: Anchor Books, 1961.
2. Ivan Belknap, *Human Problems of a State Mental Hospital,* New York:

McGraw-Hill Book Co., Inc., 1956; H. Warren Dunham and S. Kirson Weinberg, *The Culture of the State Mental Hospital*, Detroit: Wayne State University Press, 1960.

3. Peter Townsend, *The Last Refuge, A Survey of Residential Institutions and Homes for the Aged in England and Wales*, London: Routledge and Kegan Paul, 1962.

4. See Ann Cartwright, *Human Relations and Hospital Care*, London: Routledge and Kegan Paul, 1964 and Rose L. Coser, *Life in the Ward*, East Lansing, Mich.: Michigan State University Press, 1962.

5. For example, English patients who can afford it may go to a private specialist in order to get a hospital bed quicker than they would from a National Health Service specialist, as reported in Cartwright, *op. cit.*

6. See "The Moral Career of the Mental Patient" in Goffman, *op. cit.*

7. Anselm Strauss, Leonard Schatzman, Rue Bucher, Danuta Ehrlich and Melvin Sabshin, *Psychiatric Ideologies and Institutions*, New York: The Free Press of Glencoe, 1964.

8. Alfred H. Stanton and Morris S. Schwartz, *The Mental Hospital, A Study of Institutional Participation in Psychiatric Illness and Treatment*, New York: Basic Books, Inc., 1954.

9. William Caudill, *The Psychiatric Hospital as a Small Community*, Cambridge: Harvard University Press, 1958.

10. Ideologically connected with this movement is Maxwell Jones, *The Therapeutic Community, A New Treatment Method in Psychiatry*, New York: Basic Books, Inc., 1953.

11. Robert Rubenstein and Harold D. Lasswell, *The Sharing of Power in a Psychiatric Hospital*, New Haven: Yale University Press, 1966.

12. Ivan Belknap and John G. Steinle, *The Community and Its Hospitals, A Comparative Analysis*, Syracuse: Syracuse University Press, 1963.

13. Ezra Stotland and Arthur L. Kobler, *Life and Death of a Mental Hospital*, Seattle: University of Washington Press, 1965.

14. As an occupational grouping in the state mental hospital, the psychiatric aides are so much better able to control treatment than anyone else simply because of the long-term commitment some of them have to the hospital, other occupational groups turning over more completely.

15. Basil S. Georgopoulos and Floyd C. Mann, *The Community General Hospital*, New York: The Macmillan Co., 1962, p. 394.

16. *Ibid.*, p. 401.

17. For a more elaborate and stronger statement of this assessment see Charles Perrow, "Hospitals: Technology, Structure and Goals," in James G. March (ed.), *Handbook of Organizations*, Chicago: Rand-McNally, 1965, pp. 910–970.

18. Cartwright, *op. cit.*, p. 173.

19. Julius Roth, *Timetables*, Indianapolis: Bobbs-Merrill Company, 1963.

# Community Psychiatry and Social Power

## RONALD LEIFER

**O**ne of the most recent threats to our individual
freedoms posed by "expert knowledge" is the powerful
Community Psychiatry Movement. Psychiatrists, with
their official powers to certify sanity and insanity, are
increasingly moving out into society to try to prevent
mental illness. They are becoming increasingly involved in
(urban) social planning to carry out these preventive
measures. Yet psychiatrists cannot even agree among
themselves about what constitutes mental illness; and
there are literally hundreds of psychiatric theories of the
causes. This is an ideal situation for using science as a tool
of political control.

As with all medical programs, this one is especially
effective and especially difficult to criticize because it is
presented entirely under the aegis of doing what is helpful
for the public. There are undoubtedly many problems that

*Reprinted from Ronald Leifer, "Community Psychiatry and Social
Power,"* Social Problems, *14 (1966), 16–22, by permission of the
author and The Society for the Study of Social Problems.*

could be solved by the use of such techniques, but we must always keep in mind that other individuals and groups can in fact wind up controlling our lives, destroying our individual freedoms, even if their intention is to help us. It is up to us to make certain that they are in fact helping us. It is not their intentions which are in question but the *actual effects* of their programs.

> Out of intimations of dissolution and insecurity has emerged an interest in the properties and values of community that is one of the most striking social facts of the present age.
>
> ROBERT A. NISBET[1]

> Contemporary prophets of the totalitarian community seek, with all the techniques of modern science at their disposal, to transmute popular cravings for community into a millennial sense of participation in heavenly power on earth.
>
> ROBERT A. NISBET[2]

Professional "revolutions" are not simply alterations in professional practices which have no broader social and historical relevance; they are intimately linked to the problems and processes of an era. The "Third Psychiatric Revolution"[3] is a complex social movement.[4] It promises to alter the profession of psychiatry and the communities in which and on which it operates. It is therefore vital that we understand the origins, character, and directions of this movement and their relationship to modern social and political life.

## What Is Community Psychiatry?

While there is little consensus about the precise nature of community psychiatry, there is a general agreement that it represents an extension beyond the traditional psychiatric concerns with hospital and private practice. This transformation cannot be viewed simply as the result of expanding medical technology. Although psychiatry is considered to be a medical specialty, it differs from other medical specialties in a number of important respects.[5] The aim of medical intervention is to alter the structure and function of the body in order to eliminate, reduce, or avoid pain, physical disability, and death. The aim of psychiatric intervention is to alter patterns of individual behavior and social arrangements in order to promote personal development, social adjustment, domestic tranquility, and other social ideals.

The social matrix of psychiatry was noticed in 1938 by Kingsley Davis[6] who suggested that the Capitalist-Protestant ethic inherent in our society was the "unconscious system of premises" upon which the "scientific" concepts of psychiatry were based. He characterized this ethic as: 1) democratic, in favoring equal opportunity; 2) secular, in emphasizing worldly values such as wealth and status; 3) ascetic, in stressing thrift, industry and prudence; 4) individualistic, in placing responsibility on the individual for his destiny and stressing ambition and self-reliance; 5) rationalistic and empirical; and 6) utilitarian. He also suggested that the mental health movement adopted a psychological approach to human conduct and a "medico-authoritarian" mantle in order to disguise its ethical basis and to obtain public support for its social functions.

In 1938, American psychiatry consisted largely of privately conducted, psychoanalytically oriented therapy (to the values of which Davis was undoubtedly referring) and hospital practice. In the past three decades, there have been striking changes in the character of American culture, and consequently, in the character of American psychiatry. The number of persons who are being labelled mentally ill and confined to psychiatric institutions is increasing. Since tranquilizing drugs came into general use in 1956, the mental hospital population has declined by 9.7%; but the number of admissions has climbed 6.8% and the number of discharged patients has doubled.[7] There are a number of reasons for this rise: the greater strain placed on the individual by the complexity of modern society; the absolute increase in persons labelled mentally ill as a result of the growth in population; and the growing tendency to "psychiatrize" human problems.

Community psychiatry has developed partly in response to the predicament of persons finding themselves displaced from family, job, and community as a result of their psychiatric hospitalization. It has also developed in response to a period of rapid economic growth in which an increasingly complex system of technology, distribution, and organization requires a manpower pool which is highly trained in technical and social skills. Finally, community psychiatry has developed "because of the increasing assumption of responsibility by government for the personal welfare of citizens." [8]

Community psychiatry programs have four distinguishable aims: 1) to minimize the separation and to facilitate the re-integration of the hospitalized mental patient into his family and community; 2) to obviate the need for hospitalization where possible and to reduce the incidence of rehospitalization; 3) to reduce the incidence, duration, and disability due to mental disorder; and 4) to promote the positive mental health of the community.[9] These aims are to be achieved by four related but distinguishable types of community psychiatry programs.

1. *The modification of psychiatric hospitals.* There is a trend away from the construction of large, rural custodial institutions. Facilitated by tranquilizing drugs which act as chemical restraints,[10] the administrative and treatment policies of psychiatric hospitals are changing in the direction of the open door and the therapeutic community.[11] Security measures are being relaxed, patients are permitted greater freedom of movement, visiting privileges are being liberalized, improved interior decoration is being utilized to simulate home or hotel settings and, in some cases, the sexes are permitted to live and mingle on the same ward. Relations between staff and inmates and among inmates are improved by means of "milieu" therapy, group therapy, and patient government programs. Patient activity is promoted by means of social and occupational therapy facilities. The aim of these changes is to stimulate the access of the community and the hospital inmates to each other; and to ease the transition from society to hospital and back.

2. *Community mental health centers.* With the Community Mental Health Services Act of 1963, the federal government launched a massive program to finance the construction and staffing of community mental health centers.[12] These centers provide a wide range of programs which include: inpatient and outpatient facilities, day and night care services, emergency services, follow-up and rehabilitation clinics, halfway houses, foster home placement services, consultation and educational functions, and facilities for training, research, and the evaluation of programs.

3. *The coordination and integration of mental health facilities.* It has become apparent to community psychiatrists that the separate and unplanned development of public and private agencies dealing with psychiatric patients leads to the duplication, omission, and inefficiency of services. Comprehensive mental health planning thus attempts to coordinate

and integrate mental health facilities with each other, with ancillary facilities, such as social welfare agencies, and with nonpsychiatric institutions, such as the courts.[13] The degree of community organization desired is illustrated in the following statement by a prominent community psychiatrist:

> This system [of organization] must include not only the governmental psychiatric services, both mental hospitals and community clinics, but also the voluntary psychiatric services and the other community services which are not labelled psychiatric, but which play a large part in preventing and treating mental disorders—the general medical services including hospitals, nursing homes, nursing agencies, public health services, family doctors; the social welfare agencies; the recreational services; the religious services; the educational system; the courts and correctional agencies; and so on.[14]

In this system of organization, the psychiatrist is to play a leading role as an organizer, an administrator, an educator, a consultant, and a therapist.

4. *The prevention of mental illness and the promotion of positive mental health.* It is the primary theoretical orientation of the community mental health movement that social conditions are crucial determinants in the etiology, treatment, and prevention of mental illness. The reduction of mental illness and the promotion of positive mental health are therefore to be accomplished by the establishment of broad programs in the health, educational, social, economic, and political spheres.[15] These programs are aimed at improving education and employability; eliminating poverty, malnutrition, and other deprivations; providing recreation and medical care; interrupting "pathogenic" trains of events (by such means as the "temporary relocation of agitating and sparking personalities" in order to "permit the neighborhoods to restore some sort of emotional balance" [16]); and generally ameliorating the stresses and crises associated with the life cycle.[17] One psychiatrist states that "Juvenile delinquency, school problems, problems of urban areas, community conflicts, marriage and family counselling, and well-being programs all can be seen as reasonably in the province of the psychiatrist, who formerly limited his interest to psychopathology." [18] Other psychiatrists envision the "therapeutic" application of their knowledge in order to prevent nuclear war and reduce international conflict.[19]

## Community Psychiatry as a Collectivist Social Movement

Community values, interests, and power have always been relevant to the definition of and response to mental illness. In communities which are small and highly integrated, the response to mentally ill persons most often involves the mobilization of their family or clan in activities which are designed to restore them to the desired level of social functioning.[20] Failing this, the mentally ill may be relieved of their social obligations and privileges and retained in the custody and care of their family. As communities become large, cosmopolitan, and differentiated, the family and clan are superseded by the collective and the individual as the important social units.[21] Thus, such social change not only increases the strain on the individual, but it leads to the State's assuming the function of defining and controlling deviant behavior, including mental illness.

Today, an increasing portion of psychiatric activity is supported by government funds.[22] Only 54% of psychiatrists spend some time in private office practice and only 40% of these spend more than 35 hours a week. The majority of psychiatrists (73%) spend some time working for the government.[23] This is in contrast with the remainder of medicine in which the vast majority of doctors practice privately. Moreover, in New York State all public and private psychiatric facilities (except privately conducted practice) fall under the regulatory powers of the Department of Mental Hygiene.[24] These facilities are stringently regulated; state hospital staffs are organized in a hierarchy of power with the director in total command, a situation which has much to do with the total character of state institutions.

Community mental health centers, which are to be financed with government funds, will become a part of this vast operation; they will therefore be subject to the same processes of bureaucratization, specialization, and impersonality which characterize other large public enterprises. The extension of psychiatric activities into all aspects of community life carries the threat of the widening use of state sanctioned psychiatric power. As psychiatric services interdigitate with other community functions, increasing numbers of persons will come under its influence, including growing numbers of hospital dischargees, mental health clinic clients, welfare recipients, juvenile delinquents, criminals, students, and the families of these persons. The privacy, dignity, and liberty of the individual may be increasingly encroached upon by public and private agencies which employ psychiatrists, under the rubric of medical investigation and treatment, for the purpose of personnel management, the promotion of the middle class ethic, and social control.

The possibility of the extension of coercive mental health practices may be appreciated by referring to the writings of community psychiatrists. For instance, Dr. Harold Visotsky, Illinois Commissioner of Mental Hygiene, advocates that a "benignly aggressive approach should be made to reach out and seek these people rather than sit and wait for them to come through [psychiatric] programs." [25] Dr. Gerald Caplan writes: "He [the psychiatrist] cannot wait for patients to come to him, because he carries equal responsibility for all those who do not come. A significant part of his job consists of finding out who the mentally disordered are and where they are located in his community, and he must deploy his diagnostic and treatment resources in relation to the total group of sufferers rather than restrict them to the select few who ask or are referred for help." [26] In another place, Dr. Caplan has suggested that the problem of persons who "exert a noxious mental health influence" might be handled "by obtaining sanctions for the psychiatrist to exercise surveillance over key people in the community and to intervene in those cases where he identifies disturbed relationships in order to offer treatment or recommend dismissal." [27]

## Involuntary Treatment and Social Control

Underlying the expanding influence of community psychiatry is an important difference between psychiatrists and other medical physicians: medical doctors very rarely treat persons without their consent; psychiatrists often do. Indeed, the diagnosis of mental illness may justify detaining an individual involuntarily and subjecting him to measures designed to alter his behavior. Since the meaning of terms cannot be divorced from the consequences of their use, involuntary institutionalization and behavior modification and the stigmatization associated with them must be included in the meanings of the terms "mental illness" and "psychiatric treatment."

A good deal of psychiatric influence is charismatic and is based on the psychiatrist's claim to be able to ameliorate a wide range of personal and social suffering. However, psychiatric claims are far more widely acknowledged than their successes and remain, with few exceptions, without serious challenge from the intellectual community.[28] A substantial degree of the psychiatrist's power is based on his ability to socially deface an individual by "diagnosing" him as "mentally ill" and, in effect, to imprison him by means of psychiatric commitment. The modification of psychiatric hospitals under the community psychiatry mandate does not alter their function. The "liberalization" of psychiatric commitment procedures, which tend to skirt court hearings in favor of direct certification by physicians, simply makes it easier to admit persons to mental hospitals. Once committed, the patient falls almost completely under the influence of the psychiatrist. As long as such a person cannot leave the hospital when he wishes, as persons in medical hospitals may do, he is frozen into the role of "patient" and may be subjected to techniques designed to alter his behavior against his will. The alterations of psychiatric practices must be viewed in the context of the changing patterns of deploying psychiatric and social power as well as in terms of a complex society's manifest need for institutionalized procedures to palliate personal and social troubles.

The sponsorship of psychiatric services by the state and the central role of psychiatric power in "treating" involuntary "patients" tend to suggest that psychiatric services are becoming grounded in the (crypto) ideology of group rather than individual values. Psychiatrists who are involved in public programs are paid by the state and must be considered the agents of the state rather than of their patients. The patient's self-defined interests will be respected only when they do not conflict with those of the group.[29] Psychiatric power, as a political instrument, is particularly well suited for use against the individual. Since groups cannot be defined as mentally ill and committed, they are safe from psychiatric power. Thus, in operation (as opposed to in theory) psychiatric power can only have an anti-individualistic ideology and, unlike other political ideologies, constitutes no direct threat to the state.

Described in non-medical terms, community psychiatry is a quasi-political movement which, by means of social interventions and state sanctioned social power, attempts to palliate personal troubles, to foster the orderly and productive functioning of individuals in their community, to alleviate certain disturbances of domestic tranquility, to organize and integrate community programs, to implement the dominant social ideology, and, in accordance with this ideology, to promote the development of social conditions which are thought to be maximally compatible with human desires and requirements.

## Community Psychiatry and the Obfuscation
## of Social Problems

A number of modern psychiatrists and social scientists have conceptualized the problems of mental illness under the rubric of alienation: in terms of the disrupting, isolating, disaffiliating, disintegrating stresses of modern, mass, industrial society.[30] In this context, community psychiatry must be construed as one of a number of modern social movements attempting to alleviate these stresses by means of comprehensive social planning. It is, as its name un-self-consciously implies, one segment of the modern quest for community, in the sense of the term which indicates a coherent, ordered, integrated social system. It is the therapy of alienation.

As we have learned from other contemporary examples, the modern quest for community, undertaken with the instrument of state power, is the greatest enemy of the open society. It is more likely to lead, in varying degrees, to homogenization rather than to individuation, to the extinction of human resources rather than to their development, and to obedience rather than to freedom and responsibility.

This does not imply that all of the scientific concerns and social services which psychiatry provides are without value. However, the problems with which psychiatry deals are not medical; they are social, ethical, economic, and political. There is need for inquiry and concern about the problems of the individual in mass society, about the difficulties of life even under the best of circumstances, about the possibilities of transcending the fragmenting effects of alienation, about fostering a humanistic community, and about the clarification of social ideals and the means for achieving them. Proposing solutions to these problems in the language of medicine, in terms of the prevention of mental illness and the promotion of positive mental health, serves only to obscure both the problems and the alternatives.[31] It permits the advocates of certain approaches to these problems to promote their cause under the banner of medical progress; and it permits them to justify the exercise of power for social control in the name of helping the suffering.[32]

# NOTES

1. Robert A. Nisbet, *Community and Power,* New York: Oxford University Press, 1962, p. 23.
2. *Ibid.,* p. 23.
3. The First Psychiatric Revolution, symbolized by Pinel's striking the chains from the inmates of the Bicetre in 1793, consisted of liberal and humane reforms in the treatment of the hospitalized mentally ill. The Second Psychiatric Revolution consisted of the introduction of psychoanalysis into psychiatry by Sigmund Freud and his followers. See Leopold Bellak, "Community Psychiatry: The Third Psychiatric Revolution," in L. Bellak (ed.), *Handbook of Community Psychiatry and Community Mental Health,* New York: Grune and Stratton, 1964.
4. Max Pepper, Fritz Redlich, and Anita Pepper, "Social Psychiatry," *American Journal of Psychiatry,* 121 (January, 1965), pp. 662–666.
5. Thomas S. Szasz, *Pain and Pleasure,* New York: Basic Books, 1957; and *The Myth of Mental Illness,* New York: Paul B. Hoeber, 1961.
6. Kingsley Davis, "Mental Hygiene and the Class Structure," *Psychiatry,* 1 (February, 1938), pp. 55–65.
7. *Community Mental Health Advances,* United States Department of Health, Education, and Welfare, Public Health Service Pamphlet No. 1141, April, 1964.
8. Gerald Caplan, "Community Psychiatry—Introduction and Overview," in *Concepts of Community Psychiatry: A Framework for Training,* United States Department of Health, Education, and Welfare, Public Health Service Publication No. 1319, 1965, p. 3.
9. Gerald Caplan, *Principles of Preventive Psychiatry,* New York: Basic Books, 1964.
10. Thomas S. Szasz, "Some Observations on the Use of Tranquilizers," *American Medical Association Archives of Neurology and Psychiatry,* 77 (January, 1957), pp. 86–92.
11. Maxwell Jones, *Social Psychiatry: A Study of Therapeutic Communities,* London: Tavistock Publications, 1952; Robert N. Rapoport, *Community As Doctor: New Perspectives on a Therapeutic Community,* London: Tavistock Publications. 1960; *Research Conference on Therapeutic Community,* Herman C. B. Denber (ed.), Springfield: Charles C Thomas, 1960; John Cumming and Elaine Cumming, *Ego and Milieu,* New York: Atherton Press, 1962; and Ivan Belknap, *Human Problems of a State Mental Hospital,* New York: McGraw-Hill, 1956.
12. John F. Kennedy, "Message From the President of the United States Relative to Mental Illness and Mental Retardation," *American Journal of Psychiatry,* 120 (February, 1964), pp. 729–737; Lucy D. Ozarin and Bertram S. Brown, "New Directions in Community Mental Health

Programs," *American Journal of Orthopsychiatry,* 35 (January, 1965), pp. 10–17; and Robert H. Felix, "Community Mental Health," *American Journal of Orthopsychiatry,* 33 (October, 1963), pp. 788–795.

13. *Community Resources in Mental Health,* Joint Commission on Mental Illness and Mental Health Monograph Series, No. 5, New York: Basic Books, 1960; Seymour Perlin and Robert L. Kahn, "The Overlap of Medical and Non-Medical Institutions in a Community Mental Health Program," *Comprehensive Psychiatry,* 4 (December, 1963), pp. 461–467.

14. Gerald Caplan, *Principles of Preventive Psychiatry, op. cit.,* p. 139.

15. See, for instance, Leon Eisenberg, "If Not Now, When?" *American Journal of Orthopsychiatry,* 32 (October, 1962), pp. 781–793; Frank T. Rafferty, "Symptoms and Process in the Multidisciplined Community," *American Journal of Orthopsychiatry,* 32 (March, 1963); Alfred M. Freedman, "Beyond Action for Mental Health," *American Journal of Orthopsychiatry,* 32 (October, 1963), pp. 799–805.

16. Leonard J. Duhl, "The Changing Face of Mental Health," in *The Urban Condition,* Leonard Duhl (ed.), New York: Basic Books, 1963, p. 68.

17. Gerald Caplan, *op. cit.*

18. Harold M. Visotsky, "Community Psychiatry: We Are Willing To Learn," *American Journal of Psychiatry,* 122 (December, 1965), p. 692.

19. M. G. Raskin, "Political Anxiety and Nuclear Reality," *American Journal of Psychiatry,* 120 (March, 1964), pp. 831–836; and Stewart Meachum, "The Social Aspects of Nuclear Anxiety," *American Journal of Psychiatry,* 120 (March, 1964), pp. 837–841.

20. Robin J. Fox, "Witchcraft and Clanship in Cochiti Therapy," in *Magic, Faith and Healing: Studies in Primitive Psychiatry Today,* Ari Kiev (ed.), New York: The Free Press of Glencoe, 1964, pp. 174–200; Claude Levi-Strauss, *Tristes Tropiques,* New York: Atheneum, 1964, p. 386; and Joseph W. Eaton and Robert J. Weil, *Culture and Mental Disorders,* Glencoe, Ill.: The Free Press, 1955.

21. Robert A. Nisbet, *op. cit.*

22. One third of the total budget of New York State, more than three hundred million dollars, is usually allotted to mental hygiene programs. See Paul H. Hoch, "Public and Private Responsibility for Psychiatric Care," *American Journal of Psychiatry,* 121 (February, 1965), pp. 742–745.

23. Robert F. Lockman, "Nationwide Study Yields Profile of Psychiatrists," *Psychiatric News,* 1 (January, 1966), p. 2.

24. State of New York, Department of Mental Hygiene, Mental Hygiene Law and General Orders, Section 7, General Powers and Duties of Commissioner and Department, Utica: State Hospitals Press, 1964.

25. Harold Visotsky, "Social Psychiatry Rationale: Administrative and Planning Approaches," *American Journal of Psychiatry,* 121 (November, 1964), pp. 433–441.

26. Gerald Caplan, "Community Psychiatry—Introduction and Overview," *op. cit.,* pp. 4–5.

27. Gerald Caplan, *Principles of Preventive Psychiatry, op. cit.,* p. 79.
28. In some circles, challenges to psychiatric claims or practices are automatically associated with the political right, in the hope they will then be ignored. This simply indicates that the political interests of psychiatry are to the left. This, in itself is not reprehensible, but the denial that psychiatry has a political character is. See Manfred S. Guttmacher, "Critique of Views of Thomas Szasz on Legal Psychiatry," *American Journal of Psychiatry,* 121 (March, 1964), pp. 230–245; and Zelda Teplitz, book review of the ethics of psychoanalysis, *The New Republic,* August 7, 1965.
29. Thomas S. Szasz, "Ethics and Psychiatry," paper presented to the Department of Philosophy, University of Kansas, Lawrence, Kansas, February 25, 1965 (to be published).
30. See for instance Israel Zwerling, "Some Implications of Social Psychiatry for Psychiatric Treatment and Patient Care," *Institute of Pennsylvania Hospital Strecker Monograph Series,* No. 11, 1965; J. Sanbourne Bockoven, "The Moral Mandate of Community Psychiatry in America," *Psychiatric Opinion,* 3 (Winter, 1966), pp. 24–39; Robert Merton, "Social Structure and Anomie," *American Sociological Review,* 3 (October, 1938), pp. 672–682; and George Devereaux, "A Sociological Theory of Schizophrenia," *Psychoanalytic Review,* 26 (June, 1939)', p. 315–342.
31. Frank Riessman, and S. M. Miller, "Social Change Versus the Psychiatric World View," *American Journal of Orthopsychiatry,* 34 (January, 1964), pp. 29–38.
32. *Cf.* the observation of Kingsley Davis that: "Mental hygiene turns out to be not so much a science for the prevention of mental disorder, as a science for the prevention of moral delinquency." Kingsley Davis, *op. cit.,* p. 60.

PART VI

# The Future of Freedom
# and Tyranny in the
# Technological Society

# Technological Change in Industry

---

I R E N E  T A V I S S  and
W I L L I A M  G E R B E R

**I**n this essay Irene Taviss and William Gerber
analyze the fundamental and sweeping changes that are
taking place in the nature of work in our society, which is
increasingly becoming a knowledge society. They show the
effects likely to be produced on our society by these
fundamental changes in the nature of work.

Technological change has not resulted in the kind of
alienation that many sociologists have always expected of
industrial production. In many ways the increasing pace of
technological change in American industry is leading to
the general upgrading of jobs. Many menial jobs are being
eliminated, but new, more knowledge based jobs are being
created. This essay, then, shows some of the more ''positive''
effects of technology on our lives and suggests ways in
which these positive benefits could increase greatly in the
years ahead.

*Reprinted from Irene Taviss and William Gerber,* Research Review
No. 2 *(Winter, 1969), Harvard University Program on Technology
and Society, by permission of the author.*

The pace of technological change in industry has been a source of much public concern. In the late 1950's and early 1960's the literature on the subject was often characterized by the extremes of grave pessimism concerning the masses of people who would be "thrown out of work by machines" and utopian optimism about the "leisure society" in which man would at last be freed from "the burdens of labor." By the mid- and late 1960's more sober views began to prevail. In 1966 the National Commission on Technology, Automation, and Economic Progress issued a comprehensive report on the subject. It concluded that although technological change plays a major role in determining the particular persons who will be displaced, the rate of economic growth rather than technological change *per se* is the principal determinant of the general level of employment. To keep the level of unemployment to a minimum, therefore, "aggressive fiscal and monetary policies to stimulate growth" are needed.[1]

The significance of economic policy in determining the employment effects of technological change serves to illustrate the general importance of social structures and attitudes in mediating between technology and its effects. The impact of technology on occupational structure and on patterns of work behavior is rarely a direct one. The frequently noted discrepancies in the literature concerning whether automation raises or lowers skill requirements, whether it increases or decreases job satisfaction result from this fact. The same technology may have different effects depending upon the reaction of the specific organization or social structure into which it is introduced. It has been noted, for example, that the reduction in middle-level white collar positions often results not from automation directly but "from the re-organization of the office resulting from automation, such as the centralization of the office work."[2] Yet such centralization is itself not a necessary consequence of office automation. For organizational structure—the division of labor, levels of hierarchy, and channels of communication—intervenes between automation and its effects. Thus, it is only in traditional "line" organizations which do not allow for horizontal channels of communication that disputes between the computer experts and the line managers will tend to be resolved by the head of the organization, thereby leading to a high degree of centralization of control. When "an organization can dispense with the concept of a rigid chain of command and allow horizontal interchange, then automation will have little impact on its members' ability to co-operate with one another," and such centralizing tendencies will not emerge.[3]

Such large-scale changes in the occupational structure as the growth of the service sector and the increased importance of education are again the result of an interaction between social and technological factors. Although there is some dispute about the magnitude of these changes, it is generally acknowledged that technological advance in the production and processing of goods has allowed the growing demand for goods to be fulfilled quite adequately by an increasingly smaller proportion of the total work force. At the same time, the introduction of advanced technology into the service sector has not resulted in a reduction of labor needs, so that there has been some growth in service sector employment as the demand for labor elsewhere has decreased. But technology is only indirectly responsible for the growth in demands for services. This demand has grown as the society has become more affluent. Generally, as income has risen, the demand for services has increased more rapidly than the demand for goods. Moreover, growing affluence has supplied the basis for expanded efforts to provide a greater proportion of the population with such services as health and education.

The enhanced importance of education as a prerequisite to employment is likewise a product of both social and technical factors. For in a society with sufficient wealth to allow large numbers of people to postpone entry into the labor force so that they may receive more education, employers often have a sizeable pool of educated manpower at their disposal. Given the value placed upon education in our society and the ease with which educational credentials may serve as a screening device, employers will often prefer to hire the more educated, even though the intrinsic requirements of the job do not call for such education. It is certainly true that as technological advances have diminished the need for unskilled manual labor, the newer jobs tend to require more education and training. Education also tends to produce a greater flexibility in the worker, although there has been some recognition that "overqualified" manpower may create problems. There are many indications, however, that the educational requirements for a given job are often exaggerated. The most frequently cited and well-known example is that of computer programming. Initially, only college graduates—and usually those with training in mathematics—were hired as programmers. Today, high school graduates—and in some instances even high school dropouts—are being trained for the job. James Bright has been so impressed with the interaction between social and technical factors in the work sphere that he argues that while automation affects the skill level required for certain jobs, the available pool of manpower skills in turn influences the progress of automation. In his "law of automation evolution," he asserts that machinery evolves to provide the degree of automatic operations which is "economically supportable by the level of skill that can be made readily available in the existing work force." Thus, "when the machine manning needs have been reduced to a standard that is normally available in the loacl work force, . . . the economic incentive for automation progress disappears." [4]

As industrial society has moved through the stages of technological development from mechanization to mass production to automation, new tensions and accommodations between the technology and the social structure have appeared at each stage. While we are still in the transition towards an automated society, with only a small percentage of the labor force employed in automated industries,[5] some of the trends of the emerging "postindustrial society" have come to be visible. Thus it appears that the major issues confronting our society as a result of technological developments and occupational change will center about the nature of the "knowledge society" and the new social choices and decisions that it requires, and the changing patterns of work and leisure.

## The Knowledge Society

The basic change which technology has effected in the occupational structure is most often symbolized in the distinction between the pyramid-shaped structure of the early industrial labor force and the diamond-shaped structure of the modern industrial system. As the repetitive manual labor which constituted the base of the pyramid has been replaced by machine power, the base has shrunk and there has been a widening near and below the top which reflects the need for white collar workers and technicians, salesmen and managers, administrative and co-ordinating personnel, and the scientists, engineers, and other professionals who generate and implement the knowledge and technology so important to a modern society.

As Daniel Bell has observed, our society may be characterized as a "knowledge society" in two senses: "first, the sources of innovation are increasingly derivative from research and development (and more directly, there is a new relation between science and technology because of the centrality of *theoretical* knowledge); and second, the 'weight' of the society —measured by a larger proportion of Gross National Product and a larger share of employment—is increasingly in the knowledge field." [6] The number of professional and technical workers in the United States labor force

more than doubled between 1947 and 1964. "By 1975, manpower requirements for this occupational group are expected to rise by more than half,
to 13.2 million persons. If one assumes a total labor force at that time of
88.7 million, then the professional and technical group would make up
14.9 per cent of the working population. If one adds in, as well, an estimated 9.2 million managers, officials, and proprietors, then the total group
would make up 25.3 per cent of the working population. In effect, one
out of every four persons would have had about four years of college—the
educational average for the group—and this 25.3 per cent would comprise
the educated class of the country." [7] Within this educated class, "the most
crucial group, of course, in the knowledge society is scientists, and here the
growth rate has been the most marked of all professional groups . . .
whereas between 1930 and 1965 the work force increased by about 50 per
cent, the number of engineers increased by 370 per cent and that of scientists, by 930 per cent." [8]

What do these developments mean for the future of the occupational and
class structure of our society? Many writers of science fiction or utopian
novels have portrayed a two-class future society composed of the educated
and the uneducated. John Kenneth Galbraith has expressed a similar notion: "When capital was the key to economic success, social conflict was
between the rich and poor. . . . In recent times education has become
the difference that divides." [9]

The increased importance of educational attainments for entry into
higher level positions does not, however, ipso facto produce a rigid two-
class society. The technological changes which have altered the occupational distribution and increased the need for more educated manpower
provide, in the long run, expanded opportunities for upward mobility as the
bottom level of the occupational hierarchy contracts and the upper levels
expand. And indeed, a recent large-scale study of occupational mobility
in the United States finds no evidence of increasing rigidity in the occupational structure.[10] But if the occupational structure is to continue to be an
open and fluid one, a major social effort will have to be made to insure
that all individuals in the society are educated to the limits of their ability
and that the most effective use is made of the talents of the existing labor
force.

The goal of maintaining a fluid occupational structure coincides with
the economic and technological requirements of an advanced industrial society. The failure to make the most effective use of existing talents often
results in a lack of co-ordination between labor supply and demand which

is responsible for unemployment and economic loss. The inadequacies of current education and training systems likewise help to produce unemployment by failing to keep pace with the changing demands for labor. For "while few employees actually lose their jobs when radical technological improvements are introduced, it is likely that jobs which otherwise would have been available for young people when they were ready to begin work will not be there. The suspiciously high unemployment rate for young people—about three times that for older age groups—suggests the validity of this hypothesis." [11]

The provision of adequate education and the proper identification of talent are essential not only for the reduction of unemployment and economic loss, but also for the very maintenance and growth of a system dependent upon advanced technology. In the past and in many of the less developed countries economic development has required large amounts of capital. "Tomorrow, however, the long-range economic expansions of the society will be limited by shortages in technical and scientific manpower. Such problems are novel. We know, from economic theory, how to raise money capital . . . but the source of brainpower is limited in part by the genetic distributions of talent and also by cultural disadvantages. The process of identifying and husbanding talent is long and difficult, and it involves the provision of adequate motivation, proper counselling and guidance, a coherent curriculum, and the like. The 'time-cycle' in such planning, a period of from fifteen to twenty years, is vastly different from that required in the raising of money capital." [12]

The requirements of modern technology and the values of an egalitarian social system thus converge to produce a need for revisions in our educational system and the establishment of some system of manpower planning. In the short run, it is incumbent upon the government to assure that jobs or income will be available to those workers who are displaced from their present employment. To this end, the Automation Commission has recommended: "(1) fiscal policy calculated to provide at all times a brisk demand for labor; (2) direct employment of any long-term residue of unemployed workers; and (3) income maintenance for families with inadequate earnings." [13] But in the longer run, new public policies must be devised to overcome present rigidities in the labor market (arbitrary retirement and hiring practices, racial discrimination, relocation problems), to provide a flexible system of education and training (on-the-job training systems, sabbatical leaves for educational purposes, new mechanisms for occupational guidance), and to secure a better match between labor supply and demand.

The re-allocation of resources that would be required for such institutional changes to occur poses many dilemmas of social choice. It has been estimated, for example, that in 1980, "given a $4,413 per capita GNP . . . , achieved with a 37½-hour workweek, a 48-week workyear, and providing retraining for 1 per cent of the labor force, society could choose to retrain much more heavily (4.25 per cent of the labor force per year) or, alternatively, could add 1½ weeks per year in vacation. In 1985, when per capita GNP should reach about $5,000, the choice could be between retraining almost 7 per cent of the labor force annually or taking an additional 3 weeks of vacation. Obviously, other choices could be made, involving a further reduction in the workweek, a lowering of retirement age, or an increased educational span for those entering the labor force." [14] The value issues involved in such choices include the following: "If the rate of technological change begins to exceed our ability to adjust to it, to what extent should the introduction of new production techniques be controlled? What price in individual freedom of action would we be willing to pay in order to eliminate unemployment among teen-age Negroes in urban ghettos? Although it seems obvious that we are becoming an increasingly leisure-oriented society, it is not nearly so apparent that we *should* become so. The increased national product resulting from a continuation of the present pattern of working hours plus increased productivity could be used to improve a wide variety of services, such as public education, that are not now adequately financed." [15]

Whatever the nature of the social choices that will be made to help minimize the disruptive effects of technological change and to maintain mobility and fluidity in the occupational structure, technological change in industry has resulted in the blocking of certain older paths of mobility. In industry, because of "the need for managerial personnel to have a broad educational and technological background, . . . a moat [has been established] between the workers and their foremen and all other supervisory personnel. It is increasingly rare for a working man to advance more than one step up the managerial ladder. He can become a foreman, but that is all." [16] Mobility in office work appears to be similarly blocked as "the middle step in the old promotion ladder"—positions requiring experience and seniority, but beneath the managerial level—appears to be growing smaller with the introduction of automation.[17] And among managerial and supervisory personnel in industry, "a 'gap' is forming between lower and higher levels of management. . . . Yet in the wide number of areas where promotional paths are being modified the extent to which modified job and work environments call for the (technical) degree is not clearly established. There is a clear tendency to overestimate its relevance. In addition, where higher level skills are indicated, the development potential of existing company personnel is frequently overlooked." [18]

Such inability to move up within the hierarchy of an employing organization has been a source of frustration to many workers; and since the blockage often results from exaggerated notions of the importance of formal education, there is an underutilization of existing talents. In many instances on-the-job training has been used quite effectively to permit the existing work force to assume the new roles and responsibilities. Furthermore, in the face of rapid technological change, even recent college graduates suffer from the problem of knowledge obsolescence.

For these reasons, some analysts have been advocating the establishment of "new careers" which would allow a worker to move from a nonskilled entry position to intermediate sub-professional functions and then on to full professional status through a sequence of on-the-job training and formal education, with new types of accreditation that would reward experience gained on the job. Currently, Arthur Pearl and Frank Riessman argue, "society insists that training take place prior to job placement. Such a system made sense (although it reinforced inequality) when only a small percentage of the population was engaged in highly skilled occupations, while most of the work force required little formal training. This condition no longer exists. Most of the needs of society can be satisfied only by the highly-skilled and the well-trained. In an era of rapid technological development even the skills of the professional rapidly become obsolete. Training cannot be considered a prerequisite for employment." [19]

The "new careers" concept thus focuses on those occupations in which on-the-job training could replace advance preparation. It departs also from the observation that societies need as much health, education, and welfare services as they can afford. There is room for expansion of existing careers in these service areas. Many more people could become qualified teachers, for example, if a process of moving up from the position of teacher's aide through a series of steps allowed them to become certified teachers. In addition, various social service "activities not currently performed by anyone, but for which there is a readily acknowledged need and which can also be satisfactorily accomplished by the unskilled worker" could be developed.[20] The attempt to design new types of careers is thus also responsive to the problem of providing meaningful work for the increasing numbers of workers who will not be able to find gainful employment in the labor force of the future.

## Changing Patterns of Work and Leisure

The perceived rapidity of technological change has often called forth exaggerated notions of the development of a "leisure society." Although more careful research has shown that "average hours worked per year have been declining slowly and sporadically for a long time, with the average yearly decrease about 0.3 to 0.4 per cent," [21] the consequences of a significant increase in leisure time are sufficiently important to merit early attention. Of equal—if not greater—importance, however, are the changes in work life that have been occurring at all levels of the occupational hierarchy in the wake of technological change.

The technological change which has resulted in the relative decline of unskilled and standardized jobs has not eliminated the need for routine and dull work. "In the complex and diversified manufacturing sector of an advanced industrial society, at least three major kinds of blue-collar factory work exist at the same time: the traditional manual skill associated with craft technology; the routine low-skilled manual operations associated with machine and assembly-line technologies; and the 'non-manual' responsibility called forth by continuous-process technology. Although craft skill will continue to play a significant role, the shift from skill to responsibility is the most important historical trend in the evolution of blue-collar work." [22]

The role of technology in allowing the worker to exercise greater responsibility runs counter to the frequently stated generalization that industrial technology produces alienation in the worker. Modern automated technology is a very different entity from the assembly-line technology portrayed in Chaplin's "Modern Times." A study by Robert Blauner of alienation among workers in diverse types of industry concludes that: "In the early period, dominated by craft industry, alienation is at its lowest level and the worker's freedom at a maximum. Freedom declines and the curve of alienation . . . rises sharply in the period of machine industry. . . . But with automated industry there is a countertrend, one that we can fortunately expect to become even more important in the future. The case of the continuous-process industries, particularly the chemical industry, shows that automation increases the worker's control over his work process and checks the further division of labor and growth of large factories. The result is meaningful work in a more cohesive, integrated industrial climate." [23]

Likewise, the introduction of electronic data processing into offices has resulted in an upgrading of the responsibility of a proportion of the white-collar labor force. In both the white- and blue-collar situations, the positive consequences of this heightened responsibility in decreasing alienation and increasing the worker's sense of importance have often been offset by the tensions which it generates. The more serious consequences of error and the need for greater concentration and alertness in handling automated machinery have caused strain for some workers. White-collar workers also resent the necessity for shift work that often accompanies the introduction of computers.

The introduction of shift work for office workers is but one indication of the growing convergence between blue-collar and white-collar work. Technological change has resulted in "a narrowing of traditional differentiation in terms of job content. What have hitherto been manual jobs, albeit with a high degree of skill, have an increasing conceptual content, and an increasing emphasis upon formal knowledge. On the other hand some clerical jobs have an increasing manual content with the advent of computers." [24] Moreover, "where the ratio of capital to labour costs is high, maximum utilisation of plant becomes extremely important. It becomes even more necessary to avoid breakdowns and to have a reliable labour force. Granting such 'white-collar' conditions as an annual salary, improved fringe benefits is then seen partly as the price to pay for dependability. . . . It is also in such industries that technology has had, and is likely to have most effect upon the content of the job. The dividing line between the skilled plant operator who is 'blue-collar,' and the technologist who is 'white-collar' becomes very narrow indeed." [25] But if technological factors are fostering the convergence of white- and blue-collar jobs, social factors rooted in the historical differences between the two groups continue to inhibit such convergence.

Just as blue- and white-collar workers experience some similar tensions as a result of the new responsibilities accompanying automation, so workers in different occupational strata have similar problems as a result of the growth in the complexity of employing organizations. As technological advance has brought more levels of supervision and a more differentiated and specialized division of labor, role ambiguity is a frequent problem. This has been well documented in a national survey of 725 employed persons (matched by sex, age, education, and occupation with the employed persons reported in the 1961 census). Forty-eight per cent of the sample reported that "from time to time they are caught in the middle between two sets of people who want different things from them, and 15 per cent indicate this to be a frequent and serious problem. Thirty-nine per cent report being bothered at times by thinking that they will not be able to satisfy the conflicting demands of the various people over them." [26] The subjects also reported a lack of clarity about the scope and responsibilities of their jobs (35%) and ambiguity about what their co-workers expect of them (29%).[27] In the case of professionals, the ambiguities are compounded by competing loyalties—loyalty to the employing organization versus loyalty to the profession or discipline.

In addition to role ambiguity, there is another problem in the modern work situation which cuts across different occupational strata: the rapid obsolescence of knowledge and skills. This problem is particularly intense for the professionals whose expertise is no longer secure once acquired. If they are to retain their status, they must assimilate the new knowledge which is constantly being generated. The difficulty of this task has led to various proposals for instituting systems of continuing education and has raised questions about the adequacy of tenure and licensing systems. Should a doctor, for example, be licensed to practice medicine and retain that right automatically even if he has not kept up adequately with the more recent knowledge and techniques?

The progressive specialization and division of labor coupled with the need for greater cooperation and co-ordination between specialties exacerbates the problem. Professionals today are often faced with the need not only to keep abreast of new developments in their own specialties but also, to some extent, of those in related fields. Researchers in interdisciplinary teams, doctors in public health, and certain types of consultants serve as examples.

In management there is some tension between the need for specialists and the need for generalists. The advent of office automation has raised much discussion of "how specialised managers ought to be and how far 'professionalisation' of management should be allowed, or encouraged to go. . . . The prevalent view seems to be that technical background is not likely to become a prerequisite for top managers. While some students of the subject incline to the view that top managers must understand mathematical concepts, it is not generally thought that they themselves need particular skills in their application. It is coming to be generally accepted that top executives need the best possible general educational background." [28] Yet Jay Gould finds that "new men are beginning to emerge at the very highest levels of command of America's leading corporations, men who speak the language not only of science and engineering but of business as well." [29] And he attributes the increasing prominence of technical managers to the fact that "key managerial decisions today rest increasingly on technical and scientific premises that impinge upon and frequently override financial, marketing, and other business considerations." [30]

There is one work problem which is peculiar to the upper occupational strata. This is what might be called their "over-commitment" to work. While most workers have experienced some increase in leisure, the upper strata have probably lost leisure during the twentieth century. It would be difficult to determine how much of this loss of leisure has been due to the requirements of the work itself and how much to the preferences and values of the workers. But the result has been a certain alienation or disengagement from non-work activities comparable to the traditional nonconcern with work activities that is manifested by blue-collar workers. As one observer has commented: "Shall we deplore the worker's lack of interest in his occupation, or the intellectual's excessive interest in work?" [31]

Most projections assume that the trend will continue so that while workers will increasingly have free time, the upper echelons will not. If the increases in leisure time for the non-elite become significant, some serious problems would be raised by this duality. As Donald Michael has expressed it: "How do we educate one segment of society to expect to have and use productively more free time and, at the same time, educate another segment to expect to have little or no free time and not to want it?" [32] The problem may be particularly pressing in view of the fact that many workers do not really want more free time. Studies have shown that "it is primarily the worker's fear of unemployment that prompts him to press for a reduced workweek, and not a desire for increased leisure. . . . In the absence of the unemployment threat workers would place a higher value on additional goods than on additional leisure, and . . . given a choice between an increase in hourly wage rates . . . and a reduction in working time, they would choose the former." [33]

Since future leisure time will probably take the form of lengthened vacations rather than shortened workweeks, we have had little experience to date that might indicate how this time might be filled. The only groups to-day who have extended free time at their disposal are the unemployed and the retired. The former suffer from a lack of resources and the psychological pains of being unemployed. The latter are often unable to make the necessary adjustment away from the work ethic. "Moreover, for many, retirement—especially early retirement—will imply that somehow one's contribution to the work-force is no longer needed . . . , that one is not socially valuable as one's contemporaries who have remained in the work-force or been enticed back into it." [34] The limited evidence that we do have from steelworkers with extended vacation periods indicates that there might be some increase in travel, but no substantial increase in educational pursuits, community activities, or hobbies.[35]

While some commentators take such evidence as an indication that modern man is ill-prepared for extended leisure, others maintain that leisure provides a potential for creative self-fulfillment that should be developed through appropriate planning and education. It is well to remember, how-ever, that many social choices must be made for such leisure to become a reality—choices between increased productivity, leisure, and training pro-grams for example. Perhaps too, a rather different solution will be found to the "leisure problem": the deliberate creation of new jobs. Such jobs would not be modelled on the make-work activities supported during the depression of the 1930's. Rather they would be set up to exploit existing individual talents and to provide new or better services to the population. Some of these jobs might take the form of payment for services that are currently rendered on a voluntary basis.

While economically useful jobs might become scarce in some future "leisure society," it may be possible for socially useful jobs to be created. A prototype of this kind of job might be that of "hand-holder" for the aged or the sick. Persons holding such jobs would serve to provide sympathetic company for persons who otherwise have little social contact. These jobs thus would serve the dual function of filling unwanted or excessive leisure time and of providing the kind of social services that will become possible in a highly productive and affluent society.

Before any such development might come to pass—if indeed it ever does—many changes are likely to occur in the patterns of work and leisure. But the most pressing problems of the immediate future concern the al-terations that will have to be made in the educational and occupational structures in order to take care of those workers who are displaced by technological change and to assure the maximum possible mesh between the needs of the individual workers and the technological and economic needs of the society at large.

# NOTES

1. National Commission on Technology, Automation, and Economic Progress, *Technology and the American Economy* (Washington, D.C.: Government Printing Office, 1966), Vol. I, p. 109.

2. Albert A. Blum, "Computers and Clerical Workers" (Oberhausen, Germany, 1968), Document D 1-68 of the Third International Conference on Rationalization, Automation and Technological Change, sponsored by the Metalworkers' Industrial Union of the Federal Republic of Germany), p. 15.

3. Marshall W. Meyer, "Automation and Bureaucratic Structure," *American Journal of Sociology,* 74 (November 1968), p. 264.

4. James R. Bright, "The Relationship of Increasing Automation and Skill Requirements," in National Commission on Technology, Automation, and Economic Progress, *The Employment Impact of Technological Change,* Appendix Volume II to *Technology and the American Economy* (Washington, D.C.: Government Printing Office, 1966), p. 221.

5. See William A. Faunce, *Problems Of An Industrial Society* (New York: McGraw Hill, Inc., 1968), pp. 51–61.

6. Daniel Bell, "The Measurement of Knowledge and Technology," in Eleanor Bernert Sheldon and Wilbert E. Moore, eds., *Indicators of Social Change* (New York: Russell Sage Foundation, 1968), p. 198.

7. *Ibid.,* p. 200.

8. *Ibid.,* pp. 201–202.

9. John Kenneth Galbraith, *The New Industrial State* (Boston: Houghton Mifflin Co., 1967), p. 244.

10. See Peter M. Blau and Otis Dudley Duncan, *The American Occupational Structure* (New York: John Wiley & Sons, Inc., 1967).

11. Eli Ginzberg and Hyman Berman, *The American Worker In The Twentieth Century* (New York: The Free Press, 1963), p. 353.

12. Bell, *op. cit.,* pp. 158–59.

13. National Commission on Technology, Automation, and Economic Progress, *Technology and the American Economy, op. cit.,* p. 43.

14. Juanita M. Kreps and Joseph J. Spengler, "The Leisure Component of Economic Growth," in *The Employment Impact of Technological Change,* Appendix Vol. II to *Technology and the American Economy, op. cit.,* p. 365.

15. Faunce, *op. cit.,* pp. 82–83.

16. Ginzberg and Berman, *op. cit.,* pp. 333–34.

17. See Blum, *op. cit.*

18. Elmer J. Burack and Thomas J. McNichols, "Management and Automation Research Project, Final Report" (Chicago: Illinois Institute of Technology, 1968), processed, p. 2.
19. Arthur Pearl and Frank Riessman, *New Careers For the Poor* (New York: The Free Press, 1965), p. 3.
20. *Ibid.,* p. 13.
21. National Commission on Technology, Automation, and Economic Progress, *Technology and the American Economy, op. cit.,* p. 10.
22. Robert Blauner, *Alienation and Freedom* (Chicago: University of Chicago Press, 1964), p. 169.
23. *Ibid.,* p. 182.
24. Dorothy Wedderburn, "Are White-Collar and Blue-Collar Jobs Converging?" (Oberhausen, Germany, 1968), Document P 12–68 of the Third International Conference on Rationalization, Automation and Technological Change, sponsored by the Metalworkers' Industrial Union of the Federal Republic of Germany, p. 11.
25. *Ibid.,* p. 20.
26. Robert L. Kahn, Donald M. Wolfe, Robert P. Quinn, and J. Diedrick Snoek, *Organizational Stress: Studies in Role Conflict and Ambiguity* (New York: John Wiley & Sons, Inc., 1964), pp. 55–56.
27. *Ibid.,* p. 74.
28. H. A. Rhee, *Office Automation in Social Perspective* (Oxford: Basil Blackwell, 1968), pp. 130–31.
29. Jay M. Gould, *The Technical Elite* (New York: August M. Kelley, 1966), p. 77.
30. *Ibid.,* p. 84.
31. James R. Bright, "Technology, Business, and Education," in Walter J. Ong, S.J., ed., *Knowledge And the Future Of Man: An International Symposium* (New York: Holt, Rinehart, and Winston, 1968), p. 214.
32. Donald N. Michael, "Free Time—The New Imperative in Our Society," in William W. Brickman and Stanley Lehrer, eds. *Automation, Education, and Human Values* (New York: School and Society Books, 1966), p. 303.
33. Kreps and Spengler, *op. cit.,* p. 371.
34. Michael, *op. cit.,* pp. 299–300.
35. See W. J. Klausner, "An Experiment in Leisure," *Science Journal,* 4 (June 1968), pp. 81–85.

# Can We Survive Abundance?

ROBERT THEOBALD

In this essay Robert Theobald argues that the scientific
and technological revolution now taking place with such
great rapidity in the Western world both poses a profound
challenge to our society and provides us with a great hope.
It is a challenge primarily because it demands new forms
of social planning, whereas our socio-economic system has
thus far involved a fundamental opposition to large-scale
planning. It is entirely problematic whether our society
will choose the path of increasingly complex and
centralized social planning which Theobald believes the
present situation demands. It is very possible that the
members of our society will reject the path of planning.
They will thereby refuse to accept the challenge and will
fail to meet it.

The scientific-technological revolution gives us hope of

freeing ourselves from dull and demeaning labor, freeing ourselves for more creative, productive pursuits.

Theobald argues that it is the great challenge for this generation to find ways of solving the conflict between the promise and the danger of technology. The few who have carefully observed American response to technology in recent years have little faith that the challenge will be met. Again and again, Americans, especially at federal and state government levels, have refused even to consider the fundamental challenge of social planning. Our society has chosen, perhaps by default, to stumble along blindly from one decision to another, rarely trying to put these decisions rationally together into a more general pattern of planning.

Theobald sees our problems as caused not by selfishness, bourgeois greed, or any such Marxian demons, but by corporate heads, union leaders, government officials, and so on, each acting in a perfectly rational fashion within the present context of our socio-economic system to produce the best or greatest welfare for his group. The problem is that there is no way of assuring that these "rational" efforts will go together to serve the best interests of the whole society. Only individuals striving for utopian goals are today really practical. Only the man who seeks to change the general nature of society is acting in a practical and realistic fashion to solve our problems.

Theobald is not, of course, calling for a political upheaval; he is calling for the same kind of government change in social planning which is called for in the succeeding selections from Shubik and Mannheim.

In our present world of interlocking paradoxes, the concept of Free Men and Free Markets in a single unity seems to be one more paradox—with a Utopian appearance. The reader will have to judge for himself whether or not it is a paradox, after consideration of the evidence and argument presented in these pages; the Utopian appearance, however, is misleading. All Utopian thought is the product of dissatisfaction with an existing socioeconomic structure and a desire for a better one. However, Utopian thought does *not* contain two elements vital to the discussion presented here: recognition that flexibility and a capacity for change must be present in any socioeconomic system if it is to continue, and concern with finding a dynamic route to the desired goals. Utopian thought concentrates on ends and ignores means.

A contrasting approach to socioeconomic problems ignores ends and concentrates on means; in this view the manifest day-to-day deterioration in our situation is indeed a matter for grave concern; but the approach advocated, although admittedly practical, is one of slight adjustments in the functioning of the socioeconomic system—the employment of a mosaic of small measures in order to restore a supposed former condition. Those who support this nostalgic approach, while vehemently denying any intention of *planning* a socioeconomic structure, are in effect acting with a plan of the socioeconomic structure in mind. They could be considered Sub-Utopians, for their practical action is oriented towards the re-establishment of a socioeconomic structure which in fact was never fully realized in the past, while the dreams of the Utopians are concentrated on a socioeconomic structure which is impossible of realization in the future. Until very recently, it seemed that it might be possible to realize both the Utopian and the Sub-Utopian ideals because a demonstration of their unreality was lacking, but we are now witnessing the initial stages of that demonstration: the dynamic organizing force of the scientific and technological revolution is becoming apparent.

The scientific revolution of the mid-twentieth century is neither merely an unpleasant fact which can be safely ignored, nor an exciting subject for euphoric discussions: it is a real and urgent problem. It poses a challenge to the viability of Western socioeconomic systems and it provides an opportunity for a demonstration of the strength behind their basic philosophy. Unfortunately, little fundamental thought has yet been given to the changes which the scientific revolution will require in the socioeconomic system of Western countries.

The object is to discover the new significance, in present conditions, of the two main principles in Western thought: the desire to achieve freedom for the individual and the belief in the necessity for free markets. The concept of the dignity and rights of the individual citizen and the duty of the state to protect these rights has come down to us from the Greeks. Eighteenth-century thinkers widened this concept into a fundamental belief in the rights of *all* men to life, liberty, and the pursuit of happiness. They also argued that each man should have the right to participate in decisions that affected him. The belief in the free operation of the market is more recent but it has been central to Western thought for the better part of two hundred years. It has been argued that the functioning of the economic system is so complex that it is impossible for the bureaucrat to second-guess it effectively. The more extreme, Adam Smith version of this thesis was that the "invisible hand" of the market mechanism would harmonize the selfish interests of all into the good of the total society. This comfortable, yet dynamic, philosophy gained greater acceptance in the United States than in any other country.

For a brief period of a century and a half, Western governments followed a policy of nonintervention in the socioeconomic system: this policy resulted from the belief that the efficient operation of free markets also provided the individual with increasing freedom. However, the favorable effect of the efficient operation of the market on the freedom of the individual was never as great as was assumed by much of the economic and political thought of the nineteenth century.

The great Depression of the 1930's forced the final abandonment of the extreme, Adam Smith version of the free-market mechanism. Western governments found that they had to intervene increasingly in the socioeconomic system as it became obvious that the operation of the market, however efficient, would not furnish enough employment; public opinion forced action to provide for those who could not find work. However, the abandonment of *complete* reliance on the free-market mechanism did *not* mean the abandonment of a general belief in the free-market mechanism. Governments therefore found themselves compelled to balance two goals: the preservation of the free-market mechanism and the safeguarding of the basis for individual freedom. The problem of deciding on appropriate policies was greatly complicated by the fact that many of the actions that can be taken to safeguard the basis for individual freedom tend to destroy the free-market mechanism, while many of the steps which can be taken to strengthen the free-market mechanism tend to limit the freedom of the individual.

The fact that many existing policies are designed *either* to support the continuance of the free-market mechanism *or* to protect the individual, has resulted in increasingly polarized fears about the direction in which the socioeconomic system is moving. Conservatives fear that the market, which they believe has been responsible for past dynamism, is being hamstrung and that the potential for complete government control is being installed. Liberals fear that continuance of the *laissez-faire* attitude held to be necessary to encourage the profit drive and promote growth is allowing the activities of the large corporation to dominate the socioeconomic system. While conservative and liberal thinkers are therefore moving ever farther apart in their philosophies, the policy proposals of political parties throughout the Western world, which try increasingly to be all things to all men, move ever closer to dead center.

The confused and immobile dead-center philosophies of Western political parties are not capable of developing the energetic policies which we will need to deal with the transformation being brought about by science and technology. The purpose is to suggest a new synthesis of the fundamental and valid principles in Western thought which can be restated in the following terms: *It is the goal of all Western societies to ensure that each individual has the maximum of freedom in his choice of action compatible with the needs of the society. Such a degree of freedom can only be obtained if the individual is provided with sufficient resources to enable him to live with dignity. No attempt should, however, be made to provide the required resources through government control of the market mechanism, for not only will such an attempt fail but it will also prevent the realization of the original goal: it will restrict individual freedom rather than advance it.*

Although governments cannot and should not *control* the market mechanism, they do have major socioeconomic responsibilities in today's world. One of the most important tasks of the coming decade is to discover ways in which these responsibilities can be most competently carried out. The demonstrably muddled way in which governments are currently discharging their responsibilities is not primarily attributable to administrative incompetence but to the piecemeal way in which measures are introduced; and this in turn should be seen as a response to the inherent contradiction in current beliefs about the proper role of government.

At the present time there exists an implicit belief that governments are, at the very least, responsible for providing each person with enough resources to live as a member of society. At the same time there exists a conviction, particularly in America, that it is improper for government to run the economy, that government intervention in the socioeconomic system should be limited, and that it is still "consumer sovereignty" which determines the allocation of resources through the supply-and-demand mechanism, exactly as set forth in traditional economic theory. Any government, however, must deal with realities. The overwhelming reality regarding the allocation of resources is that the government has been forced to intervene. In addition, it has been forced to carry out extensive programs designed to meet the over-all needs of the socioeconomic system: it tries to provide minimum subsistence for all through unemployment and Social Security payments and through welfare benefits; it is responsible for keeping the economy in balance and preventing a slump; it influences the direction in which the socioeconomic system moves through the legislation it passes and the consequent allocation of its funds. The implications of this latter fact have been little studied. We have not yet considered how to develop methods of controlling the actions of an Administration which has the power to decide whether national resources should be allocated to put a man on the moon or to abolish poverty.

[We are] primarily concerned with the effects of the technological revolution on the distribution of income, but before passing on to an extensive examination of this relationship, it is essential that we recognize the extraordinary scope and pervasiveness of the scientific revolution now taking place in the world. The knowledge we are gaining is already being used and will increasingly be employed to reorder the world in which we live. In particular, it provides us with the possibility of developing many kinds of machinery to take the place of human labor and skills. We are moving beyond the "industrial" revolution, which was based on the combination of the *power of the machine with the skill of the human being*. We have now entered a new revolutionary era in which the *power of the machine is combined with the skill of the machine* to form a productive system of, in effect, unlimited capacity. The basis of this new revolution is a greatly increased understanding of the processes of communication between men and machines and between machines themselves, and the change can therefore justly be called the cybernetic revolution, after the word invented by Norbert Wiener and adapted by Donald Michael. According to Michael's definition, cybernation includes both the use of computers and the use of automatic machinery and tools. This is the usage followed in this book because a certain degree of ambiguity is now associated with the word automation, which is *usually* employed to cover the use of automatic machinery and tools but is *sometimes* extended to cover the use of computers.

Michael's definition was made in his pamphlet *Cybernation—the Silent Conquest,* published by the Center for the Study of Democratic Institutions. In this pamphlet he describes developments in the cybernated equipment becoming available:

There are two important classes of devices. One class, usually referred to when one speaks of "automation," is made up of devices that automatically perform sensing and motor tasks, replacing or improving on human capacities for performing these functions. The second class, usually referred to when one speaks of "computers," is composed of devices that perform, very rapidly, routine or complex logical and decision-making tasks, replacing or improving on human capacities for performing these functions. . . .

Cybernated systems perform with a precision and a rapidity unmatched in humans. They also perform in ways that would be impractical or impossible for humans to duplicate. They can be built to detect and correct errors in their own performance and to indicate to men which of their components are producing the error. They can make judgments on the basis of instructions programmed into them. They can remember and search their memories for appropriate data, which either has been programmed into them along with their instructions or has been acquired in the process of manipulating new data. Thus, they can learn on the basis of past experience with their environment. They can receive information in more codes and sensory modes than men can. They are beginning to perceive and to recognize.

As a result of these characteristics, automation is being used to make and roll steel, mine coal, manufacture engine blocks, weave cloth, sort and grade everything from oranges to bank checks. More versatile automatic fabricators are becoming available. . . .

At the other end of the continuum, computers are being used rather regularly to analyze market portfolios for brokers; compute the best combination of crops and livestock for given farm conditions; design and "fly" under typical and extreme conditions rockets and airplanes before they are built; design, in terms of costs and traffic-flow characteristics, the appropriate angles and grades for complex traffic interchanges; keep up-to-date inventory records and print new stock orders as automatically computed rates of sales and inventory status indicate.

Predictions about the startling effects of cybernation are now made frequently and usually have a very matter-of-fact air. Here are three chosen more or less at random. Dr. John W. Mauchly, one of the inventors of computers, has argued: "There is no reason to suppose the average boy or girl cannot be master of a personal computer," and suggested that this could occur within about a decade. A British engineering professor has suggested that it will be possible during the 1970's to buy an efficient robot "housemaid" for $2,000, which will set the table, make beds, push a vacuum cleaner, and do other household chores. Professor John E. Gibson of Purdue informed the National Electronics Conference that he was preparing to couple two types of computer: one with high calculating speeds and the other with the potential for storing large amounts of data. He believed that the combination of the two would lead to the development of solutions to new types of problems, where the computer has so far been of little use.

The evidence is overwhelming. The United States and the other rich countries will shortly have the technological capability to install a productive system based primarily on *machine* power and *machine* skills within the next two decades; market forces will compel both government and business to use cybernated equipment. Since the beginning of the industrial revolution we have witnessed a growing replacement of manpower by machine power, but man's skills were still essential to the utilization of machine power. The coming replacement of man's skills by the machine's skills will destroy many jobs and render useless the work experience of vast numbers now employed. The possibility of obtaining employment in one of the restricted number of new fields will depend to a very large extent on the level of skill and education of the job applicant. It follows that the decline in job opportunities will be most severe for those who perform repetitive tasks and whose work can most easily be done by machines. This conclusion implies the *complete* breakdown of our present socio-economic system, which depends on the ability to provide jobs for all who require them. The resulting situation is paradoxical. We are going to be able to produce more goods than ever before and we therefore have the ability to provide a standard of living compatible with the maintenance of human dignity for everybody. However, because we still believe that the income levels of the vast majority of the population should depend on their ability to continue working, over 20 per cent of the American population is exiled from the abundant economy and this percentage will grow, rather than decline, in coming years.

We are trapped by "the dismal science"—economics. The founders of economic theory believed that we could *never* achieve abundance and therefore defined economics as the art of "distributing scarce resources." Today we already have large-scale agricultural surpluses and we have the ability to produce more than $60 billion in additional goods and services with our *presently* existing productive capacity; it is therefore ludicrous to continue to define economics as the art of distributing scarce resources.

Abundance has arrived. Up to the present time, we have merely been made a little uncomfortable by the incongruities of juxtaposed abundance and scarcity within the same socioeconomic system. However, we are already aware of the fact that available resources could be used to abolish poverty and that we have so far failed to find a way to liberate resources for this purpose. We see manufacturers of products spending more to sell their goods than to produce them—we know that advertising, packaging, premiums, etc., account for more than half the total cost of many products. We wonder whether we have to put up with depressing, repetitious advertising, or whether a new and more rational system could be developed. Occasionally a writer such as Michael Harrington sharpens our misgivings into a definite sense of acute, if temporary, discomfort by revealing the tragedies behind the ironies. In *The Other America,* Harrington showed how 40 to 50 million Americans have been cut off not only from any possibility of sharing in economic abundance but also from any chance of becoming an American in good standing.

Despite our peripheral recognition of the awkwardness caused by our failure to use abundance, we have not yet become concerned by the fact that our unwillingness to concede the existence of abundance could lead to a reversal of the successful social revolution in America. Herman P. Miller, special assistant in the Bureau of the Census, has argued: "It is conceivable . . . that in the absence of remedial action, this nation may soon be faced with an increase in the disparity of incomes caused by the existence of a large block of untrained and unwanted men. Unless we are careful, we may then discover that our 'social revolution' not only has been marking time for nearly twenty years, but is beginning to move backward." Nor have we considered the prospect that growing abundance could lead to a worldwide slump the dimensions of which would be even greater than that of the thirties. We will see in this volume that these results will inevitably follow unless we make the necessary changes in our socioeconomic system.

If the coming of abundance raises the possibility of reversal of the hitherto successful social revolution and threatens a severe worldwide slump, why have we failed to recognize these threats? Our failure results from the extreme difficulties experienced by individuals and societies in changing their patterns of thought. This is, of course, the basic thesis that Arnold Toynbee, the noted historian, presents. In this form, however, the thesis is not constructive, for its closed nature indicates no avenues of advance toward new solutions. However, once we act upon a critical recognition that our *past* patterns of thought are expressed in the *present* pattern of institutions, the necessary steps become clearer.

Our present pattern of institutions was developed at a time when the most urgent need of the socioeconomic system was defined in terms of an increase in production, and many of the institutions developed at this time were therefore designed for maximum efficiency in promoting growth in production. Corporations can only maintain their profit levels if they sell an ever-increasing quantity of goods: the manager of the corporation must therefore act to promote further growth, for this is the *only* way in which he can ensure the continued existence of his corporation. The unions must try to raise wages and therefore purchasing power; when men are competing with machines for jobs, this will cause growing unemployment. The government must encourage further investment; since the new equipment installed will usually be more cybernated than the old, this will also mean growing unemployment. In effect, therefore, the separately "rational" actions of the various parts of society are the *same* actions that combined are shaking our total socioeconomic system apart.

It is not the selfish actions of evil men that are causing today's major problems, but the "rational" decisions of the highly respected corporate head, the energetic union leader, and the concerned cabinet member. Each finds that he can *only* meet his own responsibilities, as they are presently defined, by acting in a particular way; few of these people have the time or opportunity to step back and consider the effects of their actions on the over-all socioeconomic system. When describing the actions of such people it will therefore be necessary to make much use of such words as "must," "forced," and "compelled." The use of these words will reflect the fact that those in control of most types of organizations will have little freedom of choice in their actions until the socioeconomic system is changed. This book is written in the belief that most of these individuals are fundamentally more concerned with the achievement of the West's basic goals than with the preservation of their present roles, with their attached rights and obligations. It follows that recognition of the realities of the present situation will lead them to support the necessary measures. It should be noted, however, that the *over-all* importance of these highly trained and highly skilled individuals will *not* decline as we adapt our socioeconomic system to today's realities: on the contrary, society's need for such people will increase.

New policy formation must not only ensure that government, business, and the unions alter their patterns of action and interaction but must also recognize the need for new attitudes in foreign policy: it must take account of the fact that abundance is a worldwide problem. Such a statement appears nonsensical; only America appears to have both considerable surplus capacity and unemployed workers in early 1963. It is generally forgotten that abundance was created in America during the ten-year period after World War II. It therefore seems almost certain that the full effects of abundance will be felt in Europe within the next decade, for the economic position of many European nations is now considerably more advanced than that of America at the end of World War II. In addition, the latest study of Russia suggests that the industrial production in the Soviet Union was already 75 per cent as large as United States production in 1960. Europe and Russia will probably have to wrestle with the problems America is now facing by the end of the sixties, and will certainly be forced to take vigorous action before 1975. The poverty of the remainder of the world does not shield it from the effects of abundance: the poor nations are suffering from the effects of the scientific and technological progress in the rich countries, for the highly advanced machinery they are installing in their new industries provides few jobs for their unemployed. The International Labor Office recently stated that unemployment and underemployment is rising in almost all the poor countries.

Up to the present time we have made no effort to employ abundance fruitfully; instead our policy has been a resolute determination to try to suppress its growth. Nevertheless we are failing even in this attempt. We have allowed a ridiculous situation to arise. The goal of nineteenth- and twentieth-century economic growth was to develop abundance; having achieved this we now appear determined to reap only the problems while suppressing the benefits. We could now have a productive system which would toil for us, but we still demand that everybody should continue to toil. Further, the coming of abundance not only permits, but also requires, the new synthesis of the liberal and conservative philosophies: that all Western societies should ensure that each individual obtains sufficient resources to allow him freedom in his choice of actions, and that these resources should be distributed without government intervention in the market mechanism. The coming of abundance allows and requires the support of non-market-created activities; it allows and requires that we provide everybody with the resources they need to live with dignity; in short, it allows and requires that we develop the good life. It is not hyperbole to suggest that we could be the modern Greeks, with mechanical slaves taking the place of human toil.

The coming of abundance should liberate our ideas, hitherto painfully constricted by the necessity to economize "scarce resources"; the allocation of material resources should no longer be the chief factor in our societal decisions. In these circumstances it is the Sub-Utopian, the "practical man," pragmatically using recent historical evidence to argue for small adjustments to our present policies, who is unrealistic. The realistic observer has understood that there are, in effect, no limits to our present actions except those imposed by a failure of our imaginations. Once we recognize the changed nature of the world, the required policy measures appear not only essential but also socially and morally desirable; only the continued hold of the dismal science prevents us from moving forward.

We have always had the ability to "dream dreams." The coming of abundance gives us the power to make them come true, for the implementation of our societal dreams is now a way of dealing with reality rather than a fight from it. This should be a time of strenuous intellectual activity and unlimited commitment. Instead the atmosphere is one of fear and hesitation. The legend of the emperor's clothes might be rewritten in the following terms: There was once a nineteenth-century emperor, for whom a superb set of robes was woven. Unfortunately, this was long before the invention of insect-proofing, and the clothes were steadily reduced to shreds by moths, agents of change and decay. Each successive emperor wore the garments despite their tatters, for nobody liked to call attention to their decrepit state, and the patched-up clothes continued to be worn although the royal domain grew rich and had the ability to produce as many fine new sets as the emperor cared to acquire. It is *our* decisions which will write the end to this legend: either we acquaint the Emperor Society with the realities of abundance, or he will die of exposure as a result of the chill winds entering through the holes in his clothing.

A few of the people reading this [article] began their working life at a time when Henry Ford was introducing his five-dollar day. What an incentive to hard work and what satisfaction was felt in the increased rewards! Many readers will remember the vital necessity of an all-out productive effort during World War I and II. Almost all readers recall the argument introduced to justify full employment as a societal goal, and the determination that the misery of the 1930's should not recur. Today we still feel that we have the inalienable right to work, and any suggestion that the market might not be able to provide enough conventional jobs to go round is akin to heresy. But cybernation has arrived, and abundance with it; any timidity in our approach to this giant, any regretful backward glances at dwindling *conventional* job opportunities, will only mean a reduction in the concentration of the energies so necessary to deal with the *new* problems of living.

*Theoretical* backward glances are equally out of place in the present situation, and a radical alteration in a way of thinking can be quite as painful as a change in a way of doing. I was trained within the great tradition of economic theory taught at Cambridge in England and Harvard in the United States. Along with a belief in the strength and virtue of the free enterprise system and the right of the individual to labor, I was taught that answers to economic problems—past, present, and future—could be found by a careful application of the Keynsian neoclassical synthesis. However, matters became more complicated when my professors, particularly Richard Goodwin, showed me how to use the tools developed by economists during the process of economic theory formation. The extension of the use of these tools from an analysis of a theoretical "scarcity economy" to an examination of the real "abundance economy" produced the series of *un*traditional economic observations presented here. Although clearly untraditional, they are equally clearly economic. This does not mean that it is necessary to be an economist to understand the argument; anyone acquainted with the terminology used to chronicle our growing economic abundance in the daily papers will be on familiar ground when reading the discussion of it in these pages.

The reverse side of an economy of abundance is the fact that a large proportion of the population will have to be provided with resources even if they are not carrying out a conventional market job—a somewhat sobering thought to many. A large number will not only consider this thought sobering but also shocking, and will consider that any book containing this debilitating concept should bear a title such as *The Lifelong Vacationer's Guide,* or *The Great Giveaway,* or maybe *The Whole-Hearted Handout or Passing the Buck.* This kind of satire is easy but it is irrelevant. The present socioeconomic system was formed at a time when the vital need was to encourage both productivity and production, and it naturally reflects this necessity; today, the productive system can grow fast enough to meet *any* demand which is likely to be placed on it. Financial incentives and inducements will play a limited role in the socio-economic system of the future.

While I believe that the problem of finding non-market methods of providing incomes is so immediate and vital to the continuance of Western societies as to make wholly negative criticism of this concept irrelevant, I am not suffering from the delusion that the answers to the problems proposed here are final, nor that other parts of the discussion in this book are so complete and correct as to be beyond criticism. The paucity of information on the subject of abundance would alone ensure that many aspects of its effect on present or future socioeconomic systems remain unexamined. Indeed some of them are unknown and some probably unknowable in advance of their emergence. This book is an agenda for discussion, presented because of the writer's conviction that although the coming of abundance provides *all the potential* for evolution into a new and better society, it can also destroy us unless we use it intelligently. I believe that many forces threaten to break loose during the sixties and could have the potential to sweep us irresistibly towards a type of society completely alien to our basic beliefs. We will need all the time we now have if we are to examine the implications of abundance and make the necessary changes in our socioeconomic system so that it can benefit from abundance rather than be destroyed by it.

# Information, Rationality, and Free Choice in a Future Democratic Society

## MARTIN SHUBIK

**I**n this selection Shubik carries further some of the ideas about changes in government necessitated by the rapid development of technology. Shubik argues that the basic assumptions of our earlier laissez-faire democracy no longer hold. As a consequence, we must both expect and seek to bring about basic changes in our society, if we are to maintain a democratic form of government.

*Reprinted from Martin Shubik, ''Information, Rationality, and Free Choice in a Future Democratic Society,''* Daedalus, Journal of the American Academy of Arts and Sciences, 96 (Summer, 1967), by *permission of the publisher.*

Underlying the concepts of the free market and the democratic voting process are some implicit models of man both as a rational, informed individual and as a decision-maker with an important freedom of choice. The rational utilitarian man, the Invisible Hand, and the democratic vote may be regarded as forming a trinity for an economic and political faith in a free-enterprise democracy.

Changes in society and in knowledge have caused us to question all of these concepts. The behavioral sciences, especially psychology and economics, and to some extent political science, sociology, and anthropology, have provided new tools with which one may examine them.

What are the economic and political values that a democratic society wishes to foster and preserve? What conditions must be imposed on institutions designed to obtain and maintain these values? What assumptions have been made implicitly or explicitly in current doctrines concerning the role and the nature of the individual?

Numbers, communication, the growing importance of joint property and services, as well as the speed of change in knowledge and information, force a reconsideration of our concepts. In terms of the democratic state and its citizens, we must re-examine power, equality, freedom of choice, ownership, centralization, "fair shares for all," "to each according to his needs, from each according to his ability," and many other appealing yet ill-defined words and slogans.

Both implicitly and explicitly much of our economic and political thought draws upon the peculiarly rationalistic basis of utilitarianism. Rational economic man in the economists' model is someone who knows what he wants, what his choices are, what his resources are. His value system is assumed to be well defined; his cool, consistent mind quickly and costlessly scans the myriads of alternatives facing him. His flawless discernment enables him to spy subtle differences in quality. He even calculates the value differences between the "giant economy size" and the regular pack. Many an economist realizes, however, that this is not so; that gaps in information exist; that *homo economicus* is not always certain of his desires. Yet it has been felt that the utilitarian model of the maximizing man with complete information is a good approximation. How good an approximation and of what are questions that remain to be answered. As technology grows, markets expand, and societies grow in size, the individual's share of the knowable decreases drastically. More and more the question becomes: How much should one pay for information the worth of which cannot be evaluated until it has been obtained?

Given clear preferences and complete knowledge, rational behavior amounts to following a consistent plan of action toward one's goals. The optimal program may be very complex, but it is well defined. Modern decision theory, economics, psychology, and game theory recognize, as a basic case, clearly motivated individual choice under conditions of complete information. It is also recognized that two unfortunate facts of life remove us from the relative simplicity of this basic case. The first concerns man as an information processor and the second the conflict of individual with group preferences.

Man lives in an environment about which his information is highly incomplete. Not only does he not know how to evaluate many of the alternatives facing him, he is not even aware of a considerable percentage of them. His perceptions are relatively limited; his powers of calculation and accuracy are less than those of a computer in many situations; his searching, data processing, and memory capacities are erratic. As the speed of transmission of stimuli and the volume of new stimuli increase, the limitations of the individual become more marked relative to society as a whole. *Per se* there is no indication that individual genius or perceptions have changed in an important manner for better or worse in the last few centuries, but the numbers of humans, the size of the body of knowledge, and the complexity of society have grown larger by orders of magnitude.

Perhaps the eighteenth and nineteenth centuries will go down as the brief interlude in which the growth of communications and knowledge relative to the size of population, speed of social and political change, and size of the total body of knowledge encouraged individualism and independence. By its very success, this brought about the tremendous need for and growth of knowledge reflected in the research monasteries, colleges of specialists, and cloisters of experts of the twentieth century's corporate society.

Dr. Johnson observed that there were two types of knowledge: knowing something oneself or knowing who knows it. In bureaucracies it is often said pejoratively that "it is not what you know but whom you know." Both of these observations are reasonable in terms of a world in which the gathering and evaluation of information is costly. As the number of individuals, things, and concepts grows, it becomes more and more difficult to maintain a constant relative level of information. The languages of signs, sounds, and motions provide us with methods of coding vast amounts of information in a compact manner. An experience shared can often be called to view at a glance by those who shared it. Yet even with our ingenuity for coding, the overload grows, especially if we wish to maintain values that stress individual men not as small component parts of the social intelligence, but as individuals.

If we believe that our political and economic values are based on the individual who understands principles, knows what the issues are, and has an important level of knowledge and understanding of his fellow citizens, then the twentieth and twenty-first centuries pose problems never posed before. Quantitative change has brought important qualitative distinctions. Specifically, how viable is the jury system for cases with technical evidence? How close must we move to formalizing concepts of statistical justice where the costs and time in the process, together with impersonal probabilities of being caught, become more important considerations than the case itself?

In spite of growth in communications, has there been any considerable change in the number of individuals that a person can get to know well? Since spatial distribution has changed, the individual may select his friends from a larger set. Yet regardless of the growth of modern science and the speeds of transportation, an evening with a friend, except for the transportation factor, will still call for the same amount of time to be expended in the twenty-first century as in the nineteenth. It has been suggested that 7! (5,040) citizens is the optimum size for the city state. Span of control literature suggests 7 as the largest span. George A. Miller's "magical number $7 \pm 2$" discusses the data-processing implications of this number.[1]

Taking a few crude calculations we observe that if half a day a year is needed to maintain contact with a relatively good friend, then there is an upper bound of seven hundred people with whom we could have much personal interaction. How many cases can the judge handle? How many patients can the psychiatrist treat? Is personal interaction becoming a luxury that modern mass society cannot afford, or are there new social forms and institutions that will foster and preserve it?

In voting do we have criteria other than a blind faith in the "stolid common sense of the yeoman"? The growth in the size of the electorate and in the numbers and complexities of issues is only exceeded by the torrents of writings in which the public may be buried if it so chooses. In the jungle of municipal politics, even the well-educated and relatively more articulate part of the population is woefully under-informed. At what point does a division of labor become a division of values and of social responsibilities?

The second fact of life that limits any simple view of individual rational men with freedom of choice, who wisely select actions so that their private welfare coincides with the public welfare, is that, given the preferences of all, market mechanisms and voting procedures will only succeed if very special conditions prevail (even assuming complete information). These conditions were indicated in writings from Adam Smith onwards. They call for certain technical properties to hold for the production processes in society; it is necessary to consider that the preferences of the individual are either completely independent of the welfare of others or subject to very strict limitations (such as being identical). Furthermore, the conditions go against intensive specialization, as many individuals are needed in all walks of life in order to avoid the dangers of monopolization. It is doubtful that conditions for the smooth functioning of the price system were ever applicable to the majority of the economy of any society; in general, they do not hold. As the size of the population and cities grows and as modern communication and information technologies weld previously independent groups together, the chances for the conditions to hold become even more diminished.

The aggregation of individual wants and powers into social wants and powers is one of the central problems of political science, economics, and sociology. We are currently in the position where we need to, and may be able to, answer certain fundamental questions concerning the possibility of constructing institutions to satisfy desired properties for the relation between the individual and his society. In particular, we are at least able to formulate in several different ways concepts such as equality, centralization, and power, and to ask if it is at least logically possible to discover methods for making diverse aims of a society consistent. It is neither obvious nor true that there may be any institutions that enable our desires for decentralization, dispersion of power, and equality (or equity) of distribution to be simultaneously satisfied.

These casual comments should be taken merely as preliminary and somewhat disjointed notes calling for the rethinking of some of our models of political and economic man so that they fit the pattern of the uncertain decision-maker acting under severely restricted conditions of information embedded within a communication system upon which he is becoming increasingly more dependent. His freedom of scope is limited by the powers of others; as these powers become more numerous and technology permits quicker communication, his actions become more deeply intertwined with those of others. Given our view of man, and for the moment assuming no great biological changes, we need to explore the arithmetic of economics and politics for the restrictions on the societies of the future.

Where will we be in the year 2000 or 2100 is far more a problem in control and anticipation than in prediction. Man has succeeded so far because of his incredible flexibility and adaptability. Now that he has learned to control fantastic sources of energy and to create devices in the form of computers and communication equipment that promise to aid his intellectual and organizational abilities, his power to manipulate the future has grown tremendously.

Knowledge has grown, and our abilities to analyze have increased. Has there been a like increase in either individual or social wisdom? Additions to human power without like additions to wisdom could set up the conditions for the destruction of civilization. The case has not yet been proved in either direction. Whether this society will destroy itself or not cannot be answered even with the proliferation of modern weaponry.

We may not be able to specify sufficient conditions to guarantee the preservation of values and of man. It is possible, however, to consider some necessary conditions. These involve a thinking-through of a political economy for the modern world. We need to touch upon conceptual problems dealing with measurements and the logic of society's control of itself, and to re-examine both the values to be preserved in our society and the role of modern technology in the attainment of its goals.

Problems are often complex and cannot be explained in a few sentences. The market mechanism is not sufficient to solve the problems of optimum allocation in our society. The voting mechanism in combination with the price system may provide a way, though not necessarily an optimal one, for the achievement of society's goals. Our beliefs and desires may call for a preservation of both the market and voting mechanisms at the federal, state, municipal, and corporate levels. Nevertheless, many modifications are possible. The period from 1930 to the present can be characterized by a tremendous growth in the means and measures of economic control. National income accounting, input-output tables, gross national income figures, and other monetary measures came to the fore. The next thirty years must be characterized by the development of social statistics and measures for the control of the services and joint processes of society. What are the measures by which to judge the performance of the police, education, social services, justice, and so forth? Such measures will undoubtedly be complex and subject to dangerous misinterpretation. (For example, how are the police to be credited for crime prevention?) Because of the difficulties involved in constructing suitable measures, it may easily require decades of devising and revising the appropriate indices and processes for obtaining them.

Compulsory levels of sanitation and education are not regarded by any except a small minority as limitations on freedom. Does this also hold for the draft, Medicare, taxation, or fluoridation of the water supply? In the next few years, birth control and possibly even genetic control must be considered seriously. The nature of government for a multi-billion-person world (and, eventually, planetary system) is neither quantitatively nor qualitatively the same as that required for an isolated New England village. What freedoms do we intend to preserve? Perhaps it would be more accurate to ask: What new concepts of freedom do we intend to attach the old names to?

The purely academic economic, social, or political theorist may claim that we can scarcely define values, can hardly measure them, and cannot compare them. Only the Philistine or the administrator faced with the problem dares to ask the question, "What price should we pay to increase the safety level for an astronaut?" In spite of themselves, the behavioral sciences have been forced to become applied sciences. Measurements have been and will be made that many claim are impossible. Even the crudest approximation provides a guide for behavior where a decision *has* to be made.

The influence of the high-speed digital computer upon society cannot be underestimated. If we wish to preserve even modified democratic values in a multi-billion-person society, then the computer, mass data processing, and communications are absolute necessities. It must be stressed again that they are necessary, but not sufficient. Using an analogy from the ballet, as the set becomes more complex and the dancers more numerous, the choreography required to maintain a given level of co-ordination becomes far more refined and difficult. The computer and modern data processing provide the refinement—the means to treat individuals as individuals rather than as parts of a large aggregate.

The treatment of an individual as an individual will not be an unmixed blessing. Problems concerning the protection of privacy will be large. Once established, the universal identification number will mean a great release from the drudgery of having to use a dozen cards to establish one's credit rating. A computer check of central files could supply the individual with an extensive dossier whenever he needed it. It could, however, also supply the dossier to others unless appropriate checks on availability are established.

Devices on automobiles or other property may be invented in order to keep track of their use. This would enable societies to enforce tax schemes for the use of joint assets that are closely related to individual use—such as parking space and roads. Computers would do the accounting, meter reading, and billing. Once more we are confronted with questions concerning privacy. At what point do we wish to stop "Big Brother" from watching our every move?

Voting patterns could change by use of the "instant referendum." With the availability of a computer console as a standard consumer good as commonly available as a television set, it would be feasible to present the electorate with the opportunity to vote directly and immediately on a variety of issues. Not only could they be asked to vote, but they could be supplied with information by direct library interrogation prior to casting their vote.

Computer and other modern information technology can make it possible to preserve or even to extend the treatment by society of the individual as an individual. His own memory and internal data processing may not change, but information technology will increase by several orders of magnitude his ability to obtain information and to store and retrieve it externally.

The growth of numbers of people, amounts of knowledge, and speed of change in technology work against the individual being in a position to exercise free, reasonably well-informed, rational, individual choice concerning much of his destiny. The advent of computing and communications devices to aid both in the obtaining and analysis of information has provided the possibility of preserving and possibly extending the individual's freedom. Technology is necessary, but it is not enough. Sophisticated devices and sophisticated measures and methods for the co-ordination of behavior in a complex free society may call for a sophisticated society with sophisticated individual members. If we wish to preserve and extend our freedoms, to permit the growth of world population to tens of billions, to increase the world's standard of living, to explore and possibly colonize space, then the next changes may well have to be within ourselves.

# N O T E

1. George A. Miller, "The Magical Number Seven, Plus or Minus Two—Some Limits on Our Capacity for Processing Information," *Psychological Review,* Vol. 63, No. 2 (1956), pp. 81–97.

# Diagnosis of Our Time

KARL MANNHEIM

Mannheim argues in this work, as in so many of his works, that the complex social relations resulting from the growth of the mass society and the technological mode of production make centralized social planning absolutely necessary. The question that remains is whether this social planning will be totalitarian or democratic.

If social planning is not itself the result of rationally planned action, if it is done in a piecemeal, hit-or-miss fashion, then very likely the form of social planning which will come about will be totalitarian. However, there is no reason why we should see democracy and social planning as basically opposed to each other. If the planning itself is done for the purpose of increasing our individual freedom and supporting our democratic institutions, it can become

*Reprinted from Karl Mannheim,* Diagnosis of Our Time: Wartime Essays of a Sociologist, *by permission of Humanities Press, Inc., and Routledge & Kegan Paul, Ltd.*

a fundamental force supporting democracy and leading to greater individual freedom.

If we are able, through the use of social-scientific knowledge, to gain the objective and reliable understanding needed to make rational plans for such a highly complex society, and if we act with courage and wisdom, we should be able to plan for democracy and individual freedom. If we plan well and act wisely, modern technological knowledge, like knowledge in the past, can lead to greater individual freedom, as well as greater economic affluence, for all. The technological society can be a society of wealth and freedom, or it can be a terribly efficient tyranny worse than any man has known. The militant democracy called for by Mannheim could be of fundamental importance in the realization of these hopes and in guaranteeing that the technicist projection will remain only a nightmare.

## I. The Significance of the New Social Techniques

Let us take the attitude of a doctor who tries to give a scientific diagnosis of the illness from which we all suffer. There is no doubt that our society has been taken ill. What is the disease, and what could be its cure? If I had to summarize the situation in a single sentence I would say: "We are living in an age of transition from laissez-faire[1] to a planned society. The planned society that will come may take one of two shapes: it will be ruled either by a minority in terms of a dictatorship or by a new form of government which, in spite of its increased power, will still be democratically controlled."

If that diagnosis be true, we are all in the same boat—Germany, Russia, Italy, as well as Britain, France and U.S.A. Although in very many respects still different, we are all moving in the same direction towards a kind of planned society, and the question is whether it will be a good sort of planning or a bad one; for planning with dictatorship or on the basis of democratic control will emerge. But a diagnosis is not a prophecy. The value of a diagnosis does not mainly consist in the forecast as such, but in the reasons one is able to give for one's statements. The value of a diagnosis consists in the acuteness of the analysis of the factors which seem to determine the course of events. The main changes we are witnessing to-day can ultimately be traced to the fact that we are living in a Mass Society. Government of the masses cannot be carried on without a series of inventions and improvements in the field of economic, political and social techniques. By "Social Techniques" [2] I understand the sum of those methods which aim at influencing human behaviour and which, when in the hands of the Government, act as an especially powerful means of social control.

Now the main point about these improved social techniques is not only that they are highly efficient, but that this very same efficiency fosters minority rule. To begin with, a new military technique allows a much greater concentration of power in the hands of the few than did the technique of any previous period. Whereas the armies of the eighteenth and nineteenth centuries were equipped with rifles and guns, our armies work with bombs, aeroplanes, gas and mechanized units. A man with a rifle threatens only a few people, but a man with a bomb can threaten a thousand. That means that in our age the change in military technique contributes a great deal to the chances of a minority rule.

The same concentration has occurred in the field of government and administration. Telephone, telegraph, wireless, railways, motor-cars and, last but not least, the scientific management of any large-scale organization—all these facilitate centralized government and control. Similar concentration can also be observed in the means of forming public opinion. The mechanized mass production of ideas through press and wireless works in this direction. Add to this the possibility of controlling schools and the whole range of education from a single centre, and you will realize that the recent change from democratic government to totalitarian systems is due here also not so much to the changing ideas of men as to changes in social technique.

The new science of Human Behaviour brings into the service of the Government a knowledge of the human mind which can either be exploited in the direction of greater efficiency or made into an instrument playing on mass emotions. The development of the social services, especially of social work, allows the exertion of an influence which penetrates into our private lives. Thus, there is a possibility of subjecting to public control psychological processes which formerly were considered as purely personal.

The reason why I lay such emphasis on these social techniques is that they limit the direction in which modern society can develop at all. The nature of these social techniques is even more fundamental to society than the economic structure or the social stratification of a given order. By their aid one can hamper or remould the working of the economic system, destroy social classes and set others in their place.

I call them techniques because, like all techniques, they are neither good nor bad in themselves. Everything depends on the use that is made of them by the human will. The most important thing about these modern techniques is that they tend to foster centralization and, therefore, minority rule and dictatorship. Where you have bombs, aeroplanes and a mechanized army at your disposal, telephone, telegraph and wireless as means of communication, large-scale industrial technique and a hierarchic bureaucratic machinery to produce and distribute commodities and manage human affairs, the main decisions can be taken from key positions. The gradual establishment of key positions in modern society has made planning not only possible but inevitable. Processes and events are no longer the outcome of natural interplay between small self-contained units. No longer do individuals and their small enterprises arrive at an equilibrium through competition and mutual adjustment. In the various branches of social and economic life there are huge combines, complex social units, which are too rigid to reorganize themselves on their own account and so must be governed from the centre.

The greater efficiency, in many respects, of the totalitarian states is not merely due, as people usually think, to their more efficient and more blatant propaganda, but also to their instant realization that mass society cannot be governed by techniques of the homespun order, which were suited to an age of craftsmanship. The terror of their efficiency consists in the fact that by co-ordinating all these means they enslave the greater part of the population and superimpose creeds, beliefs and behaviour which do not correspond to the real nature of the citizen.

In this description of the concentration of social techniques I consciously refer to changes which characterize the very structure of modern society. That means, if the main reason for what happened in Germany, Italy, Russia and the other totalitarian countries is to be sought in the changed nature of social techniques, it is only a question of time and opportunity when some group in the so far democratic countries will make use of them. In this connection a catastrophe like war, rapid depression, great inflation, growing unemployment, which make extraordinary measures necessary (i.e., concentration of the maximum power in the hands of some Government), is bound to precipitate this process. Even before the outbreak of the war the present tension brought about by the existing totalitarian states forced the democratic countries to take measures very often similar to those which came into force in the totalitarian countries through revolution. It goes without saying that the tendencies towards concentration must greatly increase in a war when conscription and the co-ordination of food and other supplies becomes necessary.

After this brief description of the social techniques you might rightly say: "What a gloomy prospect. Is there a remedy for this? Are we simply the victims of a process which is blind but stronger than all of us?" No diagnosis is complete unless it seeks for a kind of therapy. It is only worth studying the nature of society as it is, if we are able to hint at those steps which, taken in time, could make society into what it should be. Fortunately, a further attempt at a diagnosis reveals to us some aspects of the situation which not only free us from the feeling of frustration but definitely call upon us to act.

## II. The Third Way: A Militant Democracy

What I have so far described are social techniques. Like all techniques, they are neither good nor bad in themselves. Everything depends on the use that is made of them by human will and intelligence. If they are left to themselves and develop unguarded they lead to dictatorship. If they are made to serve a good purpose and are continually checked, if they do not master men but are mastered by men, they are among the most magnificent achievements of mankind. But we shall be able to turn the flow of events and avert the fate of Germany, Italy and Russia only if we are vigilant and use our knowledge and judgment for the better. The principle of laissez-faire will not help us any further, we shall have to face the forthcoming events at the level of conscious thought in terms of concrete knowledge of society. Such an analysis will have to start with some preliminary clarifications which might help us in defining our policy.

First of all—not all planning is evil. We shall have to make a distinction between planning for conformity and planning for freedom and variety. In both cases co-ordination plays a great rôle, co-ordination of the means of social techniques such as education, propaganda, administration, etc.; but there is a difference between co-ordination in the spirit of monotony and co-ordination in the spirit of variety. The conductor of an orchestra co-ordinates the different instruments and it rests with him to direct this co-ordination to the achievement of monotony or of variety. The goose-step co-ordination of the dictators is the most primitive misinterpretation of the meaning of co-ordination. Real co-ordination in the social sphere means only a greater economy and a more purposeful use of the social techniques at our disposal. The more we think about the best forms of planning, the more we might arrive at the decision that in the most important spheres of life one should deliberately refrain from interference, and that the scope for spontaneity should rather be kept free than distorted by superfluous management. You might plan the time-table of a boarding-school and come to the decision that at certain hours the pupils should be left entirely free—it is still planning if you are the master of the whole situation and decide that with certain fields of life one should not interfere. This sort of deliberate refraining from interference by a planner will radically differ from the purposeless non-interference of the laissez-faire society. Although it seems obvious that planning should not necessarily mean goose-step co-ordination, it was the bureaucratic and militaristic spirit of the totalitarian states which distorted the meaning of planning in that way.

There is a simple reason why in the long run great society cannot survive if it only fosters conformity. The French sociologist Durkheim first pointed out in *The Division of Labour in Society*[3] that only very simple societies like those of primitive peoples can work on the basis of homogeneity and conformity. The more complex the social division of labour becomes, the more it demands the differentiation of types. The integration and unity of great society is not achieved through uniform behavior but through the mutual complementing of functions. In a highly industrialized society people keep together because the farmer needs the industrial worker, the scientist, the educationist, and vice versa. Besides this vocational differentiation, individual differentiation is needed for the sake of inventions and efficient control of the new developments. All this only corroborates our statement that the bureaucratic and military ideal of planning must be replaced by the new ideal of the planning for freedom.

Another necessary clarification is that planning need not be based upon dictatorship. Co-ordination and planning can be done on the basis of democratic advice. There is nothing to prevent parliamentary machinery from carrying out the necessary control in planned society.

But it is not only the abstract principle of democracy which must be saved as well as recast in a new form. The increasing demand for social justice has to be met if we wish to guarantee the working of the new social order. The working of the present economic system, if left to itself, tends in the shortest possible time to increase the differences in income and wealth between the various classes to such an extent that this itself is bound to create dissatisfaction and continuous social tension. But as the working of democracy is essentially based upon democratic consent, the principle of social justice is not only a question of ethics but also a pre-condition of the functioning of the democratic system itself. The claim for greater justice does not necessarily mean a mechanical concept of equality. Reasonable differences in income and in the accumulation of wealth to create the necessary stimulus to achievement might be maintained as long as they do not interfere with the main trends in planning and do not grow to such an extent as to prevent co-operation between the different classes.

This move towards greater justice has the advantage that it can be achieved by the existing means of reform—through taxation, control of investment, through public works and the radical extension of social serv-ices; it does not call for revolutionary interference, which would lead at once to dictatorship. The transformation brought about through reform instead of revolution also has the advantage that it can reckon with the help of former leading democratic groups. If a new system starts with the destruction of the older leading groups in society, it destroys all the traditional values of European culture as well. Ruthless attacks on the Liberal and Conservative intelligentsia and the persecution of the Churches are designed to annihilate the last remnants of Christianity and humanism and to frustrate all efforts to bring peace to the world. If the new society is to last, and if it is to be worthy of the efforts humanity has made so far, the new leadership must be blended with the old. Together they can help to rejuvenate the valuable elements in tradition, continuing them in the spirit of creative evolution.

But it is obvious that a new social order cannot be brought about simply by a more skilful and human handling of the new social tech-niques—it needs the guidance by the spirit, which is more than a system of decision on technical issues. The system of laissez-faire Liberalism could leave the final decisions to chance, to the miracle of the self-equilibrating forces of economic and social life. The age of Liberalism, therefore, was characterized by a pluralism of aims and values and a neutral attitude towards the main issues of life.

Laissez-faire Liberalism mistook neutrality for tolerance. Yet, neither democratic tolerance nor scientific objectivity means that we should refrain from taking a stand for what we believe to be true or that we should avoid the discussion of the final values and objectives in life. The meaning of tolerance is that everybody should have a fair chance to present his case, but not that nobody should ardently believe in his cause. This attitude of neutrality in our modern democracy went so far that we ceased to believe, out of mere fairness, in our own objectives; we no longer thought that peaceful adjustment is desirable, that freedom has to be saved and democratic control has to be maintained.

Our democracy has to become militant if it is to survive. Of course, there is a fundamental difference between the fighting spirit of the dictators on the one hand, who aim at imposing a total system of values and a strait-jacket social organization upon their citizens, and a militant democracy on the other, which becomes militant only in the defence of the agreed right procedure of social change and those basic virtues and values— such as brotherly love, mutual help, decency, social justice, freedom, respect for the person, etc.—which are the basis of the peaceful functioning of a social order. The new militant democracy will therefore develop a new attitude to values. It will differ from the relativist laissez-faire of the previous age, as it will have the courage to agree on some basic values which are acceptable to everybody who shares the traditions of Western civilization.

The challenge of the Nazi system more than anything else made us aware of the fact that the democracies have a set of basic values in common, which are inherited from classical antiquity, and even more from Christianity, and that it is not too difficult to state them and to agree on them. But militant democracy will accept from Liberalism the belief that in a highly differentiated modern society—apart from those basic values on which democratic agreement will be necessary—it is better to leave the more complicated values open to creed, individual choice or free experimentation. The synthesis of these two principles will be reflected in our educational system in so far as the agreed basic virtues will be brought home to the child with all the educational methods at our disposal. But the more complex issues will be left open to save us from the evil effects of fanaticism.

The main problems of our time can be expressed in the following questions. Is there a possibility of planning which is based upon co-ordination and yet leaves scope for freedom? Can the new form of planning deliberately refrain from interfering except in cases where free adjustment has led not to harmony but to conflict and chaos? Is there a form of

planning which moves in the direction of social justice, gradually eliminating the increasing disproportion in income and wealth in the various
strata of the nation? Is there a possibility of transforming our neutral
democracy into a militant one? Can we transform our attitudes to valuations so that democratic agreement on certain basic issues becomes possible, while the more complex issues are left to individual choice?

## III. The Strategic Situation

Our diagnosis would be incomplete if we examined the possibilities in
the abstract only. Any sociological or political therapy must devote special
attention to the concrete situation in which we find ourselves. What is
then the strategic situation? There are a number of forces which seem to
be moving automatically in the direction which I have indicated above.
First, there is a growing disappointment with laissez-faire methods. It is
gradually being realized that they have been destructive, not only in the
economic field where they produced the trade cycle and devastating mass
unemployment, but that they are partly responsible for the lack of pre-
paredness in the liberal and democratic states. The principle of letting
things slide cannot compete with the efficiency of co-ordination—it is
too slow, is based too much upon improvization and encourages all the
waste inherent in departmentalization. Secondly, there is a growing disappointment about Fascism for, although it seems to be efficient, its efficiency is that of the devil. Thirdly, there are grave doubts concerning
Communism, even in the minds of those to whom—as a doctrine—it
first meant the panacea for all the evils of Capitalism. Not only are they
forced to ponder upon the chances of Communism if it were to be introduced by revolutionary methods into the Western countries with their
differentiated social structure, but they cannot close their eyes to certain
changes which took place in the time between Lenin and Stalin. The
more they have to admit that what has happened was an inevitable compromise with realities, the more they have to take into account the presence of these realities also elsewhere. What these realities teach us is,
briefly, that Communism works, that it is efficient and has great achievements to its credit as far as the state of the masses goes. The miscalculation
begins with the fact that neither Dictatorship nor the State seems to wither
away. Marx and Lenin believed that dictatorship was only a transient
stage, which would disappear after the establishment of a new society.

To-day we know that this was a typical nineteenth-century delusion. When Marx conceived this idea, one could point to the fate of absolutism which everywhere was slowly giving way to democracy. But this process, in the light of our analysis, was due to the fact that in the nineteenth century social techniques were still very inefficient and those in power had to compromise with the forces working from below. In a modern totalitarian state once the whole apparatus is appropriated by a single party and its bureaucracy, there is little chance that they will give it up of their own accord.

Thus there is at least a chance that out of the general fear and disillusionment a more reformist attitude may develop. War automatically created a united front—a kind of natural consensus which is needed for such reform. Ultimately it depends on us whether we can take full advantage of this unanimity. The question of the moment is whether we understand the deeper meaning of the so-called Emergency Measures. These are a step towards the necessary co-ordination of the social techniques at our disposal without giving up democratic control based upon the co-operation of all parties. Of course, many of these emergency measures cannot, and should not, remain permanent. But some of them must endure, as they are simply an expression of the basic fact that the vital needs of the community should everywhere and always override the privileges of individuals. On the other hand, if we are to preserve the great traditions of Western civilization, we must vigorously defend those rights of the individual upon which real freedom depends. In this struggle for a new and stronger authority combined with new forms of freedom we must base our selection upon conscious principles in the building up of a new system.

To this analysis of the strategical situation one may object that the political unity engendered by the war cannot be expected to last, once the threat of the common enemy is removed. The advantage of a war emergency from the standpoint of planning is that it creates a unity of purpose. My answer to this is that, whatever the outcome of this war may be, the menace of social and economic chaos will be imminent and may replace the threat of Fascist aggression. Of course this threat will only produce co-operation between groups and parties if under the pressure of the situation they are capable of creative adjustment, if they are capable of a type of response which is on a higher level of morality and based upon a fuller understanding of the situation than is required under normal conditions. If this happens there could well be co-operation and agreement upon certain basic, long-range issues, and the transition to a higher stage of civilization could be planned. As in the life of the individual, so in the life of nations, the hour of crisis reveals the presence of fundamental vitality. We must prepare the ground now for a full realization of the significance of the hour.

The unbridled criticism of the form of freedom and democracy which has existed in the past decades must therefore cease. Even if we agree that freedom and democracy are necessarily incomplete as long as social opportunities are hampered by economic inequality, it is irresponsible not to realize what a great achievement they represent and that through them we can enlarge the scope of social progress. Progressive groups will be readier to advocate reformist measures, as it is becoming obvious that recent revolutions tend to result in Fascism and that the chances of a revolution will be very slight as soon as a united party has co-ordinated all the key positions and is capable of preventing any organized resistance.

The depressing experiences of the past few years have taught us that a dictatorship can govern against the will of even a large majority of the population. The reason is that the techniques of revolution lag far behind the techniques of government. Barricades, the symbols of revolution, are relics of an age when they were built up against cavalry. This means that there is a high premium on evolutionary methods. As to the ruling classes, there is a chance that the more intelligent sections within them may, under changed conditions, prefer a gradual transition from the present unplanned stage of Capitalism to a democratically planned society with social aims to the alternative of Fascism. Although Fascism does not formally deprive them of their property, State interference is growing and will ultimately subjugate them. The strategical problem in their case consists in splitting their ranks in such a way that the would-be Fascists among them are severed from those who have only to lose in a Fascist experiment.

In my opinion, a new social order can be developed and the dictatorial tendencies of modern social techniques can be checked if our generation has the courage, imagination and will to master them and guide them in the right direction. This must be done immediately, while the techniques are still flexible and have not been monopolized by any single group. It rests with us to avoid the mistakes of former democracies, which, owing to their ignorance of these main trends, could not prevent the rise of dictatorship, and it is the historical mission of this country on the basis of her long-standing tradition of democracy, liberty and spontaneous reform to create a society which will work in the spirit of the new ideal: "Planning for Freedom."

# NOTES

1. In this book, the terms "laissez-faire" and "Liberalism" are used as ideal types, i.e. the term does not exactly designate reality as it is or ever was, but it deliberately emphasizes certain features which are relevant for the purposes of the presentation and for the valuations prevailing in the latter. Without focussing on such ideal types for developing clear-cut antinomies, it would be impossible to make one's points in a political discussion.

   On the other hand, justice to the source from which we draw so much of our sustenance is restored, if we remind the reader that Liberalism, neither in its philosophy nor in its practice, ever completely corresponded to what could be called pure laissez-faire, that is to say the belief that self-adjustment both in the economic field and in the other spheres of social activity spontaneously leads to an equilibrium. Especially classical English Liberalism never demanded the complete absence of controls.

   Nevertheless, after these reservations have been made it is still true that the laissez-faire ideology hoped for something like spontaneous self-adjustment, and in its exaggerated form it was partly responsible for the disintegration of communal controls in the later phases of capitalist Democracy in the course of which not equilibrium but crises and monopolies developed.

2. Cf. my *Man and Society in an Age of Reconstruction: Studies in Modern Social Structure* (3rd ed., London, 1942), especially part v. This chapter is a brief restatement and further development of that book, where the reader can find a more detailed treatment of many of the problems presented here. Furthermore, the author is working on a book, "Essentials of Democratic Planning," which will deal in a more systematic manner with the different aspects of planning.

3. E. Durkheim, *On the Division of Labour in Society* (transl. by G. Simpson: New York, 1933).

*A Note on the Type*

The text of this book was set on the Linotype in a face called TIMES ROMAN, designed by Stanley Morison for The Times (London), and first introduced by that newspaper in 1932.

Among typographers and designers of the twentieth century, Stanley Morison has been a strong forming influence, as typographical advisor to the English Monotype Corporation, as a director of two distinguished English publishing houses, and as a writer of sensibility, erudition, and keen practical sense.

*Composed, printed, and bound by*
*The Colonial Press, Inc., Clinton, Massachusetts*

*Designed by*
*Al Burkhart*